INFORMATICS PRACTICES
for CBSE Class XII

Reema Thareja
Assistant Professor
Department of Computer Science
Shyama Prasad Mukherji College
University of Delhi

All rights reserved. No part of this book may be modified, reproduced or utilised in any form, or by any means, electronic or mechanical, including photocopying, recording or by any information storage and retrieval system, in any form of binding or cover other than in which it is published, without permission in writing from the publisher.

INFORMATICS PRACTICES FOR CBSE CLASS XII

UNIVERSITIES PRESS (INDIA) PRIVATE LIMITED

Registered Office
3-6-747/1/A & 3-6-754/1, Himayatnagar, Hyderabad 500 029, Telangana, India
info@universitiespress.com; www.universitiespress.com

Distributed by
Orient Blackswan Private Limited

Registered Office
3-6-752 Himayatnagar, Hyderabad 500 029 Telangana, India

Other Offices
Bengaluru, Chennai, Guwahati, Hyderabad, Kolkata,
Mumbai, New Delhi, Noida, Patna, Visakhapatnam

© Universities Press (India) Private Limited 2022

ISBN 978-93-89211-93-1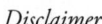

Cover and book design:
© Universities Press (India) Private Limited 2022

Typeset in Adobe Garamond Pro 10.5 points *by*
Cameo Corporate Services Limited, Coimbatore

Printed in India by
Yash Printographics, Greater Noida 201 310

Published by
Universities Press (India) Private Limited
3-6-747/1/A & 3-6-754/1, Himayatnagar, Hyderabad 500 029, Telangana, India

Disclaimer
Care has been taken to confirm the accuracy of the information presented in this book. The author and the publisher, however, cannot accept any responsibility for errors or omissions or for consequences from the application of the information in this book, and make no warranty, express or implied, with respect to its contents. This textbook does not constitute a standard, specification or regulation. The trademarks or manufacturers' names appear/are used in this book only because they are considered essential to the object of subject discussion and do not necessarily constitute endorsement of the product/standard by the author or publisher. All products and company names are trademarks™ or registered® trademarks of their respective holders. Use of them does not imply any affiliation with or endorsement by them.

*I dedicate this book to my family and my uncle Mr B L Theraja,
who is a well-known author himself*

Contents

Preface   *xiii*
About the Author   *xv*

Chapter 1: Introduction to Python Pandas — 1

- 1.1 Introduction to Data Handlining Using Python — 1
- 1.2 Introduction to Arrays, 2-D Arrays (or Matrices) and *N*-D Arrays — 1
  - 1.2.1 One-dimensional Arrays — 1
  - 1.2.2 Matrices or Two-dimensional Arrays — 2
  - 1.2.3 Multi-dimensional Arrays — 4
- 1.3 Introduction to Numpy Module — 5
  - 1.3.1 Creating NumPy Arrays — 5
  - 1.3.2 Attributes of NumPy Array — 7
  - 1.3.3 The `head()` and `tail()` Methods of NumPy Array — 7
  - 1.3.4 Accessing NumPy Arrays — 8
- 1.4 Starting with Pandas — 8
- 1.5 Series — 9
  - 1.5.1 Creating Series — 10
  - 1.5.2 Create an Empty Series — 10
  - 1.5.3 Create a Series from `ndarray` — 10
  - 1.5.4 Create a Series from `dict` — 10
  - 1.5.5 Create a Series from Scalar — 11
- 1.6 Accessing Data from Series with Position — 11
- 1.7 Series Object Attributes — 12
- 1.8 The `in` and `not in` Operators with Python Series — 13
- 1.9 Python Series Nulls — 14
- 1.10 The `all()` Function — 15
- 1.11 Arithmetic Operations on Python Series — 15
- 1.12 Filter Data — 16
- 1.13 Some More Series Functions — 17
- 1.14 Pandas Series vs. Python List — 17
- 1.15 Data Frame — 18
  - 1.15.1 Creating a Data Frame — 18
  - 1.15.2 Creating Data Frame from Dictionary — 19

Programmer's Zone   19

1.16	Pandas DataFrame Functions and Attributes	22
1.17	Mathematical Operations on DataFrame	24
1.18	Matching/Broadcasting Operations	25
1.19	Missing Data and Operations with Fill Values	26
1.20	Flexible Comparisons	27
1.21	Boolean Reductions	28
1.22	Comparing if Objects are Equivalent	29
1.23	Comparing Array-like Objects	29
1.24	Combining Data Frames	30
1.25	Descriptive Statistics	31
1.26	Summarizing or Describing Data	34
1.27	Index of Min/Max Values	35
1.28	Value Counts and `mode()` Function	37
1.29	Other Statistical Functions	38
1.30	Row- or Column-wise Application of Functions	39
1.31	Comparison of Different Data Structures	40
1.32	Transfer Data Between CSV Files/SQL Databases, and Data Frame Objects	41
	1.32.1 Loading CSV Data into Pandas	41
	1.32.2 Reading a CSV File	42
	1.32.2 Writing Data to a CSV File	43

Key Terms | Chapter Highlights | Review Questions | Programming Exercises | Fill in the Blanks | State True or False | Multiple Choice Questions | Give the Output | Find the Error | Answers

Chapter 2: More on Python Pandas Module   57

2.1	Quick Review of Pandas	57
2.2	Pivoting Data Frame	58
2.3	Sorting a DataFrame	59
	2.3.1 Sorting by Labels	60

Programmer's Zone   61

2.4	Combining Data Frames	62
2.5	Histogram	63
2.6	Quantiles	66
2.7	Function Apllication	69
	2.7.1 Table-wise Function Application: `pipe()`	69
	2.7.2 Row- or Column-wise Function Operations: `apply()`	70
	2.7.3 Element-wise Function Application: `applymap()`	71

	2.8	Aggregation (Group By)		72
		2.8.1	Group by One Column	72
		2.8.2	Grouping by Multiple Columns	73
	2.9	Transform Function in Python		74
	Programmer's Zone			*75*
	2.10	Reindexing in Pandas Data Frame		78
	2.11	Replacing the Missing Values		81
	2.12	Altering Column Labels		82
	2.13	Importing/Exporting Data Between MySQL Database and Pandas		83
		2.13.1	Exporting Data from Pandas to MySQL	83
		2.13.2	Reading/Importing Data from MySQL Database Table into Pandas Data Frame	84

Key Terms | Chapter Highlights | Review Questions | Programming Exercises | Explain the Instructions | Fill in the Blanks | State True or False | Multiple Choice Questions | Give the Output | Answers

Chapter 3: Plotting Graphs — 97

	3.1	Visualizing Data Through Plots		97
	3.2	Bar Chart		97
		3.2.1	Drawing a Bar Graph in Python	97
	Programmer's Zone			*99*
		3.2.2	Some Important Miscellaneous Functions	101
	3.3	Plotting Histograms		102
	Programmer's Zone			*104*
	3.4	Frequency Polygon		106
	3.5	Boxplot		107
		3.5.1	Understanding a Boxplot	107
		3.5.2	Use of Boxplot Graph	107
		3.5.3	Creating a Boxplot	108
	3.6	Pie Chart		109
		3.6.1	Plotting a Pie Chart	110
		3.6.2	Customizing a Pie Chart	110
	3.7	Scatter Plot		112
	Programmer's Zone			*113*

Key Terms | Chapter Highlights | Review Questions | Programming Exercises | Fill in the Blanks | State True or False | Multiple Choice Questions | Fill in the Blanks to Complete the Code | Answers

Chapter 4:	Structured Query Language (SQL)		121
4.1	Introduction to MySQL Database		121
4.2	Introduction to Structured Query Language (SQL)		121
	4.2.1	How MySQL Works	121
	4.2.2	Uses of SQL	122
	4.2.3	Types of SQL Queries	122
4.3	SQL Data Types		122
4.4	Date and Time Types		123
4.5	Operators in SQL		123
4.6	Performing Simple Calculations with SELECT Statement		124
4.7	SQL Numeric Functions		125
4.8	String Functions		127
4.9	Retrieving Data from Table		130
4.10	The WHERE Clause		130
4.11	SQL AND and OR Operators		131
4.12	The WHERE BETWEEN Clause		132
4.13	The SQL WHERE IN Clause		132
4.14	The SQL SELECT DISTINCT Statement		133
4.15	ORDER BY Clause		134
4.16	The WHERE LIKE Clause in SQL		135
4.17	SQL SELECT MIN, MAX Statement		137
4.18	SELECT COUNT, SUM, AVG		138
4.19	The SQL GROUP BY Statement		139
4.20	The Having Clause		139
4.21	Column Aliases		140
4.22	SQL JOIN		141
	4.22.1	INNER JOIN	141
	4.22.2	LEFT JOIN	142
	4.22.3	RIGHT JOIN	143
	4.22.4	FULL JOIN	143
4.23	Relational Algebra in DBMS		144
	4.23.1	SELECT Operator	144
	4.23.2	PROJECT Operator (Π)	145
	4.23.3	UNION Operator	145
	4.23.4	INTERSECTION Operator	146
	4.23.5	SET DIFFERENCE Operator	146
	4.23.6	CARTESIAN PRODUCT Operator	147

| | | 4.23.7 | RENAME Operator | 147 |

Key Terms | Chapter Highlights | Review Questions | Programming Exercises | Fill in the Blanks | State True or False | Multiple Choice Questions | Give the Output | Answers

Chapter 5: Computer Networks — 157

5.1	Introduction		157
	5.1.1	Limitations of Computer Network	158
5.2	Types of Network		158
	5.2.1	LAN – Local Area Network	158
	5.2.2	WAN – Wide Area Network	158
	5.2.3	MAN – Metropolitan Area Network	160
	5.2.4	CAN – Campus Area Network or Corporate Area Network	160
	5.2.5	PAN – Personal Area Network	161
5.3	Network Devices		161
	5.3.1	MODEM (MOdulator DEModulator)	161
	5.3.2	Switch	162
	5.3.3	Repeater	162
	5.3.4	Hub	163
	5.3.5	Router	164
	5.3.6	Gateway	165
	5.3.7	Wi-Fi Card	166
5.4	Network Topology		167
	5.4.1	Bus Topology	167
	5.4.2	Star Topology	167
	5.4.3	Ring Topology	168
	5.4.4	Mesh Topology	168
	5.4.5	Tree Topology	169
	5.4.6	Hybrid Topology	169
5.5	Internet		170
5.6	Uniform Resource Locator or Universal Resource Locator		170
5.7	World Wide Web		171
5.8	Communication on the Internet		172
	5.8.1	Electronic Mail	172
	5.8.2	Chatting	173
	5.8.3	Internet Conferencing	173
5.9	Voice Over Internet Protocol (VoIP)		174
	5.9.1	How VoIP / Internet Voice Works	174
	5.9.2	What Kind of Equipment Do I Need?	174

	5.9.3	Advantages of VoIP	175
	5.9.4	Disadvantages of VoIP	176
5.10	Web Page		176
5.11	Website		176
	5.11.1	Static and Dynamic Websites	177
5.12	Web Servers		178
5.13	Web Hosting		178
	5.13.1	Types of Web Hosting Services	179
	5.13.2	Selecting the Right Web Hosting Package	180
5.14	Web Browser		181
	5.14.1	Popular Web Browsing Software	181
	5.14.2	Add-on and Plug-in	181
5.15	HTTP Cookie		182
	5.15.1	Types of Cookies	182
	5.15.2	Security Concerns	183
	5.15.3	Removing Cookies	183
5.16	Web Browser Settings		183

Key Terms | Chapter Highlights | Review Questions | Fill in the Blanks | State True or False | Multiple Choice Questions | Answers

Chapter 6: Societal Impacts — 189

6.1	Digital Footprint	189
6.2	Netiquette	190
6.3	Ethics in Computing	191
6.4	Data Protection	191
	6.4.1 Key Information Privacy Principles	192
6.5	Intellectual Property Rights (IPR)	192
6.6	Plagiarism	194
6.7	Software Licensing	196
6.8	Free and Open-source Software (FOSS)	196
	6.8.1 Difference Between Open-source Software and Other Types of Software	197
	6.8.2 Benefits of Open-source Software	197
6.9	Computer Fraud	198
6.10	Internet Frauds and Scams	198
6.11	Information Technology Act 2000	200
6.12	Hacking	201
6.13	Spreading Rumour and Cyber Bullying	201
6.14	Phishing	202

6.15	E-waste Management		203
	6.15.1	Development of Waste Recycling Technologies	204
	6.15.2	Formal vs. Informal Recycling	204
	6.15.3	Alternative Solutions of Disposal	205
6.16	Awareness About Health Concerns Related to the Usage of Technology		206
	6.16.1	Digital Eye Strain	206
	6.16.2	Sleep Disorders	207
	6.16.3	Physical Inactivity	207
	6.16.4	Musculoskeletal Problems	207
	6.16.5	Mental Health	208
	6.16.6	Technology Affecting Children	208

Key Terms | Chapter Highlights | Review Questions | Fill in the Blanks | State True or False | Multiple Choice Questions | Answers

Preface

We all know that Information Technology (IT) is the buzzword of the 21st century. We use computers to store, retrieve, transmit and manipulate data. Today, computers are used to perform every other task such as publishing a newspaper, designing a building, coaching sports players and training pilots in flight simulators. Computers have become so widespread that almost every electrical and electronic device (like washing machines, air conditioners, etc.) has a small embedded computer within it. Even the mobile phones that we use are smart phones (phones with computing technology) that are connected to the Internet. Information technology has revolutionized our lifestyle. Thus in today's scenario, learning about computers is mandatory not only for students pursuing a career in engineering and technology but also for those in other professions like journalism, nursing, archaeology, construction and management, to name a few.

Computing skills always help one to be more productive and self-sufficient. Therefore, a basic knowledge of computers and their underlying technology will pay rich dividends in the future. In this context, Python is an open-source, excellent, easy, high-level, interpreted, interactive, object-oriented and a reliable language that uses English-like words. It is also a versatile language that supports development of a wide range of applications ranging from simple text processing to WWW browsers to games. Moreover, programmers can embed Python within their C, C++, COM, ActiveX, CORBA, and Java programs to give 'scripting' capabilities for users.

Python has a huge user base that is constantly growing. The strength of Python can be understood from the fact that this programming language is the most preferred language of companies like Nokia, Google, YouTube and even NASA for its easy syntax. The support for multiple programming paradigms, including object-oriented programming, functional Python programming, and parallel programming models makes it an ideal choice for the programmers.

However, no student can learn to program just by reading a book; rather, it is a skill that must be developed by practice. So, after learning the rudiments of program writing, students will find in this book, a number of examples and exercises that would help them learn to design efficient programs. The book presents various programming examples that have already been implemented and tested using Python 3.8.3.

KEY FEATURES

This book is aimed at serving as a textbook for the commerce and humanities students enrolled in Class XII of CBSE. It explores how Python can be used for numerical data analysis and data visualization. It also discusses the basics of computer networking to familiarize students with how computers are interconnected in the real world for data transfer and information exchange. The book includes several student-friendly features:

Comprehensive Coverage: The book provides comprehensive coverage of all important topics from the examination point-of-view.

Easy to Understand: The book uses very simple language to explain the concepts and breaks down technical jargons to simpler terms for the student's benefit.

Pictorial Approach: Numerous well-labelled diagrams are provided throughout the text for clear understanding of the concepts.

Practical Orientation: Replete with solved examples and chapter-end exercises in the form of objective type questions and review questions, the book's well-defined pedagogy enables students to check their understanding of the concepts.

Glossary: A list of key terms is provided at the end of each chapter to facilitate easy revision.

Informative Textboxes: Important concepts are highlighted throughout the text for a quick recap.

Programmer's Zone examples are used in context to help the students understand the technique of programming.

Complementary App for CUCET: Students can download the free mobile app Jruma from Google Play Store or Apple Store for additional learning resources. The app would help them to recapitulate and test their understanding of the concepts learnt in Classes XI and XII. The app will also be useful for the students to hone their Computer Science (CS) and Logical Reasoning (LR) skills. CS and LR is a mandatory section in the CUCET and all other entrance exams the students may take throughout their professional career.

ACKNOWLEDGMENTS

The writing of this text book was a mammoth task for which a lot of help was required from many people. Fortunately, I have had the fine support of my family, friends and fellow members of the teaching staff at the Shyama Prasad Mukherji College.

My special thanks would always go to my father Late Sh. Janak Raj Thareja, my mother Smt. Usha Thareja, my brother Pallav and sisters Kimi and Rashi who were a source of abiding inspiration and are a divine blessing for me. I am especially indebted to my son Goransh, who has been very patient and cooperative in letting me realize my dreams. I am obliged to my uncle Mr B L Theraja for his inspiration and guidance in writing this book.

Last but not the least, my acknowledgements will always be incomplete if I do not thank the team at Universities Press (India) Private Limited that gave me this brilliant opportunity to utilize my writing skills.

Reema Thareja
reema_thareja@yahoo.com

About the Author

Reema Thareja is Assistant Professor at Shyama Prasad Mukherji College, University of Delhi. She has over 15 years of experience, teaching computer science for various courses including BA, BSc, MSc, BBA, MBA, BCA and MCA. She has authored several books, including those on Computer Fundamentals, C Programming, OOPS with C++, Data Structures, Data Warehousing and Python Programming, which are well-accepted across the globe. She has also written books on Data Science and Machine Learning in R for the current academic session.

Dr Thareja has published 17 research papers in journals of national and international repute. In addition, she has got the acceptance for four more papers. A recipient of 64 Google Scholar Citations, she has launched a Computer Science Learning and Quizzing mobile app, Jruma, for both Android and iOS devices.

A recipient of the Nobel Laureate Maria Goeppert–Mayer Inspiring Woman of the Year 2021 Award in the field of Computer Science by International Multi-disciplinary Research Foundation (IMRF), Dr Thareja was also among "India's Top 50 Women Leaders in the Education Industry" recognized by uLektz Wall of Fame for the year 2020. She has conducted several faculty development programs, student workshops and webinars in India and the US, and participated in the International Dialogue on Empowered Future – Women's Role on the eve of International Women's Day 2021.

A member of the Computer Society of India and Editorial Board and Keynote Speaker of the IMRF Conference Board, Dr Thareja is a skilled motivator who helps students utilize their untapped skills and reinvent themselves. She was recently conferred with the Knowledge Mobilization Award at the Seventh Annual Research Awards event organized by Shri Param Hans Education and Research Trust and has been invited as a speaker for the Global Virtual Summit to be held in New York this summer.

Introduction to Python Pandas

Chapter Objectives

In class XI, we discussed the basic concepts of programming language Python. We studied about some vital data structures like strings, lists, tuples and dictionaries. We also learnt about NumPy arrays that are far more flexible than Python lists. Although all these data structures are very useful to write solutions for real-world applications, the best thing about Python is that its capabilities do not end here. Therefore, in this chapter we will read about some more exciting features that make Python a perfect language for data sciences.

- Basics of arrays
- Creating and manipulating data stored in NumPy arrays
- Methods supported by NumPy arrays
- Introduction to Pandas data frame and series
- Creating and working on series objects
- Methods and functions supported on Pandas series object
- Creating, accessing and manipulating data stored in a data frame
- Mathematical operations on a data frame
- Matching/ broadcasting, combining and comparing data frames
- Dealing with missing values
- Boolean reductions
- Descriptive statistics and statistical functions for summarizing data
- Row- or column-wise application of functions

1.1 INTRODUCTION TO DATA HANDLINING USING PYTHON

Python is a very powerful language and it is increasingly being used for scientific applications. Matrix and vector manipulations which involve storing and analyzing data in single as well as well as multi-dimensional arrays form the backbone of scientific computations. Both NumPy and Pandas are essential libraries for applications including machine learning and data sciences due to their extensive functionalities that support high-performance matrix computation.

Pandas stands for "Python Data Analysis Library". It is an open-source, free-to-use (under a BSD (Berkeley Source Distribution) license) module that was originally written by Wes McKinney. Pandas takes data (like a CSV (comma-separated values) or TSV (tab-separated values) file, or an SQL (Structured Query Language) database and creates a Python object with rows and columns called data frame. You can think of a data frame as a table in any statistical software (like Excel or SPSS).

NumPy stands for 'Numerical Python' or 'Numeric Python'. It is an open-source module of Python which provides fast mathematical computation on arrays and matrices. NumPy, along with other modules like Scikit-learn, Pandas, Matplotlib, TensorFlow, etc., complete the Python Machine Learning Ecosystem. In this chapter, we will learn about NumPy and Pandas modules that are extensively used for data handling in Python.

1.2 INTRODUCTION TO ARRAYS, 2-D ARRAYS (OR MATRICES) AND *N*-D ARRAYS

Before getting into the details of Pandas and Numpy modules, let us first understand that basic terminology that will be frequently used in this chapter.

1.2.1 One-dimensional Arrays

To realize the need of an array, consider a situation in which there are 20 students in a class. We have been asked to write a program that reads and prints the marks of all these 20 students. In this program we will need 20 integer variables with different names, as shown in Fig. 1.1.

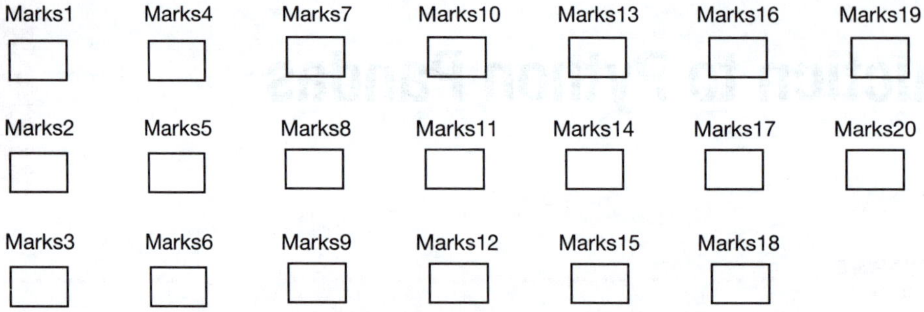

```
Marks1    Marks4    Marks7    Marks10   Marks13   Marks16   Marks19
 □          □         □          □         □         □         □

Marks2    Marks5    Marks8    Marks11   Marks14   Marks17   Marks20
 □          □         □          □         □         □         □

Marks3    Marks6    Marks9    Marks12   Marks15   Marks18
 □          □         □          □         □         □
```

Figure 1.1 Twenty variables

As per the figure, Marks1 will store marks obtained by the first student, Marks2 will store marks obtained by second student, and so on. Now, to read values for these twenty variables, we must have twenty `read` statements. Similarly, to print the value of these variables, we need 20 `write` statements. If it is just a matter of 20 variables, then it might be acceptable for the user to follow this approach. But, imagine if it will be possible to follow this approach to read and print marks of the students

- in the entire course (say 100 students)
- in the entire college (say 500 students)
- in the entire university (say 10000 students).

The answer is No, definitely not. To process large amount of data, we need a data structure known as **array**.

An array is a collection of similar data elements. These data elements have the same data type. The elements of the array are stored in consecutive memory locations and are referenced by an index (also known as the subscript). The subscript indicates an ordinal number of the element, counting from the beginning of the array.

The array index starts from zero. Consider an array of 10 elements named marks that contains 10 elements in all. The first element will be stored at 0th index and accessed as marks[0], second element at 1st index to be accessed as marks[1], and so on. Note that 0, 1, 2, 3, etc., written within square brackets, are subscripts/index. An array can thus be thought of a group of elements placed in consecutive memory locations as shown in Fig. 1.2.

1st element	2nd element	3rd element	4th element	5th element	6th element	7th element	8th element	9th element	10th element
marks[0]	marks[1]	marks[2]	marks[3]	marks[4]	marks[5]	marks[6]	marks[7]	marks[8]	marks[9]

Figure 1.2 Memory representation of an array of 10 elements

Storing the related data items in a single array enables the programmers to develop concise and efficient programs.

1.2.2 Matrices or Two-dimensional Arrays

Continuing with our problem of storing marks, imagine that we have to store marks obtained by 20 students in 5 different subjects. The problem has added one more dimension – marks in different subjects. Initially, we had one set of marks for different students. Now both parameters are different – five sets of marks for 20 sets of students.

We have read that a one-dimensional array is organized linearly in only one direction. But at times, we need to store data in the form of matrices or tables. In such situations, the concept of single-dimension arrays is extended to incorporate two-dimensional data structures. A two-dimensional array is specified using two subscripts where one subscript denotes row and the other denotes column. You may think of a two-dimensional array as an array of a one-dimensional arrays.

As evident from Fig. 1.3, a two-dimensional $m \times n$ array can store $m*n$ data elements, where m is the number of rows and n is the number of columns. Each element is accessed using two subscripts, i and j where $i<=m$ and $j<=n$, where m is the number of rows and n is the number of columns.

Introduction to Python Pandas

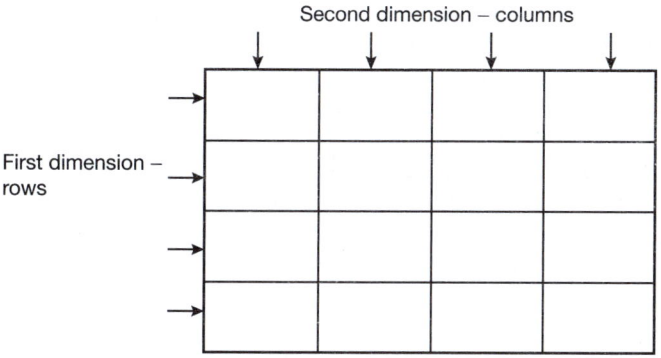

Figure 1.3 Structure of a two-dimensional matrix

In a 2-D array or a matrix named marks, the first element is denoted by marks[0][0], the second element as marks[0][1], and so on. Here, marks[0][0] stores the marks obtained by the first student in the first subject, marks[1][0], stores the marks obtained by the second student in the first subject.

The pictorial form of a two-dimensional array is given in Fig 1.4.

Rows/Columns	Col 0	Col 1	Col2	Col 3	Col 4
Row 0	Marks[0][0]	Marks[0][1]	Marks[0][2]	Marks[0][3]	Marks[0][4]
Row 1	Marks[1][0]	Marks[1][1]	Marks[1][2]	Marks[1][3]	Marks[1][4]
Row 2	Marks[2][0]	Marks[2][1]	Marks[2][2]	Marks[2][3]	Marks[2][4]

Figure 1.4 Elements in a two-dimensional array

Hence, we see that a 2D array is treated as a collection of 1D array. To understand this better, we can also represent the two-dimensional array as shown in Fig 1.5.

Marks[0]	Marks[0]	Marks[1]	Marks[2]	Marks[3]	Marks[4]
Marks[1]	Marks[0]	Marks[1]	Marks[2]	Marks[3]	Marks[4]
Marks[2]	Marks[0]	Marks[1]	Marks[2]	Marks[3]	Marks[4]
Marks[3]	Marks[0]	Marks[1]	Marks[2]	Marks[3]	Marks[4]

Figure 1.5 Two-dimensional array is an array of one-dimensional arrays

Row-major and Column-major Way of Representing Matrices

Although we have shown a rectangular picture of a two-dimensional array, in computer memory these elements are stored sequentially. There are two ways of storing a two-dimensional array in memory. The first way is row-major order and the second is column-major order.

Let us first see how the elements of a 2D array are stored in a row-major order. Here, the elements of the first row are stored before the elements of the second and third row. That is, the elements of the array are stored row by row where n elements of the first row will occupy the first n locations. This is illustrated in Fig 1.6.

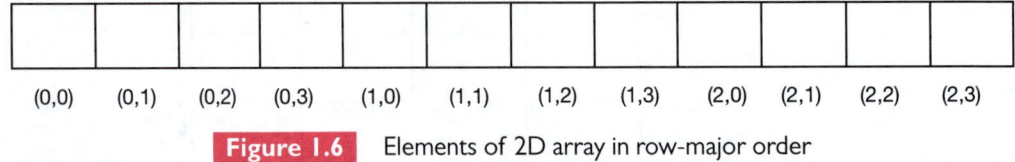

Figure 1.6   Elements of 2D array in row-major order

However, when we store the elements in a column-major order, the elements of the first column are stored before the elements of the second and third column. That is, the elements of the array are stored column by column where n elements of the first column will occupy the first n locations. This is illustrated in Fig 1.7.

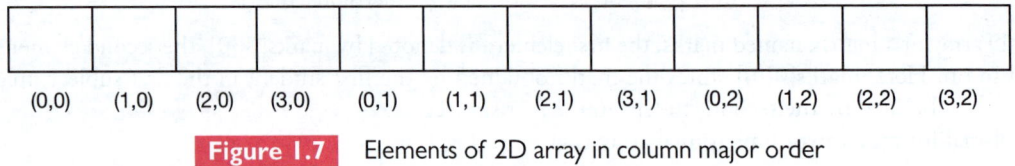

Figure 1.7   Elements of 2D array in column major order

1.2.3 Multi-dimensional Arrays

A multi-dimensional array, in simple terms, is an array of arrays. Just as we have one index in a single-dimensional array and two indices in a two-dimensional array, we have n indices in an n-dimensional array or multi-dimensional array. Conversely, an n-dimensional array is specified using n indices. An n-dimensional $m_1 \times m_2 \times m_3 \times \ldots m_n$ array is a collection of $m_1 * m_2 * m_3 * \ldots * m_n$ elements.

In a multi-dimensional array, a particular element is specified by using n subscripts as $A[I_1][I_2][I_3]\ldots[I_n]$, where, $I_1 <= M_1$ $I_2 <= M_2$ $I_3 <= M_3$ $\ldots\ldots$ $I_n <= M_n$

Here, $M_1, M_2, \ldots, M_n$ are the maximum elements permissible in that dimension. A multi-dimensional array can contain as many indices as needed and the requirement of the memory increases with the number of indices used. However, practically speaking, we will hardly use more than three indices in any program. Figure 1.8 shows a three-dimensional array. The array has three pages, four rows and two columns.

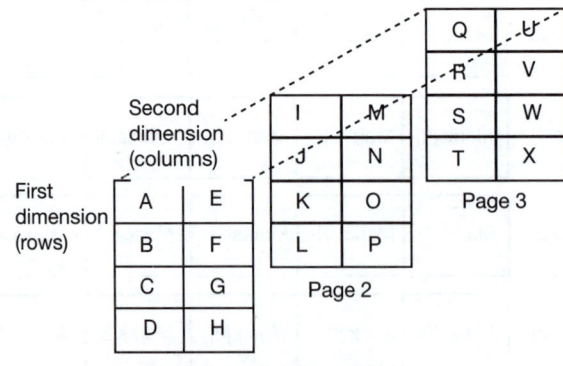

Figure 1.8   Three-dimensional matrix

Note that a multi-dimensional array is declared and initialized similar to how we declare and initialize one- and two-dimensional arrays.

Example 1.1   Consider a three-dimensional array defined as int A[2][3][2]. Calculate the number of elements in the array. Also give the memory representation of the array in row-major order and column-major order.

Note: A three-dimensional array consists of pages. Each page, in turn, contains m rows and n columns.

(a) Row-major Order

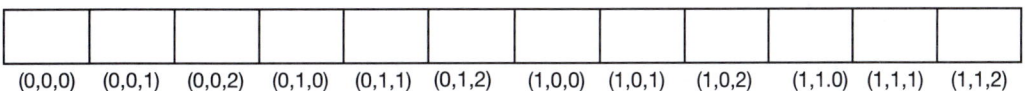

(0,0,0) (0,0,1) (0,0,2) (0,1,0) (0,1,1) (0,1,2) (1,0,0) (1,0,1) (1,0,2) (1,1.0) (1,1,1) (1,1,2)

(b) Column-major Order

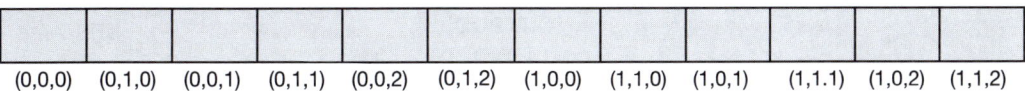

(0,0,0) (0,1,0) (0,0,1) (0,1,1) (0,0,2) (0,1,2) (1,0,0) (1,1,0) (1,0,1) (1,1,1) (1,0,2) (1,1,2)

Note that in our 3-D array, there are 2*3*2 = 12 elements

1.3 INTRODUCTION TO NUMPY MODULE

NumPy module contains a rich collection of essential functions that support computations on multi-dimensional arrays. When using NumPy, you must remember the following points.

- To use this module, we must first import it by writing, import numpy as np.
- NumPy is mainly used for creating homogeneous multi-dimensional arrays. Homogeneous means elements of same data type.
- In NumPy, dimensions are called axes.
- Number of axes is called the rank.

1.3.1 Creating NumPy Arrays

There are several ways to create an array in NumPy, such as np.array, np.zeros, no.ones, etc. Each of them provides some flexibility. Some important methods to create NumPy array are given in Table 1.1.

Table 1.1 Methods to create NumPy arrays

Function	Description	Example	Remarks
np.array	np.array is a function that allows users to create an array of elements supplied as an argument.	import numpy as np a = np.array([1,2,3]) b = np.array((5,6,7)) print(a) print(b) **OUTPUT** [1 2 3] [1 2 3] [5 6 7]	a is an array of a list of integers b is an array of a tuple of integers Likewise, we can have an array of elements that belong to other data types
np.ones	Creates a matrix of specified data type and shape (or size) filled with ones.	import numpy as np a = np.ones((4,5), dtype=np.int16) print(a) **OUTPUT** [[1 1 1 1 1] [1 1 1 1 1] [1 1 1 1 1] [1 1 1 1 1]]	a is a two-dimensional array with 4 rows and 5 columns. All elements in this array are 1.

Table 1.1 (Continued)

Table 1.1 Continued

Function	Description	Example	Remarks

`np.zeros`	Creates a matrix of specified data type and shape (or size) filled with ones.	`import numpy as np`
		`a = np.zeros((4,5), dtype=np.int16)`
		`print(a)`
		OUTPUT
		`[[0 0 0 0 0]`
		` [0 0 0 0 0]`
		` [0 0 0 0 0]`
		` [0 0 0 0 0]]`
			a is a two-dimensional array with 4 rows and 5 columns. All elements in this array are 0.

`np.full`	Returns a new array with the specified size and type. It also fills the array with specified value.	`import numpy as np`
		`a = np.full((3,2), 2.3)`
		`print(a)`
		OUTPUT
		`[[2.3 2.3]`
		` [2.3 2.3]`
		` [2.3 2.3]]`
			a is a two-dimensional array with 3 rows and 2 columns. All elements in this array have value 2.3.

`np.arange`	Returns an array with evenly spaced elements from the interval specified by the value of start and stop in the gap of step.	`import numpy as np`
		`a = np.arange(5,50,5)`
		`print(a)`
		OUTPUT
		`[ 5 10 15 20 25 30 35 40 45]`
			The syntax is: `numpy.arange([start, ] stop, [step, ], dtype=None)` Here, a is a one-dimensional array with elements from 5 to 50 in steps of 5.

`np.linspace`	Returns evenly spaced numbers over the specified interval. It is similar to arrange function but it uses the number instead of the step as an interval.	`import numpy as np`
		`a = np.linspace(1,2/3,4)`
		`print(a)`
		OUTPUT
		`[1. 0.91666667 0.83333333 0.75]`
			The syntax is: `numpy.linspace(start, stop, num, endpoint=True, retstep=False, dtype=None)`. Here, num specifies the number of values to generate.

`np.random.rand`	Creates an array of specified shape and fills it with random values.	`import numpy as np`
		`a = np.random.rand(3,2)`
		`print(a)`
		OUTPUT
		`[[0.46632055 0.19445536]`
		` [0.93474084 0.70868838]`
		` [0.18377336 0.55481711]]`
			a is a two-dimensional array with 3 rows and 2 columns. To specify a 3D array, we need to give three values within the function.

Table 1.1 (*Continued*)

Table 1.1 Continued

Function	Description	Example	Remarks

`np.empty`	Returns a new array of given shape and type, filled with random values.	`import numpy as np`
		`a = np.empty((3,2))`
		`print(a)`
		OUTPUT
		`[[ 4.35009137e-313`
		`0.00000000e+000]`
		`[ 2.71827661e-311`
		`4.46033568e-313]`
		`[-1.68577438e-037`
		`2.12510837e-311]]`
			a is a two-dimenional array with three rows and two columns filled with random values.

1.3.2 Attributes of NumPy Array

Some of the important attributes of a NumPy array are:
Ndim: displays the dimension of the array
Shape: returns a tuple of integers indicating the size of the array
Size: returns the total number of elements in the NumPy array
Dtype: returns the type of elements in the array, i.e., int64, character
Itemsize: returns the size in bytes of each item
Reshape: Reshapes the NumPy array

> The `head()` and `tail()` methods are used to view a small sample of a Series or the DataFrame object.

Example 1.2

```
import numpy as np
a = np.empty((5,3))
print("The Array is : \n",a)
print("Number of Dimensions in a : ",np.ndim(a))
print("Shape of a : ",np.shape(a))
print("Dtype of a : ",np.Itemsize(a))
```

OUTPUT
```
The Array is :
 [[6.23042070e-307 3.56043053e-307 1.60219306e-306]
 [2.44763557e-307 1.69119330e-306 1.33514617e-307]
 [3.56043053e-307 1.37961641e-306 8.06613040e-308]
 [1.24610383e-306 1.69118108e-306 8.06632139e-308]
 [1.20160711e-306 1.69119330e-306 1.39234638e+188]]
Number of Dimensions in a :  2
Shape of a :   (5, 3)
```

1.3.3 The `head()` and `tail()` Methods of NumPy Array

`head()` and `tail()` are two very frequently used methods of the NumPy array object.
head(n): Returns the first *n* rows. If the value of *n* is not specified then, by default, the first 5 rows will be displayed.
tail(n): Returns the last *n* rows. If the value of *n* is not specified then, by default, the first 5 rows will be displayed.

Example 1.3

```
import numpy as np
import pandas as pd
#Create a series with 10 random numbers
S = pd.Series(np.random.randn(10))
print("The original series is : ")
print(S)
print ("The first four rows of the data series :")
print(S.head(4))
print ("The last four rows of the data series : ")
print(S.tail(4))
```

OUTPUT

```
The original series is :
0    0.867655
1    0.989083
2    0.460942
3    0.612183
4   -1.084612
5    0.959498
6    0.110584
7   -0.881249
8    2.333609
9    1.372371
dtype: float64
The first four rows of the data series :
0    0.867655
1    0.989083
2    0.460942
3    0.612183
dtype: float64
The last four rows of the data series :
6    0.110584
7   -0.881249
8    2.333609
9    1.372371
dtype: float64
```

1.3.4 Accessing NumPy Arrays

NumPy array elements can be accessed using indices. For example,
Arr[3:6] will print elements from index 3 to 6. Index in an array starts from 0.
Arr[1::2] will print every second element from index items 1 to the end.
Arr[::-1] will print the array in the reverse order
Arr[4:] will print from index 4 to the end.

1.4 STARTING WITH PANDAS

Before using this module, it must first be installed. Once installed, the module can be imported through the Python script. Importing a module means loading it in memory for using its functionalities.

Pandas can be imported by writing **import pandas as pd**. To use any function from this module, we will write **pd.command**. Pandas deals with the following three data structures – Series, DataFrame and Panel. However, in this book, we will read only about Series and DataFrame. These data structures are built on top of NumPy array.

The best way to think of data structures is that higher dimensional data structure is a container of lower dimensional data structure. For example, a DataFrame may contain data of Series, Panel or another DataFrame. The features of these popular data structures can be summarized as given in Table 1.2.

Table 1.2 Popular data structures supported by Pandas

Data Structure	Dimensions	Description	Size mutable	Data Mutable
Series	1	1D homogeneous array.	No	Yes
Data Frames	2	2D array. Tabular structure with potentially heterogeneously typed columns.	Yes	Yes
Panel	3	3D array.	Yes	Yes

Creating and manipulating 2D or more dimensional arrays is a tedious task. But using Pandas data structures, the mental effort of the user is reduced.

All Pandas data structures are mutable. This means that their values can be changed. However, Series is an exception since it is immutable.

> DataFrame is widely used and one of the most important data structures. Panel is used much less.

Example of a Series Data

69	98	75	80	91	55	87	94	99	84

A good example is a series containing marks obtained by 10 students in a class.

Example of Data Frame: Given below is a data frame object that stores details of toppers. Note that we have both numbers and strings in the data frame. This indicates that a data frame object can store heterogeneous type of data. The data is represented in rows and columns. Each column represents an attribute and each row represents a student. Attributes of the student are RollNo., Name, Class and Marks.

Roll No.	Name	Class	Marks
001	Shreya	X-C	97
002	Anurag	XI-E	98
003	Priya	XII-A	100

1.5 SERIES

Series, in Python, is a one-dimensional array that can store data of any type (integer, string, float, python objects, etc.). A pandas Series can be created using the following constructor:

`pandas.Series( data, index, dtype, copy)`

where,
data can be a list of values, an ndarray, or constants
index values must be unique and hashable. It is of the same length as data. Pandas allows users to have non-unique index values. However, if no index is specified, then index values 0, 1, 2, 3, …, n are provided.

dtype specifies data type.
copy means to copy data. By default, its value is False.

1.5.1 Creating Series

A series can be created using various inputs like Array, Dict or Scalar values (or constant values).

1.5.2 Create an Empty Series

To create a basic empty series, the `pd.Series()` function is used without passing any arguments to it.

Example 1.4

```
#import the pandas library and aliasing as pd
import pandas as pd
S = pd.Series()
print(S)
```

OUTPUT
```
Series([], dtype: float64)
```

1.5.3 Create a Series from `ndarray`

If a series is created using an `ndarray`, then index passed must be of the same length. If no index is passed, then, by default, index will be of range(*n*) where *n* is array length, i.e., [0,1,2,3.... range(len(array))–1].

In the code given in Example 1.4, we did not pass any index. So by default, the output has indices ranging from 0 to len(data)–1, i.e., 0 to 4. We can even explicitly specify indices in the output as shown in the code given in Example 1.5.

Example 1.5

```
# Default Index
#import the pandas library and aliasing as pd
import pandas as pd
import numpy as np
data = np.array(['H','E','L','L','O'])
S = pd.Series(data)
print(S)
```

OUTPUT
```
0    H
1    E
2    L
3    L
4    O
dtype: object
```

Example 1.6

```
# Customized Index
#import the pandas library and aliasing as pd
import pandas as pd
import numpy as np
data = np.array(['H','E','L','L','O'])
S = pd.Series(data, index = ['a','b','c','d','e'])
print(S)
```

OUTPUT
```
a    H
b    E
c    L
d    L
e    O
dtype: object
```

1.5.4 Create a Series from `dict`

We can create a Series using a `dict` object that is passed as an input to `pd.Series()` function. If no index is specified, then the dictionary keys are taken in a sorted order to construct index. Otherwise, the values in data corresponding to the labels in the index will be used.

Example 1.7

```
#import the pandas library and aliasing as pd
import pandas as pd
import numpy as np
data = {'A' : 10, 'B' : 20, 'C' : 30, 'D' : 40}
S = pd.Series(data)
print(S)
```

OUTPUT
```
A    10
B    20
C    30
D    40
dtype: int64
```

Example 1.8

```
#import the pandas library and aliasing as pd
import pandas as pd
import numpy as np
data = {'A' : 10, 'B' : 20, 'C' : 30, 'D' : 40}
S = pd.Series(data, index = ['C','A','D','B'])
print(S)
```

OUTPUT
```
C    30
A    10
D    40
B    20
dtype: int64
```

1.5.5 Create a Series from Scalar

When we create a Series using scalar values, an index must be provided. The specified value will then be repeated to match the length of the index.

Example 1.9

```
#import the pandas library and aliasing as pd
import pandas as pd
import numpy as np
S = pd.Series(10, index=[1, 3, 5, 7])
print(S)
```

OUTPUT
```
1    10
3    10
5    10
7    10
dtype: int64
```

> If we add an index in a dictionary for which a key does not exist, then NaN (Not a Number) will be associated with that index.

1.6 ACCESSING DATA FROM SERIES WITH POSITION

Data in the series can be accessed similar to that in an `ndarray`. The counting of index starts from zero, which means the first element is stored at zeroth position and so on.

To retrieve the **first n** elements in the Series, we use the notation **n:**.

To retrieve values from the middle of a series, use the notation **m:n**. This extracts elements from index *m* onwards till the index *n* (not including *n*).

To retrieve values from the end of the series, we use the notation **–n:**.

Python allows users to access Series data using not only indices but also by using labels of indices. However, if the specified label is not contained in the Series object, then a KeyError exception is raised.

> If the specified label does not exist in the Series, then KeyError is raised.

Example 1.10

```
#Accessing Series elements using index
#import the pandas library and aliasing as pd
import pandas as pd
import numpy as np
data = {'A' : 10, 'B' : 20, 'C' : 30, 'D' : 40, 'E' : 50, 'F' : 60, 'G' : 70}
S = pd.Series(data)
print("First Element : ",S[0])         # print the first element
print("First Three Elements : \n", S[:3])     # prints first three elements
print("Last Three Elements : \n", S[-3:])     # prints last three elements
print("Second to fourth elements : \n", S[2:5]) # prints second, thrid, fourth elements
```

OUTPUT

```
First Element :  10
First Three Elements :
A    10
B    20
C    30
dtype: int64
Last Three Elements :
E    50
F    60
G    70
dtype: int64
Second to fourth elements :
C    30
D    40
E    50
dtype: int64
```

Example 1.11

```
# Accessing Series elements using Label Value
#import the pandas library and aliasing as pd
import pandas as pd
import numpy as np
#data = {'A' : 10, 'B' : 20, 'C' : 30, 'D' : 40, 'E' : 50, 'F' : 60, 'G' : 70}
S = pd.Series([10,20,30,40,50,60,70], index = ['I','II','III','IV','V','VI','VII'])
print("S[V] = ", S['V'])
print("Multiple Values - II, IV, VI : \n ", S[['II','IV','VI']])
```

OUTPUT

```
S[V] =  50
Multiple Values - II, IV, VI :
II    20
IV    40
VI    60
dtype: int64
```

1.7 SERIES OBJECT ATTRIBUTES

Like any other Python object, Series object also has certain attributes to store information like size, datatype. etc. Table 1.3 given below lists some of the attributes that can be used to get the information about the Series object.

> NaN is Pandas' way to represent missing values.

Table 1.3   Attributes of a series object

Attributes	Description	Example
`Series.index`	Returns an index array of the Series data.	```import pandas as pd```
`Series.name`	Used to assign a name for both the data and the indices.	```import numpy as np``` ```S = pd.Series([10,20,30,40,50,60,70,np.NaN], index = ['I','II','III','IV','V','VI','VII','VIII'])```
`Series.values`	Returns an array that has values present in the Series data.	```print("VALUES = ",S.values)``` ```print("INDEX = ",S.index)```

`Series.shape`	Returns a tuple specifying total number of elements including missing or empty values(NaN).	```print("DATA TYPE = ", S.dtype)```
		 ```print("SIZE = ", S.size)```
		 ```print("SHAPE = ", S.shape)```
		 ```print("Dimensions = ", S.ndim)```

`Series.dtype`	Returns the datatype of the data. You can use attribute dtype with Series object as `<objectname> dtype`.	```print("No. of Bytes = ",S.nbytes)```
		 ```print("Is Empty ? ", S.empty)```
		 ```print("Has NaN? ", S.hasnans)```
		 ```S.name = 'My Series'```
		 ```S.index.name = 'Scale'```
		 ```print("After Renaminh S : \n", S)```

`Series.size`	Returns the size or number of elements in Series data.	**OUTPUT** VALUES = [10. 20. 30. 40. 50. 60. 70. nan]
`Series.empty`	Returns True if Series object is empty and False otherwise.	INDEX = Index(['I', 'II', 'III', 'IV', 'V', 'VI', 'VII', 'VIII'], dtype='object')
`Series.hasnans`	Returns True if there are any NaN values and False otherwise.	DATA TYPE = float64 SIZE = 8
`Series.nbytes`	Returns the number of bytes in the data.	SHAPE = (8,) Dimensions = 1 No. of Bytes = 64
`Series.ndim`	Returns the number of dimensions in the data.	Is Empty ? False Has NaN? True After Renaminh S : Scale I 10.0 II 20.0 III 30.0 IV 40.0 V 50.0 VI 60.0 VII 70.0 VIII NaN Name: My Series, dtype: float64

1.8 THE in AND not in OPERATORS WITH PYTHON SERIES

As with any other Python object, the `in` operator can be used with Series object to check whether a particular index exists in the object or not. The `in` operator returns True if the index is present and False otherwise. Similarly, the `not in` operator returns True if the index is not present and False otherwise.

Example 1.12

```
import pandas as pd
import numpy as np
data = {'A': 10, 'B': 20, 'C': 30, 'D': 40, 'E': 50, 'F':60, 'G': 70}
S = pd.Series(data)
print("E in S : ",'E' in S)
print("J in S : ",'J' in S)
print("E not in S : ",'E' not in S)
print("J not in S : ",'J' not in S)
```

OUTPUT

```
E in S : True
J in S : False
E not in S : False
J not in S : True
```

1.9 PYTHON SERIES NULLS

The Pandas module has `isnull()` and `notnull()` functions to check if any of the data value in the Series object has a Null value (denoted by NaN). These functions return a Boolean value – True or False.

The `isnull()` function returns True is a particular value is null and False otherwise. The `notnull()` function returns True if the element has any other value except null and False otherwise.

Example 1.13

```
import pandas as pd
import numpy as np
data = {'A': 10, 'B': 20, 'C': 30, 'D': np.NaN, 'E': 50, 'F':60, 'G': 70}
S = pd.Series(data)
print("isnull S? ", S.isnull())
print("isnotnull S? ", S.notnull())
```

OUTPUT

```
isnull S?  A    False
B    False
C    False
D    True
E    False
F    False
G    False
dtype: bool
isnotnull S? A True
B    True
C    True
D    False
E    True
F    True
G    True
dtype: bool
```

1.10 THE `all()` FUNCTION

The `all()` function is used to check whether all elements in the Series object are True.

Example 1.14

```
import numpy as np
import pandas as pd
print(pd.Series([True, True]).all())
print(pd.Series([False, True]).all())
print(pd.Series([]).all())
print(pd.Series([np.nan]).all())
print(pd.Series([np.nan]).all(skipna=False))
```

OUTPUT

```
True
False
True
True
True
```

1.11 ARITHMETIC OPERATIONS ON PYTHON SERIES

Arithmetic operations can be performed on data stored in Series object. We can add, subtract, multiply or divide a scalar value with a Series object. The operation will be individually applied on items of the Series object. We can also perform these operations on two or more series objects.

We can also use mathematical functions to perform tasks like finding the exponent, square root and absolute value of items that form a part of the Series object. Functions like sqrt, exp, fabs, etc are supported by the NumPy module.

Example 1.15

```
data = pd.Series([1,-2,3,-4])
print(data)
print(data + 5)
print(data- 3)
print(data * 10)
print(data/ 2)
print(data > 0)
```

OUTPUT

```
0    1
1   -2
2    3
3   -4
dtype: int64
0    6
1    3
2    8
3    1
dtype: int64
0   -2
1   -5
2    0
3   -7
dtype: int64
0    10
1   -20
2    30
3   -40
dtype: int64
0    0.5
1   -1.0
2    1.5
3   -2.0
dtype: float64
0     True
1    False
2     True
3    False
dtype: bool
```

Example 1.16

```
import pandas as pd
import numpy as np
data = pd.Series([1,-2,3,-4])
print(data)
print("EXP FUNCTION")
print(np.exp(data))
print("FABS FUNCTION")
print(np.fabs(data))
print("SQRT FUNCTION")
print(np.sqrt(data))
```

OUTPUT
```
0    1
1   -2
2    3
3   -4
dtype: int64
EXP FUNCTION
0     2.718282
1     0.135335
2    20.085537
3     0.018316
dtype: float64
FABS FUNCTION
0    1.0
1    2.0
2    3.0
3    4.0
dtype: float64
SQRT FUNCTION
0    1.000000
1         NaN
2    1.732051
3         NaN
dtype: float64
```

1.12 FILTER DATA

We can filter data values of a Series object by listing specific indices whose value(s) have to be displayed.

Example 1.17

```
import pandas as pd
import numpy as np
data = pd.Series([1,-2,3,-4])
print(data[data>0])
```

OUTPUT
```
0    1
2    3
dtype: int64
```

Example 1.18

```
import pandas as pd
import numpy as np
data = pd.Series([10,20,30,40,50], index = ['a','b','c','d','e'])
i = ['a','c','e']
for x in i:
    print(data[x])
```

OUTPUT
10 30 50

1.13 SOME MORE SERIES FUNCTIONS

get() method: The get() method is used to return the value associated with a specified label. If the label does not exist in the Series object then None or the default value is returned.

rename() method: The pandas.Series.rename() method is used to rename a series.

Example 1.19

```
# get method
import pandas as pd
import numpy as np
S = pd.Series([10,20,30,40,50,60,70,np.NaN], index =
['I','II','III','IV','V','VI','VII','VIII'])
print('S[III] =', S.get('III'))
print('S[VIII] =', S.get('VIII'))
 print('S[IX] =', S.get('IX'))
print('S[IX] =', S.get('IX', 'NA'))
```

OUTPUT
```
S[lll] = 30.0
S[VIII] = nan
S[IX]= None
S[IX]= NA
```

Example 1.20

```
# rename() method
import pandas as pd
import numpy as np
S = pd.Series([10,20,30,40,50,60,70,np.NaN], index
['I','II','III','IV','V','VI','VII','VIII'])
S.name = 'My Series'
print('Series Name = ',S.name)
S= S.rename('The same old Series')
 print('Series Name = ',S.name)
```

OUTPUT
```
Series Name = My Series
Series Name = The same old Series
```

There are some important functions that make Series a powerful data structure. Table 1.4, given below, lists some of them.

Table 1.4 Miscellaneous methods used with Pandas object

Functions	Description
Pandas Series.map()	Map the values from two series that have a common column.
Pandas Series.std()	Calculate the standard deviation of the given set of numbers, dataframe, column, and rows.
Pandas Series.to_frame()	Convert the series object to the dataframe.
Pandas Series.value_counts()	Returns a Series that contain counts of unique values.

1.14 PANDAS SERIES VS. PYTHON LIST

From the above discussion, we can conclude that a list differs from a Series data structure in the following ways.
- Series has homogeneous elements. List may have data values of same or different types.
- Series have labelled indices that can be customized. This is not possible in a Python list.

1.15 DATA FRAME

A data frame is a two-dimensional data structure in which data is organized in a tabular fashion using rows and columns. The basic features of data frame are as follows:

- Columns are of different data types.
- Size is mutable.
- Data frame has labelled axes for rows and columns.
- Arithmetic operations can be performed on rows and columns.

1.15.1 Creating a Data Frame

A Pandas DataFrame can be created by using the pandas.DataFrame function. The syntax of this function can be given as,

pandas.DataFrame(data, index, columns, dtype, copy)

where,
data can be an ndarray, series, map, lists, dictionay, constants or any other data frame.
index denotes the row labels for the resulting frame. It is optional argument. By default, if no index is passed, then its value will be equal to np.arange(n).
column is used for specifying column labels. It is an optional argument. By default, its value is - np.arange(n), if no index is passed.
dtype specifies the data type of each column.
copy is used for copying of data, if the default is False.

Some examples of creating a data frame are given below.

Example 1.21

```
# Creating empty Dataframe
import numpy as np
import pandas as pd
import pandas as pd
df = pd.DataFrame()
print(df)
```

OUTPUT

```
Empty DataFrame
Columns: []
Index: []
```

Example 1.22

```
# Creating a Dataframe from a List
import numpy as np
import pandas as pd
import pandas as pd
data = [1,2,3,4,5]
df = pd.DataFrame(data)
print(df)
```

OUTPUT

```
    0
0   1
1   2
2   3
3   4
4   5
```

Example 1.23

```
# Creating Data From a List of Lists
import numpy as np
import pandas as pd
import pandas as pd
data = [1,['a',3],4,[5,'b'],7]
df = pd.DataFrame(data)
print(df)
```

OUTPUT

```
    0
0   1
1   [a, 3]
2   4
3   [5, b]
4   7
```

1.15.2 Creating Data Frame from Dictionary

We can also create a data frame from a dictionary containing ndarrays or lists. But when doing so, remember that all the ndarrays must be of same length. Moreover, if an index is passed, then the length of the index should be equal to the length of the arrays. In case no index is passed, then by default, index will be range(n), where n is the array length.

Key points to remember

To access a column of this data frame we just use the notation, *data_frame_object['column_name']*.

To add a column to the data frame, use the notation, *data_frame_object[key] = value*.

To delete a column from the data frame, we can either use the `del` statement by writing *del data_frame_object['column-name']* or using the `pop()` method by writing *data_frame_object.pop('key')*.

To access a particular row from the data frame using label or column name, we can use the `loc()` method. It is used by writing *data_frame_object.loc['row-name']*.

To access a particular row from the data frame, we can even pass an integer location to an **iloc** method by writing *data_frame_object.iloc[row-number]*.

To access multiple rows from a data frame, use the selection operator (:) by writing *data_frame_object.iloc[starting-row-number : ending-row-number]*.

To add new rows at the end of a data frame, use the `append()` function.

To delete or drop rows from a data frame, the `drop()` method is used. We can specify a row label or index in the `drop()` method. If a label is duplicated, then multiple rows will be dropped.

PROGRAMMER'S ZONE

1. **Write a program that creates a data frame storing names and marks of students using a list of lists. Give relevant names to the columns.**

```
import numpy as np
import pandas as pd
import pandas as pd
data = [['Ananya',67],['Nayonika',76],['Paras',91]]
df = pd.DataFrame(data, columns = ['NAME','AGGREGATE'])
print(df)
```

OUTPUT
```
       NAME  AGGREGATE
0    Ananya         67
1  Nayonika         76
2     Paras         91
```

2. **Write a program that creates a data frame from a dictionary of ndarrays and lists.**

```
import numpy as np
import pandas as pd
import pandas as pd
data = {'NAME' : ['Ananya','Shreya','Priya'],'MARKS':[98,76,45]}
df = pd.DataFrame(data)
print(df)
```

OUTPUT
```
     NAME  MARKS
0  Ananya     98
1  Shreya     76
2   Priya     45
```

3. **Write a program that creates a data frame from a list of dictionary.**
   ```
   import numpy as np
   import pandas as pd
   data =[{'Name':'Navya','Marks':90},{'Name':'Kian','Marks':88},{'Name':'Ramaira'}]
   df = pd.DataFrame(data, index = ['Stud 1','Stud 2','Stud 3'])
   print(df)
   ```

   OUTPUT
   ```
             Name    Marks
   Stud 1    Navya   90.0
   Stud 2    Kian    88.0
   Stud 3    Ramaira NaN
   ```

   > When we create a data frame from a list of dictionary, the dictionary keys are set as column names.

4. **Write a program to create a data frame from a dictionary of Series.**
   ```
   import numpy as np
   import pandas as pd
   data = {'Kiara' : pd.Series([89,90,78],index = ['M1', 'M2','M3']),
           'Meera' : pd.Series([85,87,88,92],index = ['M1', 'M2','M3','M4'])}
   df = pd.DataFrame(data)
   print(df)
   ```

   OUTPUT
   ```
        Kiara  Meera
   M1   89.0   85
   M2   90.0   87
   M3   78.0   88
   M4   NaN    92
   ```

5. **Write a program that selects a particular column from the above data frame. Also add a new column to it.**
   ```
   import numpy as np
   import pandas as pd
   data = {'Kiara' : pd.Series([89,90,78],index = ['M1', 'M2','M3']),
           'Meera' : pd.Series([85,87,88,92],index = ['M1', 'M2','M3','M4'])}
   df = pd.DataFrame(data)
   name= input("Enter the name of the student whose marks you want to see : ")
   print(df[name])    # column selection
   # adding a column
   df['Shaina'] = pd.Series([98,79,90,85],index = ['M1', 'M2','M3','M4'])
   print(df)
   ```

   OUTPUT
   ```
   Enter the name of the student whose marks you want to see : Kiara
   M1    89.0
   M2    90.0
   M3    78.0
   M4    NaN
   Name: Kiara, dtype: float64
        Kiara  Meera  Shaina
   M1   89.0   85     98
   M2   90.0   87     79
   M3   78.0   88     90
   M4   NaN    92     85
   ```

6. **Write a program that demonstrates deleting columns from a data frame using the `del` statement and `pop` method.**

```
import numpy as np
import pandas as pd
data = {'Kiara' : pd.Series([89,90,78],index = ['M1', 'M2','M3']),
        'Meera' : pd.Series([85,87,88,92],index = ['M1', 'M2','M3','M4']),
        'Shaina': pd.Series([98,79,90,85],index = ['M1', 'M2','M3','M4']),
        'Harman': pd.Series([48,52,67,71],index = ['M1', 'M2','M3','M4'])}
df = pd.DataFrame(data)
print(df)
# deleting a column
del df['Shaina']       # deleting using del statement
print(df)
# deleting another column
df.pop('Harman')       # deleting using pop method of data frame
print(df)
```

OUTPUT

```
    Kiara  Meera  Shaina  Harman
M1   89.0     85      98      48
M2   90.0     87      79      52
M3   78.0     88      90      67
M4    NaN     92      85      71
    Kiara  Meera  Harman
M1   89.0     85      48
M2   90.0     87      52
M3   78.0     88      67
M4    NaN     92      71
    Kiara  Meera
M1   89.0     85
M2   90.0     87
M3   78.0     88
M4    NaN     92
```

7. **Write a program to select a row(s) from a data frame.**

```
import numpy as np
import pandas as pd
data = {'Kiara' : pd.Series([89,90,78],index = ['M1', 'M2','M3']),
        'Meera' : pd.Series([85,87,88,92],index = ['M1', 'M2','M3','M4']),
        'Shaina': pd.Series([98,79,90,85],index = ['M1', 'M2','M3','M4']),
        'Harman': pd.Series([48,52,67,71],index = ['M1', 'M2','M3','M4'])}
df = pd.DataFrame(data)
print(df)
print("Marks obtained by students in second subject (M2) : ")
print(df.loc['M2'])
print(df.iloc[1])
print("Marks obtained by students in second subject (M2) and third subject (M3) : ")
print(df[1:3])
```

OUTPUT

```
    Kiara  Meera  Shaina  Harman
M1   89.0     85      98      48
M2   90.0     87      79      52
M3   78.0     88      90      67
M4    NaN     92      85      71
```

```
Marks obtained by students in second subject (M2) :
Kiara      90.0
Meera      87.0
Shaina     79.0
Harman     52.0
Name: M2, dtype: float64
Kiara      90.0
Meera      87.0
Shaina     79.0
Harman     52.0
Name: M2, dtype: float64
Marks obtained by students in second subject (M2) and third subject (M3) :
     Kiara   Meera   Shaina   Harman
M2   90.0     87      79       52
M3   78.0     88      90       67
```

8. **Write a program to add new rows to the above data frame. Also demonstrate the procedure to delete row(s) with a specified label.**

```
import numpy as np
import pandas as pd
df1 = pd.DataFrame([[89, 93], [67,76]], columns = ['Meera','Sheena'])
df2 = pd.DataFrame([[77, 84], [87, 92]], columns = ['Meera','Sheena'])
# Appending rows to a data frame
df1 = df1.append(df2)
print(df1)
# Deleting row(s) with specified label
df1 = df1.drop(1)
print('Data Frame after deleting row 1 : ')
print(df1)
```

OUTPUT

```
    Meera   Sheena
0    89       93
1    67       76
0    77       84
1    87       92
Data Frame after deleting row 1 :
    Meera   Sheena
0    89       93
0    77       84
```

1.16 PANDAS DATAFRAME FUNCTIONS AND ATTRIBUTES

The Pandas DataFrame has a number of column helper functions which can be used for extracting valuable information from the column. Some of these are:

Unique() : This method provides unique elements from a column by removing duplicates.
Mean() : Returns the mean value of all the items in the column.

Example 1.24

```
# unique method
import numpy as np
import pandas as pd
```

Introduction to Python Pandas

```
data = {
'Name': ["Shrey", "Gini", "Chitra", "David", "Meher","Faizal", "Geet"],
'Age': [15,16,17,15,17,16,15],
'Interest': ["Sketching", "Outdoor Games", "Cooking", "Surfing", "Reading",
"Sketching", "Surfing"]
}
df = pd.DataFrame(data)
print(df.Age.unique())
```

OUTPUT

```
[15 16 17]
```

Example 1.25

```
# mean method
import numpy as np
import pandas as pd
data = {
'Name': ["Shrey", "Gini", "Chitra", "David", "Meher","Faizal", "Geet"],
'Age': [15,16,17,15,17,16,15],
'Interest': ["Sketching", "Outdoor Games", "Cooking", "Surfing", "Reading",
"Sketching", "Surfing"]
}
df = pd.DataFrame(data)
print("MEAN AGE : %.2f"%df.Age.mean())
```

OUTPUT

MEAN AGE: 15.86

Some important attributes are

T: Returns the transpose of a data frame by interchanging rows and columns.
axes: Returns the list of row axis labels and column axis labels.
dtypes: Returns the data type of each column.
empty: Returns a Boolean value stating whether the data frame object is empty or not. A True value indicates that the object is empty.
ndim: Returns the number of dimensions of the data frame object.
shape: Returns a tuple representing the dimensionality of the DataFrame. Tuple (a,b), where a represents the number of rows and b represents the number of columns.
Size: Returns the number of elements in the DataFrame.
Values: Returns the data values stored in the data frame object as an NDarray.

Example 1.26

```
import numpy as np
import pandas as pd
data = {'Name': ["Shrey", "Gini", "Chitra", "David", "Meher","Faizal", "Geet"],
'Age': [15,16,17,15,17,16,15],
'Interest': ["Sketching", "Outdoor Games", "Cooking", "Surfing", "Reading",
"Sketching", "Surfing"]} print ("The first two rows of the data frame : ")
 print(df.head(2))
print ("The last two rows of the data series : ")
 print(df.tail(2))
```

```
#	Transposing Data Frame
 df = df.T
print(df)
#	Print Axes
 print(df.axes)
#	Print Data Type
 print(df.dtypes)
#	Check if data frame is empty
print ("Is the object empty?", df.empty)
#	Number of dimensions in data frame
 print ("Number of Dimensions: ", df.ndim)
#	Shape of Data Frame Object
print ("Shape of Data Frame object is : ", df.shape)
print ("Number of elements: ", df.size)
print ("Data Values in Data Frame are : ",df.values)
```

OUTPUT

```
The first two rows of the data frame :
    Name   Age  Interest
0   Shrey   15  Sketching
1   Gini    16  OutdoorGames
The last two rows of the data series :
    Name   Age  Interest
5   Faizal  16  Sketching
6   Geet    15  Surfing
            0        1         2    ...    4         5         6
Name        Shrey    Gini      Chitra ...  Meher     Faizal    Geet
Age         15       16        17   ...    17        16        15
Interest    Sketching Outdoor Games Cooking ... Reading Sketching Surfing [3 rows x 7 columns]
[Index(['Name', 'Age', 'Interest'], dtype='object'),
RangeIndex(start=0, stop=7, step=1)]
0    object   1    object   2    object   3    object
4    Object   5    object   6    object   dtype: object
Is the object empty? False
Number of Dimensions : 2
Shape of Data Frame object is : (3,7)
Number of elements : 21
Data Values in Data Frame are : [['Shrey' 'Gini' 'Chitra' 'David' 'Meher' 'Faizal' 'Geet'] [15 16 17 15 17 16 15] ['Sketching' 'Outdoor Games' 'Cooking' 'Surfing' 'Reading' 'Sketching' 'Surfing']]
```

1.17 MATHEMATICAL OPERATIONS ON DATAFRAME

We can easily perform mathematical operations on a single column or on the entire data frame. However, in order to broadcast, the size of the trailing axes for both arrays in an operation must either be the same size or one of them must be one. If this condition is not satisfied, then a data frame full of NaN values will be returned.

Multiplications: We can multiply DataFrame with a scalar value or with another DataFrame by writing df * num or df * df respectively.

Addition / Subtraction: We can add or subtract a scalar value to/from a data frame (ex or df1 – num). Even two data frames can be added or subtracted by writing df1 + df2.

Bitwise Operation: Bitwise operations like AND (&), OR (|), etc., can be performed on a data frame. This can be done by writing df & 0 or df | 1.

Introduction to Python Pandas

Example 1.27

```
import numpy as np
import pandas as pd
data = [[1,2,3,4], [5,6,7,8], [9,0,1,2], [3,4,5,1],  [2,4,1,0]]
df1 = pd.DataFrame(data)
df1 = pd.DataFrame(data, index = [1,2,3,4,5], columns = ["A", "B", "C", "D"] )
print(df1)
data = [[0,1,1,2], [2,3,4,4], [3,4,4,5], [5,4,3,1],  [2,1,0,3]]
df2 = pd.DataFrame(data)
df2 = pd.DataFrame(data, index = [1,2,3,4,5], columns = ["A", "B", "C", "D"] )
print(df2)
print("DF1 X DF2 : ")
print(df1 * df2)
print("DF1 X 10 : ")
 print(df1 * 10)
print("DF1 +5 : ")
 print(df1 + 5)
print("DF1 + DF2 : ")
print(df1 + df2)
```

1.18 MATCHING/BROADCASTING OPERATIONS

When performing operations with Pandas data structures, broadcasting (or matching) operations and filling missing values are two key points of interest. Broadcasting behavior can be seen between higher- and lower-dimensional objects. For example, when performing operations involving a two-dimensional data frame and a one-dimensional series.

Example 1.28

```
import numpy as np
import pandas as pd
df = pd.DataFrame({'one': pd.Series([1,2,3], index=['a', 'b', 'c']),
   'two': pd.Series([4,5,6,7], index=['a', 'b', 'c', 'd']),
   'three': pd.Series([8,9,10], index=['b', 'c', 'd'])})
print(df)
row= df.iloc[1]
column = df['two']
print("Subtracting all rows from the first row")
print(df.sub(row, axis='columns'))
print("Subtracting other column's values from column two")
print(df.sub(column, axis='index'))
```

OUTPUT

	One	two	three
a	1.0	4	NaN
b	2.0	5	8.0
c	3.0	6	9.0
d	NaN	7	10.0

```
Subtracting all rows from the first row
     One      two       three
a    -1.0    -1.0       NaN
b     0.0     0.0       0.0
c     1.0     1.0       1.0
d     NaN     2.0       2.0
Subtracting other column's values from column two
     One      two  three
a    -3.0     0    NaN
b    -3.0     0    3.0
c    -3.0     0    3.0
d    NaN      0    3.0
```

We have seen that a data frame has the methods `add()`, `sub()`, `mul()`, `div()` for performing binary operations. For broadcasting behavior, we can perform these operations between a data frame and series object by either matching the index or columns via the axis keyword.

1.19 MISSING DATA AND OPERATIONS WITH FILL VALUES

When working with Series and DataFrame, we can use arithmetic functions to input a `fill_value` that can be used to substitute missing values. This is important when we are adding two DataFrame objects. In such a case, if one of the data frame has a NaN at a particular location and a non-NaN value at the corresponding location in the other data frame, then it is better to replace NaN with 0.

Example 1.29

```python
import numpy as np
import pandas as pd
df = pd.DataFrame({'one': pd.Series([1,2,3], index=['a', 'b', 'c']),
    'two': pd.Series([4,5,6,7], index=['a', 'b', 'c', 'd']),
    'three': pd.Series([8,9,10], index=['b', 'c', 'd'])})
print("Data Frame 1 \n", df)
df2 = pd.DataFrame({'one': pd.Series([1,2,3], index=['a', 'c', 'd']),
    'two': pd.Series([4,6,7], index=['a', 'b', 'c']),
    'three': pd.Series([8,9,10], index=['a', 'b', 'd'])})
print("Data Frame 2 \n", df)
print("Adding data frames with missing values")
print(df.add(df2))
print("Adding data frames with filled values")
 print(df.add(df2, fill_value=0))
```

OUTPUT

```
Data Frame 1
     one      two       three
a    1.0      4         NaN
b    2.0      5         8.0
c    3.0      6         9.0
d    NaN      7         10.0
Data Frame 2
     One      two       three
a    1.0      4         NaN
b    2.0      5         8.0
c    3.0      6         9.0
d    NaN      7         10.0
```

```
Adding data frames with missing values
      one       two       three
a     2.0       8.0       NaN
b     NaN       11.0      17.0
c     5.0       13.0      NaN
d     NaN       NaN       20.0
Adding data frames with filled values
      One       two       three
a     2.0       8.0       8.0
b     2.0       11.0      17.0
c     5.0       13.0      9.0
d     3.0       7.0       20.0
```

1.20 FLEXIBLE COMPARISONS

Series and DataFrame have binary comparison methods including eq, ne, lt, gt, le, and ge. These operations produce a Pandas dtype bool object (data type Boolean which represents a logical entity and can have two values: True and False) which can then be used in indexing operations. The code given below demonstrates these operations.

Example 1.30

```
import numpy as np
import pandas as pd
df = pd.DataFrame({'one': pd.Series([1,2,3], index=['a', 'b', 'c']),
   'two': pd.Series([4,5,6,7], index=['a', 'b', 'c', 'd']),
   'three': pd.Series([8,9,10], index=['b', 'c', 'd'])})
print("Data Frame 1 \n", df)
df2 = pd.DataFrame({'one': pd.Series([4,5,6], index=['a', 'c', 'd']),
   'two': pd.Series([4,6,7], index=['a', 'b', 'c']),
   'three': pd.Series([7,8,4], index=['a', 'b', 'd'])})
print("Data Frame 2 \n", df2)
print("DF1 > DF2 : ")
print(df.gt(df2))
print("DF2 != DF1: ")
print(df2.ne(df))
```

OUTPUT

```
Data Frame 1
      One       two       three
a     1.0       4         NaN
b     2.0       5         8.0
c     3.0       6         9.0
d     NaN       7         10.0
Data Frame 2
      One       two       three
a     4.0       4.0       7.0
b     NaN       6.0       8.0
c     5.0       7.0       NaN
d     6.0       NaN       4.0
DF1>DF2:
      One       two       three
a     False     False     False
b     False     False     False
c     False     False     False
d     False     False     True
```

```
DF2 != DF1:
    One     two     three
a   True    False   True
b   True    True    False
c   True    True    True
d   True    True    True
```

1.21 BOOLEAN REDUCTIONS

You can apply the reductions: empty, any(), all(), and bool() to provide a way to summarize a Boolean result. For example, the following expressions reduce Boolean results to a single Boolean value.

```
pd.Series([True]).bool() returns True
pd.DataFrame([[False]]).bool() returns False
```

The any() method checks whether any element is True. It returns False unless there is at least one element within a series or along a Dataframe axis that is True or equivalent (e.g. non-zero or non-empty).

The all() method checks whether all elements are True. It returns True if all elements within a series or along a Dataframe axis are non-zero, not-empty or not-False.

Example 1.31

```python
import numpy as np
import pandas as pd
df = pd.DataFrame({'one': pd.Series([1,2,3], index=['a', 'b', 'c']),
    'two': pd.Series([4,5,6,7], index=['a', 'b', 'c', 'd']),
    'three': pd.Series([8,9,10], index=['b', 'c', 'd'])})
print("Data Frame \n", df)
print("Check if all values are greater than 0")
print((df > 0).all())
print("Check if any value is greater than 0")
print((df > 0).any())
print("Reducing to a final boolean value : ",(df > 0).any().any())
print("Data Frame is empty:", df.empty)
```

OUTPUT

```
Data Frame
    One     two     three
a   1.0     4       NaN
b   2.0     5       8.0
c   3.0     6       9.0
d   NaN     7       10.0
Check if all values are greater than 0
one     False
two     True
three   False
dtype:  bool
Check if any value is greater than 0
one     True
two     True
three   True
dtype: bool
Reducing to a final boolean value :
True
Data Frame is empty: False
```

1.22 COMPARING IF OBJECTS ARE EQUIVALENT

Often, there are multiple ways to compute the same result. For example, df + df is equivalent to df * 2. To test whether the two computations produce the same result, we can write using the expression (df + df == df * 2). To see the result row-wise, we can even write (df + df == df * 2).all(). However, you will find that the result of this expression will be False. Do not be surprised by this result. This is just because NaN on the left is not equal to NaN on the right. You can check by comparing the two NaN values.

```
>>> import numpy as np
>>> np.NaN == np.NaN
False
```

To overcome this problem, Series and Data Frame have an **equals()** method for testing equality. This method treats NaNs in corresponding locations as equal.

Example 1.32

```
import numpy as np
import pandas as pd
df = pd.DataFrame({'one': pd.Series([1,2,3], index=['a', 'b', 'c']),
    'two': pd.Series([4,5,6,7], index=['a', 'b', 'c', 'd']),
    'three': pd.Series([8,9,10], index=['b', 'c', 'd'])})
print("Data Frame 1 \n", df)
print("df + df == df*2:")
print(df + df == df * 2)
print("(df + df).equals(df * 2): ", (df + df).equals(df * 2))
```

OUTPUT
```
Data Frame 1
    One    two    three
a   1.0    4      NaN
b   2.0    5      8.0
c   3.0    6      9.0
d   NaN    7      10.0
df + df == df * 2 :
    one    two    three
a   True   True   False
b   True   True   True
c   True   True   True
d   False  True   True
(df + df).equals(df * 2): True
```

1.23 COMPARING ARRAY-LIKE OBJECTS

We can make element-wise comparisons when comparing a Pandas data structure with a scalar value. We can also perform element-wise comparisons between different array-like objects of the same length.

Example 1.33

```
#Element-wise comparisons when comparing with a #scalar value
import numpy as np
import pandas as pd
print(pd.Series(['Good', 'Morning', 'World']) == 'Good')
```

OUTPUT
```
0    True
1    False
2    False
dtype: bool
```

Example 1.34

```
#Element-wise comparisons between different array-like #objects of the same length
import numpy as np
import pandas as pd
print(pd.Series(['Good', 'Morning', 'World']) ==np.array(['Good','Evening','World']))
```

OUTPUT

```
0    True
1    False
2    True
dtype: bool
```

Remember that if we try to compare Pandas objects of different lengths, then a ValueError will be raised. This is in contrast with NumPy behavior where a comparison between different length objects can be broadcast Examples 1.35 and 1.36.

Example 1.35

```
import numpy as np
import pandas as pd
print(pd.Series(['Good', 'Morning', 'World'])==
 np.array(['Evening','World']))
```

OUTPUT

```
ValueError: Lengths must match to compare
```

Example 1.36

```
import numpy as np
import pandas as pd
print(np.array(['Good', 'Morning', 'World'])==
np.array(['World']))
```

OUTPUT

```
[False False True]
```

1.24 COMBINING DATA FRAMES

We can combine two similar data sets. This is especially important where values in one data set are preferred over the other. This situation frequently occurs when one of the two data series representing a particular economic indicator is considered to be of "higher quality". However, the lower quality series may have more complete data coverage. So, we can combine two DataFrame objects where missing values in one DataFrame are conditionally filled with like-labelled values from the other DataFrame. The `combine_first()` function is used for implementing this operation.

Example 1.37

```
import numpy as np
import pandas as pd
df1 = pd.DataFrame({'A': [1., np.nan, 3., 5., np.nan], 'B': [np.nan, 2., 3., np.nan, 6.]})
df2 = pd.DataFrame({'A': [5., 2., 4., np.nan, 3., 7.],
    'B': [np.nan, np.nan, 3., 4., 6., 8.]})
```

```
print("DATA FRAME 1: ")
print(df1)
print("DATA FRAME 2: ")
print(df2)
print("COMBINING DATA FRAMES : ")
print(df1.combine_first(df2))
```

OUTPUT
```
DATA FRAME 1:
     A      B
0   1.0    NaN
1   NaN    2.0
2   3.0    3.0
3   5.0    NaN
4   NaN    6.0
DATA FRAME 2:
     A      B
0   5.0    NaN
1   2.0    NaN
2   4.0    3.0
3   NaN    4.0
4   3.0    6.0
5   7.0    8.0
COMBINING DATA FRAMES :
     A      B
0   1.0    NaN
1   2.0    2.0
2   3.0    3.0
3   5.0    4.0
4   3.0    6.0
5   7.0    8.0
```

The `combine_first()` method used in the above code can be replaced with a more general DataFrame method `combine()`. The `combine()` method takes another DataFrame and a combiner function as an argument to perform its intended task.

1.25 DESCRIPTIVE STATISTICS

Python supports a large number of methods for computing descriptive statistics and other related operations on Series and DataFrame objects. Aggregation functions like `sum()`, `mean()`, and `quantile()` produce a lower-dimensional result. However, other functions like `cumsum()` and `cumprod()` produce an object of the same size.

All such methods have a `skipna` option specifying whether to exclude missing data or not. `skipna` is True by default. This means that by default all NaN values are skipped or ignored.

Another important argument of descriptive functions is axis. Users can specify the axis by name or integer. The default value of axis is 0 indicating indices or rows. If axis = 1, the descriptive function is applied on columns.

Example 1.38

```
df = pd.DataFrame({'A' :[1,2, 3, 5, np.NaN],
    'B': [7,8, np.NaN, 10,1],
    'C' : [np.NaN,4, 3,2,0]})
print("DATA FRAME:")
print(df)
print("CLUMN WISE MEAN : ")
print(df.mean(0))
print("ROW WISE MEAN : ")
```

```
print(df.mean(1))
print("COLUMN WISE MEAN CONSIDERING NA : ")
print(df.mean(0,skipna=False))
print("ROW WISE MEAN CONSIDERING NA : ")
print(df.mean(1,skipna=False))
DATA FRAME :
     A       B      C
0   1.0    7.0    NaN
1   2.0    8.0    4.0
2   3.0    NaN    3.0
3   5.0   10.0    2.0
4   NaN    1.0    0.0
COLUMN WISE MEAN :
A    2.75
B    6.50
C    2.25
dtype: float64
ROW WISE MEAN :
0    4.000000
1    4.666667
2    3.000000
3    5.666667
4    0.500000
dtype: float64
CLUMN WISE MEAN CONSIDERING NA :
A    NaN
B    NaN
C    NaN
dtype: float64
ROW WISE MEAN CONSIDERING NA :
0    NaN
1    4.666667
2    NaN
3    5.666667
4    NaN
dtype: float64
```

We can use broadcasting to describe various statistical procedures, such as standardization (rendering mean equal to zero and standard deviation equal to 1) by writing,

standardized = (df - df.mean()) / df.std()

Methods like `cumsum()` and `cumprod()` preserve the location of NaN values. It can be used as `df.cumsum()`. Other important commonly used functions are given in Table 1.5.

Table 1.5 Commonly used functions in descriptive statistics

Function	Description
count	Number of non-NA observations
sum	Sum of values
mean	Mean of values
mad	Mean absolute deviation
median	Arithmetic median of values
min	Minimum
max	Maximum

Table 1.5 (*Continued*)

Table 1.5 Continued

Function	Description
mode	Mode
abs	Absolute value
prod	Product of values
std	Standard deviation
var	Unbiased variance
sem	Standard error of the mean
quantile	Sample quantile
cumsum	Cumulative sum
cumprod	Cumulative product
cummax	Cumulative maximum
cummin	Cumulative minimum

Note that like Data Frame, even NumPy methods like mean, std and sum will exclude NAs on Series input by default.

Example 1.39

```
import numpy as np
import pandas as pd
df = pd.DataFrame({'A' :[1, 2, 3, 5, np.NaN],
   'B': [7, 8, np.NaN, 10,1],
   'C': [np.NaN, 4, 3, 2,0]})
print("DATA FRAME : ")
print(df)
print("MEAN OF COLUMN B : ",np.mean(df['B']))
```

OUTPUT

```
DATA FRAME :
     A     B    C
0  1.0   7.0  NaN
1  2.0   8.0  4.0
2  3.0   NaN  3.0
3  5.0  10.0  2.0
4  NaN   1.0  0.0
MEAN OF COLUMN B : 6.5
```

We can even use the `sum()` function to count the number of nulls in each column by writing, `df.isnull().sum()`.

Key points to remember

- Since DataFrame is a heterogeneous data structure, generic functions do not work with all functions.
- Functions like `sum()`, `cumsum()`, etc., work with both numeric and character or string data. However, practically, we will never use character aggregations as these functions will not throw any exception if we try to do so.
- Functions like `abs()`, `cumprod()` throw exception when the DataFrame contains a character or string data because such operations cannot be performed on non-numerical data.

1.26 SUMMARIZING OR DESCRIBING DATA

The `describe()` function computes a variety of summary statistics on a Series or the columns of a DataFrame object. This function ignores NAs. This function gives the **mean, std** and **IQR** values.

Example 1.40

```
import numpy as np
import pandas as pd
df = pd.DataFrame({'A' :[1, 2, 3, 5, np.NaN],
   'B': [7, 8, np.NaN, 10,1],
   'C' : [np.NaN, 4, 3, 2,0]})
print("DESCRIBING DATAFRAME : ")
print(df.describe())
S = pd.Series(np.random.randn(1000))
S[::3] = np.nan
print("DESCRIBING DATAFRAME : ")
print(S.describe())
```

OUTPUT

```
DESCRIBING DATAFRAME :
        A           B           C
Count   4.000000    4.000000    4.000000
mean    2.750000    6.500000    2.250000
std     1.707825    3.872983    1.707825
min     1.000000    1.000000    0.000000
25%     1.750000    5.500000    1.500000
50%     2.500000    7.500000    2.500000
75%     3.500000    8.500000    3.250000
max     5.000000    10.000000   4.000000
DESCRIBING SERIES:
count   666.000000
mean    0.038206
std     0.997166
min     -3.006498
25%     -0.657822
50%     0.013089
75%     0.753421
max     3.016491
dtype: float64
```

In the above code we could have also selected specific percentiles to include in the output by writing, series.describe(percentiles=[.05, .25, .75, .95])

For a non-numerical Series object, `describe()` will give a simple summary of the number of unique values and most frequently occurring values.

On a mixed-type DataFrame object, `describe()` will restrict the summary to include only numerical columns. If there are no numerical values, only categorical columns are included as shown in the code given in Example 1.41.

However, we can also provide a list of type of objects that can be included in the include argument of the `describe()` function. We can even specify **include = all** to include every data type for calculating the summary. This can be done by writing, frame_object.describe(include='all'). The general syntax of specifying include argument is frame_object.describe(include=['object']). For example, writing df.describe(include=['number']).

Example 1.41

```
import numpy as np
import pandas as pd
S = pd.Series(['P','Y','T','H','O','N',np.nan,'P','R','O','G','R','A','M','M','I','N'
,'G'])
print("DESCRIBING SERIES : ")
print(S.describe())
df = pd.DataFrame({'A': ['Python','Yes',np.nan,'Programming'], 'B': range(4)})
print("DESCRIBING DATA FRAME")
print(df.describe())
print("DESCRIBING DATA FRAME WITH include = all")
print(df.describe(include='all'))
```

OUTPUT

```
DESCRIBING SERIES:
Count     17
unique    11
top       P
freq      2
dtype: object
DESCRIBING DATA FRAME
B
Count    4.000000
mean     1.500000
std      1.290994
min      0.000000
25%      0.750000
50%      1.500000
75%      2.250000
max      3.000000
DESCRIBING DATA FRAME WITH include = all
         A          B
Count    3          4.000000
unique   3          NaN
top      Python     NaN
freq     1          NaN
mean     NaN        1.500000
std      NaN        1.290994
min      NaN        0.000000
25%      NaN        0.750000
50%      NaN        1.500000
75%      NaN        2.250000
max      NaN        3.000000
```

Note that the **'include'** argument of the `describe()` function is used to pass necessary information regarding what columns need to be considered for summarizing. The value of the include argument can be one of the following:

- **object** – Summarizes string columns.
- **number** – Summarizes numeric columns. This is also the default value of include.
- **all** – Summarizes all columns together (it should not be passed as a list value).

1.27 INDEX OF MIN/MAX VALUES

The `idxmin()` and `idxmax()` functions can be used with Series and DataFrame objects to compute the index labels with the minimum and maximum corresponding values.

Example 1.42

```
# For single column data frame
import numpy as np
import pandas as pd
df = pd.Series(np.random.randn(5))
print("DATA FRAME:")
print(df)
print("Index with minimum value : ",df.idxmin())
print("lndex with maximum value :", df.idxmax())
```

OUTPUT
```
DATA FRAME :
0    -0.433586
1    -1.230765
2    -0.690756
3     0.123188
4     0.354238
dtype: float64
Index with minimum value : 1
Index with maximum value : 4
```

Example 1.43

```
# For data frame having multiple rows and columns
import numpy as np
import pandas as pd
df = pd.DataFrame(np.random.randn(5,3),
columns=['A','B','C'])
print("DATA FRAME : ")
print(df)
print("Index with minimum value (column wise): ")
print(df.idxmin(axis= 0))
print("Index with maximum value (row wise): ")
print(df.idxmax(axis= 1))
print("Index with minimum value in column B : ",
df['B'].idxmin())
print("Index with maximum value in column C : ",
df['C'].idxmax())
```

OUTPUT
```
DATA FRAME :
        A          B          C
0    0.721215   -0.312569   2.053623
1    0.295069   -0.117734   1.348776
2   -0.528853   -0.034825   1.572288
3    0.613757   -0.448653  -1.060948
4    1.124058   -0.927208   0.164340
Index with minimum value (column wise):
A    2
B    4
C    3
dtype: int64
Index with maximum value (row wise):
0    C
1    C
2    C
3    A
4    A
dtype: object
Index with minimum value in column B : 4
Index with maximum value in column C: 0
```

Key points to remember

- When a particular value that is either minimum or maximum is repeated in a data frame or series object then `idxmin()` and `idxmax()` functions return the index of the first occurrence of that value. Therefore,
  ```
  df = pd.DataFrame([1,2,3,3,1,1,3], columns=['A'], index=range(7))
  print(df['A'].idxmax())
  ```
  We will give an output 2, since 3 is the maximum value which first occurs at index 2 in the data frame.

- idxmin and idxmax are called argmin and argmax in NumPy.

1.28 VALUE COUNTS AND MODE() FUNCTION

The `value_counts()` Series method and `top-level` function computes a histogram of a 1D array of values. It can also be used as a function on regular arrays.

`mode()` function is used to get the most frequently occurring value(s) (or the mode) of the values in a Series or DataFrame as shown in the code given below.

Example 1.44

```
import numpy as np
import pandas as pd
df = pd.DataFrame({"A": np.random.randint(0,7, size=10),
   "B": np.random.randint(-10,15, size=10)})
print("DATA FRAME")
print(df)
print("MODE:")
print(df.mode())
```

OUTPUT
```
DATA FRAME
   A   B
0  2  10
1  3   8
2  1  11
3  4   6
4  1  -5
5  2   1
6  1   5
7  0   2
8  5   6
9  2  10
MODE:
   A   B
0  1   6
1  2  10
```

Example 1.45

```
import numpy as np
import pandas as pd
data= np.random.randint(0,7, size=20)
s = pd.Series(data)
print(s)
print("COUNTS OF VALUES : ")
print(s.value_counts())
print("MODE:")
print(s.mode())
```

OUTPUT

```
0      3
1      4
2      2
3      4
4      1
5      0
6      3
7      3
8      2
9      4
10     5
11     4
12     6
13     0
14     0
15     1
16     5
17     6
18     5
19     3
dtype: int32
COUNTS OF VALUES :
4      4
3      4
5      3
0      3
6      2
2      2
1      2
dtype: int64
MODE :
0      3
1      4
dtype: int32
```

1.29 OTHER STATISTICAL FUNCTIONS

As discussed, statistical methods help in understanding and analyzing the behavior of data. Some other very useful statistical functions include:

Example 1.46

```
# Percent_change()
import pandas as pd
import numpy as np
s = pd.Series([1,2,3,4,5,4])
print(s.pct_change())
```

OUTPUT

```
0    NaN
1    1.000000
2    0.500000
3    0.333333
4    0.250000
5    -0.200000
```

Percent_change: Series and Data Frames have the function `pct_change()` that compares every element with its prior element and computes the change percentage.

By default, the `pct_change()` operates on columns. To apply the function on rows, use `axis=1()` argument.

Covariance (cov): Covariance is applied on series data to compute covariance between series objects. The cov method automatically excludes NA.

Example 1.47

```
# cov() method
import pandas as pd
import numpy as np
s1 = pd.Series(np.random.randn(10))
s2 = pd.Series(np.random.randn(10))
print(s1.cov(s2))
```

OUTPUT

```
-0.18450525864415426
```

Covariance method, when applied on a DataFrame, computes cov between all the columns.

Correlation: Correlation shows the linear relationship between any two arrays of values or series as wecall in Pandas. There are multiple methods to compute the correlation like pearson(default), spearman and kendall.

Example 1.48

```
# Finding Correlation
import pandas as pd
import numpy as np
frame = pd.DataFrame(np.random.randn(10, 5), columns=['a', 'b', 'c', 'd', 'e'])
print(frame['a'].corr(frame['b']))
print( frame.corr())
```

OUTPUT

```
-0.7617698565607718
     a          b          c          d          e
a    1.000000  -0.761770   0.180424  -0.292428  -0.474428
b   -0.761770   1.000000  -0.485660   0.442686   0.263709
c    0.180424  -0.485660   1.000000  -0.324710  -0.218734
d   -0.292428   0.442686  -0.324710   1.000000   0.351329
e   -0.474428   0.263709  -0.218734   0.351329   1.000000
```

1.30 ROW- OR COLUMN-WISE APPLICATION OF FUNCTIONS

Any user-defined or library function can be applied to Pandas objects, either on an entire DataFrame or Series, one or more rows, columns or elements. The `apply()` function can be used for row-wise or column-wise application of a function on a Pandas object. In this section, we will demonstrate the use of descriptive statistics using the `apply()` function with an optional axis argument.

Example 1.49

```
import numpy as np
import pandas as pd
df = pd.DataFrame({"A": np.random.randint(0,7, size=7),
"B": np.random.randint(-10,15, size=7)})
print("DATA FRAME")
print(df)
```

```
print("APPLYING MEAN WITH DEFAULT AXIS")
print(df.apply(np.mean))
print("APPLYING MEAN WITH AXIS = 1")
print(df.apply(np. mean, axis = 1))
```

OUTPUT
```
DATA FRAME
     A    B
0    4    14
1    6    3
2    3    8
3    1    10
4    4    -5
5    1    -10
6    3    2
APPLYING MEAN WITH DEFAULT AXIS
A    3.142857
B    3.142857
dtype: float64
APPLYING MEAN WITH AXIS = 1
0    9.0
1    4.5
2    5.5
3    5.5
4    -0.5
5    -4.5
6    2.5
dtype: float64
```

Like the `mean()` function, try the use of `cumsum()` and `exp()` functions, both defined in NumPy. Remember that the `apply()` function also takes an argument raw, which is False by default. This argument is used to convert each row or column into a Series before applying the function. When set to True, the passed function will instead receive an ndarray object.

1.31 COMPARISON OF DIFFERENT DATA STRUCTURES

Data structures like lists, NumPy arrays, and Pandas data frames can all be used to hold a sequence of data. Each of these data structures are built for a specific purpose. For example,

Lists are simple built-in data structures in Python, which can be easily used as a container to hold data of different data types like integer, float, and object.

A list is a simple and flexible way to deal with a small amount of data in Python. It can be created by writing values within a pair of square brackets []. Lists are mutable, so they are naturally suitable for dealing with a dynamic sequence of data.

NumPy array supports N-dimensional array objects to allow fast scientific computing. Python lists and NumPy arrays are similar to traditional arrays in other programming languages including C, C++ and Java.

While Python list focuses on flexibility, numpy.ndarray offers performance benefits. They are specifically optimized for high scientific computation as they support built-in mathematical functions and array operations. Numpy.ndarray has always been a preferred choice for working with large amount of data or high-dimensional data.

Pandas is more like an Excel spreadsheet. It provides a tabular data structure in which data is organized using rows and columns. It can be considered to be an extended form of NumPy.ndarray. pandas.DataFrame has functions that can perform mathematical computations and array operations with high performance. Similar to lists, it is a mutable data structure that can store data of different data types. A DataFrame also provides flexible access to values using integer position or index labels.

Table 1.6 given below summarizes the key differences between the three data structures.

Table 1.6 Comparison between the different data structures

	Mutability	Homogeneity	Accessibility	Others
list	mutable	heterogeneous	integer position	Python built-in data structure
numpy.ndarray	immutable	homogeneous	integer position	high-performance array calculation
pandas.DataFrame	mutable	heterogeneous	integer position or index	tabular data structure

However, despite these differences, we can at any time, transform an object from one type to another whenever the need arises. Figure 1.9 given below illustrates the built-in functions that help us to do so.

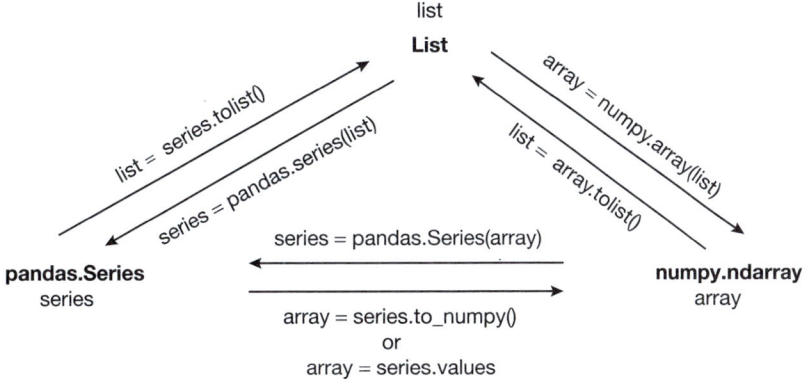

Figure 1.9 Converting one data structure to another

1.32 TRANSFER DATA BETWEEN CSV FILES/SQL DATABASES, AND DATA FRAME OBJECTS

After learning the technical details of Pandas data frames, let us see some applications of this data structure in real world.

- In a **school** system, we can create a DataFrame in which each row could represent a single student in the school, and columns can be used to store details like name (string), age (number), date of birth (date), and address (string) of the student.
- In a data frame related to **economics**, each row may represent a single city or geographical area, and columns can be used to store details like name of the area (string), population (number), average age of the population (number), number of households (number), number of schools in each area (number) etc.
- A data frame for an **e-commerce** application can be used to represent a customer in each row and number of items purchased (number), date of original registration (date), credit card number (string), etc. in the columns.

These applications usually store data in CSV files. For computational processing, data from these CSV files need to be read into data frames. Correspondingly, after processing we must write the processed data from the data frames back to CSV files.

1.32.1 Loading CSV Data into Pandas

Before learning how to read and write CSV files from python using Pandas, we must first know what a CSV file is.

CSV stands for "comma-separated values". A CSV file is a type of plain text file that uses specific structuring to arrange **tabular data**. The format used for data interchange by a CSV file is compact, simple and general. This feature facilitates websites and their users to **export** tabular data from the website into a CSV file.

CSV files can be easily opened in MS Excel. Moreover, nearly all databases can **import** from CSV file. When writing data in a CSV file, always terminate each row by a newline before beginning the next row and separate each column by a comma (,), a semicolon (;) or any other symbol. CSV files can be easily read and processed by Python.

1.32.2 Reading a CSV File

To read data from CSV files in Python, we need to use a reader function to generate a reader object.

The reader function takes each row of the file and makes a list of all columns. We can then access the column whose value has to be read.

It sounds a lot more intricate than it is. Let us take a look at this example and we will find out that working with .csv file is not so hard.

Example 1.50

```
import numpy as np
import pandas as pd
import csv
with open('AirQuality.csv','rt')as f: data = csv.reader(f)
for row in data:
    print(row)
```

SAMPLE OUTPUT

```
['Ozone "Solar.R" "Wind" "Temp" "Month" "Day"']
['1 41 190 7.4 67 5 1']
['2 36 118 8 72 5 2']
['3 12 149 12.6 74 5 3']
['4 18 313 11.5 62 5 4']
['5 NA NA 14.3 56 5 5']
['6 28 NA 14.9 66 5 6']
['7 23 299 8.6 65 5 7']
['8 19 99 13.8 59 5 8']
['9 8 19 20.1 61 5 9']
['10 NA 194 8.6 69 5 10']
```

In the above code, we have read AirQuality.csv file stored in the same folder where the Python script is saved. The program opens the file and reads the data stored in it using the `reader()` function. The data read is then displayed, row by row. Note that in the output given on the right side, only 10 rows are displayed. It is just a sample output as there were 153 rows in the file.

> If the file to be read does not exist then FileNotFoundError is returned.

Note that if your CSV file is in some other folder other than the folder in which .py file is saved, then you must specify the complete path in the `open()` function. Also remember that we can use the `read_csv()` function to read a .txt file as given below. However, before executing this code, first create a myFile.txt file and store some data in it.

Example 1.51

```
import numpy as np
import pandas as pd
import csv
print(pd.read_csv('myFile.txt'))
```

OUTPUT

```
Hello World
0     .... Welcome to the world of
1     .... PYTHON PROGRAMMING .
2     Enjoy Programming!!!
```

Note that if we have a text file having a tab as a delimiter or any other character as a delimiter like a semicolon, we must specifically mention that character as a value of the delimiter argument in the `read_csv()` function as given below.

```
pd.read_csv('myFile.txt', delimiter='\t')
```

1.32.2 Writing Data to a CSV File

To write a set of data to a CSV file so that it can be saved for future use, we need to use `writer()` function. To iterate the data over the rows (lines), the `writerow()` function is used.

We can also use the `df.to_csv()` function to write a data frame to a CSV file as shown in the code given below.

Example 1.52

```
# Writing Data to a CSV File Using the writer() Function
import numpy as np
import pandas as pd
import csv
with open('writeData.csv', mode='w') as file:
writer = csv.writer(file)
writer.writerow(['Python', 'Programming', 'is', 'fun...'])
writer.writerow(['Hello', 'World', 'Good Programming'])
writer.writerow(['I', 'love', 'Computer', 'Programming'])
writer.writerow(['Hope', 'you', 'will also', 'enjoy programming'])
```

Example 1.53

```
# Writing Data Frame to a CSV File
import numpy as np
import pandas as pd
import csv
data = [['Python', 'Programming', 'is', 'fun...'],['Hello', 'World', 'Good
Programming'], ['I', 'love', 'Computer', 'Programming'],['Hope', 'you', 'will also',
'enjoy programming']]
df = pd.DataFrame(data)
df.to_csv("MyFile.csv")
```

In Example 1.52, note that while opening the file we have specified mode = 'w' to indicate that the file is being opened for writing data to the file. The `writer()` method of the csv module returns a writer object, which is used to write data to the csv file, one row at a time using the `writerow()` method.

In Example 1.53, a data frame is written to the CSV file. The filename is specified within the `to_csv()` method of data frame object. Similarly, the `to_excel()` function is used to write a data frame object to a Microsoft Excel file.

> Pandas also allows users to read or write files from an SQL database, MS Excel (XLS / XLSX file). For this, functions like `read_xlsx()` and `read_sql()` are used.

Key Terms

Pandas: An open-source, free-to-use (under a BSD license) module that takes data (from a CSV or TSV file, or an SQL database) and creates a Python object with rows and columns called data frame.

NumPy: An open-source module of Python which provides fast mathematical computation on arrays and matrices.

Array: A collection of similar data elements (of the same data type) that are stored in consecutive memory locations and are referenced by an index (also known as the subscript).

Subscript: An ordinal number indicating the position of the element counting from the beginning of the array.

Two-dimensional array: An array of one-dimensional arrays. Every element in a 2-D array is specified using two subscripts where one subscript denotes row and the other denotes column.

Multi-dimensional array: An array of arrays.

Axes: In NumPy, dimensions of the array are called axes.

Rank: The number of axes in a NumPy array is called the rank.

Series: A one-dimensional array that can store data of any type (integer, string, float, Python objects, etc.).

Lists: Simple built-in data structures in Python, which can be easily used as a container to hold data of different data types like integer, float and object.

Chapter Highlights

- In a row-major order, elements of the first row are stored before the elements of the second and third row. In a column-major order, the elements of the first column are stored before the elements of the second and third column.
- `np.arrange()` returns an array with evenly spaced elements from the interval specified by the value of start and stop in the gap of step.
- Importing a module means loading it in memory for using its functionalities.
- All Pandas data structures are mutable. This means that their values can be changed. However, Series is an exception since it is immutable.
- Python allows users to access Series data using not only indices but also by using labels of indices. However, if the specified label is not contained in the Series object, then a KeyError exception is raised.
- The `in` operator returns True if the index is present and False otherwise. Similarly, the `not in` operator returns True if the index is not present and False otherwise.
- The `isnull()` function returns True is a particular value is null and False otherwise. The `notnull()` function returns True if the element has any other value except null and False otherwise.
- The `get()` method is used to return a value associated with a specified label. If the label does not exist in the Series object, then None or the default value is returned.
- Series and DataFrame have binary comparison methods including `eq, ne, lt, gt, le,` and `ge`. These operations produce a Pandas dtype bool object, which can then be used in indexing operations.
- Series and DataFrame have an `equals()` method for testing equality. This method treats NaNs in corresponding locations as equal.
- If we try to compare Pandas objects of different lengths then a ValueError will be raised. This is in contrast with NumPy behavior where a comparison between different length objects can be broadcast.
- The `apply()` function can be used for row-wise or column-wise application of a function on a Pandas object.
- A CSV file is a type of plain-text file that uses specific structuring to arrange tabular data. The format used for data interchange by a CSV file is compact, simple and general. This feature facilitates websites and their users to export tabular data from the website into a CSV file.

Review Questions

1. Give the full form of Pandas. Also list some of its uses.
2. What is NumPy?
3. How are elements stored in an array?
4. Differentiate between an array and a matrix.
5. Differentiate between row-major and column-major way of representing matrices.
6. Define multi-dimensional arrays.
7. Give any three ways of creating a NumPy array.
8. List some of the important attributes of a NumPy array.

9. With the help of relevant examples, explain the use of head(n) and tail(n) functions.
10. Compare Series and DataFrame.
11. With the help of an example, explain how can we filter data in a series object.
12. Identify the method for the following:
    a. Calculate the standard deviation of the given set of numbers, DataFrame, column, and rows.
    b. Convert a series object to a dataframe.
    c. Return a Series that contains counts of unique values.
    d. Compare two data frame objects
13. Compare a Pandas Series with a Python List.
14. Write instructions for the following:
    a. Print every third element from index 4 to 40 of the NumPy array.
    b. Print the NumPy array in reverse order.
    c. Print unique elements from a column by removing duplicates.
    d. Return the transpose of a data frame by interchanging rows and columns.
    e. Return a tuple representing the dimensionality of the DataFrame
    f. Combine two similar data sets.
15. With the help of example(s), explain some important attributes of data frame object.
16. Explain broadcasting behavior with the help of an example.
17. Explain how describe() function works.
18. With the help of an example, explain the use of apply() function.
19. Compare different data structures in Python.
20. What do you understand by a CSV file? With the help of an example, demonstrate how you will read and write data to such a file.
21. Differentiate between df.apply(np.mean) and df.apply(np.mean, axis=1).
22. Explain the following instructions.
    a. `frame = pd.DataFrame({'a': ['Yes', 'Yes', 'No', 'No'], 'b': range(4)})`
       `frame.describe()`
    b. `s = pd.Series(np.random.randn(5))`
       `s.idxmin(), s.idxmax()`
    c. `df = pd.DataFrame(np.random.randn(5,3), columns=['A','B','C'])`
       `df.idxmin(axis=0)`
       `df.idxmax(axis=1)`
    d. `df = pd.DataFrame([2, 1, 1, 3, np.nan], columns=['A'], index=list('edcba'))`
       `df['A'].idxmin()`
    e. `df.apply(np.cumsum)`
    f. `df.apply(np.exp)`
    g. `result = pandas.read_csv('X:\data.csv')`
       `print(result)`
    h. `pandas.read_csv('myFile.txt')`
    i. `max1 = df['Price'].max()`
    j. `pd.DataFrame(columns=list('ABC')).empty`
       `pd.Series([False]).bool()`
       `pd.DataFrame([[True]]).bool()`
    k. `from pandas import DataFrame`
       `C = {'Programming language': ['Python','Java', 'C++'],`
       `     'Designed by': ['Guido van Rossum', 'James Gosling', 'Bjarne Stroustrup'],`
       `     'Appeared': ['1991', '1995', '1985'],`
       `     'Extension': ['.py', '.java', '.cpp'],`
       `    }`

```
df = DataFrame(C, columns= ['Programming language', 'Designed by',
'Appeared', 'Extension'])
export_csv  =  df.to_csv  (r'X:\pandaresult.csv',  index  =  None,
header=True)
print (df)
```

Programming Exercises

1. Write a program that creates a NumPy array with first 20 even numbers.
2. Write a program that creates a NumPy array with four rows and five columns filled with random numbers.
3. Write a program to create a series from a list of values.
4. Write a program to create a series from an already-created dictionary in Python.
5. Create a data frame with 5 rows and 4 columns. Use a list of lists to fill the data frame.
6. Create a data frame with 5 rows and 4 columns. Use an np array to fill the data frame.
7. Write a program that creates and accesses a series using both index and label.
8. Write a program to perform calculator operations on two series objects. Also scale the resultant object by a factor of 10.
9. Write a program to perform calculator operations on data frame objects.
10. Write a program that creates a dictionary storing the name of the students as key and a list of marks in three subjects as value. Use this dictionary to create a data frame.
11. Create a data frame with three columns: Name, Age and Designation. Add at least 10 rows.
    a. Write a code to add indices to the data frame created in the above question.
    b. Write a code to insert at least three new rows to the data frame.
    c. Write a code to delete any specific row from the data frame.
    d. Write a code to display the first four rows of the data frame.
    e. Write a code to display last four rows of the data frame.
    f. Write a code to display third, fifth, seventh and nineth rows.
    g. Write a code to display fourth, fifth and sixth rows.
12. Write a program to find the square of a matrix.
13. Download the World Food production data stored in a CSV file from www.kaggle.com. Read the data from the CSV file and display it on the screen.
14. Create a text file and read its content. Also write the contents in another text file.

Fill in the Blanks

1. Pandas stands for _____.
2. _____ module provides fast mathematical computation on arrays and matrices.
3. The elements of the array are stored in consecutive memory locations and are referenced by an _____.
4. _____ is an array of one-dimensional arrays.
5. Every element in a _____ is specified using two subscripts.
6. In a _____ representation of a 2D array, element (1,0) is followed by element (1,1).
7. Before using a module, we must first _____ it.
8. _____ creates a matrix of specified data type and shape (or size) filled with ones.
9. _____ returns an array with evenly spaced elements in the interval specified by the value of start and stop in the gap of the given step.
10. _____ displays the dimension of the NumPy array.
11. _____ a module means loading it in memory for using its functionalities.
12. The _____ function is used to create an empty series object.

13. In Pandas, _____ represents a missing value.
14. The _____ function is used to check whether all elements are True.
15. The _____ method is used to return the value associated with a specified label.
16. If the label does not exist in a Series object then _____ or the _____ is returned.
17. The _____ method of series maps the values from two series that have a common column.
18. To delete a column from the data frame, we can either use the _____ statement or using the _____ method.
19. If we compare NumPy objects of different lengths, then objects can be _____.
20. The _____ function computes a variety of summary statistics on a Series or the columns of a DataFrame object.
21. The _____ and _____ functions can be used with Series and DataFrame objects to compute the index labels with the minimum and maximum corresponding values.
22. _____ function is used to get the most frequently occurring value(s) of the values in a Series or DataFrame.
23. _____ error is returned if a file to be read is not present in that location.
24. The _____ function is used to write a data frame to a CSV file.
25. Mode = 'w' indicates that the file is being opened for _____ data.

State True or False

1. Array indices are written in round brackets.
2. Array elements are placed in consecutive memory locations.
3. An m × n matrix has m columns and n rows.
4. In a row-major order, the elements of the first column are stored before the elements of the second and third column.
5. NumPy is mainly used for creating heterogeneous multi-dimensional arrays.
6. Shape returns a tuple of integers indicating the size of the array.
7. Series is a size as well as data mutable data structure.
8. A data frame can have heterogeneous data.
9. The `not in` operator returns True if the index is present and False otherwise.
10. The `isnull()` function returns False if a particular value is null and True otherwise.
11. Series have labelled indices that can be customized.
12. Data Frame has labelled axes for rows and columns.
13. To access a particular row from the data frame using label or column name, we can use the `iloc()` method.
14. NaN is equal to NaN in the context of comparing equivalent objects.
15. Descriptive statistics skips all NaN values by default.

Multiple Choice Questions

1. Pandas can be used to read data from _____.
   a. CSV File   b. Text File   c. SQL Databases   d. All of these
2. NumPy stands for _____.
   a. Number Python   b. Number Pandas   c. Numeric Python   d. Numeric Pandas
3. The array index starts from _____.
   a. 0   b. −1   c. 1   d. 10

4. An element in a multi-dimensional array is specified using _____ indices.
   a. 0   b. 1   c. n   d. 10
5. In NumPy, dimensions of the array are called _____.
   a. axes   b. rank   c. index   d. subscript
6. _____ is a function that allow users to create an array of elements supplied as an argument.
   a. `np.ones`   b. `np.zeroes`   c. `np.array`   d. `np.full`
7. _____ returns the total number of elements in the NumPy array.
   a. Shape   b. Size   c. Itemsize   d. Reshape
8. By default, `head()` function displays first _____ rows.
   a. 2   b. 5   c. 6   d. 10
9. If the specified label does not exist in a series, then which error is raised?
   a. KeyError   b. ValueError   c. IndexError   d. NameError
10. _____ returns a tuple specifying total number of elements including missing or empty values (NaN).
    a. Series.values   b. Series.size   c. Series.shape   d. Series.hasnans
11. A data frame can be created from a _____.
    a. Dictionary   b. Series   c. ndarray   d. All of these.
12. If we try to compare Pandas objects of different lengths, then which error will be raised?
    a. KeyError   b. ValueError   c. IndexError   d. NameError

Give the Output

1. ```
   import pandas as pd
   import numpy as np
   data = {'a' : 0., 'b' : 1., 'c' : 2.}
   s = pd.Series(data,index=['b','c','d','a'])
   print(s)
   ```
2. ```
   import pandas as pd
   s = pd.Series([1,2,3,4,5],index = ['a','b','c','d','e'])
   print(s[['a','c','d']])
   ```
3. ```
   series_list = pd.Series([1,2,3,4,5,6])
   series_np = pd.Series(np.array([10,20,30,40,50,60]))
   series_index = pd.Series(
   np.array([10,20,30,40,50,60]),
   index=np.arange(0,12,2)
   )
   print(series_index)
   ```
4. ```
   t_dict = {'a' : [1,2,3], 'b': [4,5], 'c':6, 'd': "Hello World"}
   series_dict = pd.Series(t_dict)
   print(series_dict)
   ```
5. ```
   import numpy as np
   a = np.ones((2,3), dtype=np.int16)
   print(a)
   ```
6. ```
   import numpy as np
   import pandas as pd
   x=pd.Series(data=[2,4,6,8])
   y=pd.Series(data=[11.2,18.6,22.5], index=['a','b','c'])
   print(x.index)
   print(x.values)
   print(y.index)
   print(y.values)
   ```

7. ```
import numpy as np
import pandas as pd
a=pd.Series(data=[1,2,3,4])
b=pd.Series(data=[4.9,8.2,5.6],
index=['x','y','z'])
print(a.ndim, b.ndim)
print(a.size, b.size)
print(a.nbytes, b.nbytes)
```

8. ```
import numpy as np
import pandas as pd
a=pd.Series(data=[1,2,3,np.NaN])
b=pd.Series(data=[4.9,8.2,5.6],index=['x','y','z'])
c=pd.Series()
print(a.empty,b.empty,c.empty)
print(a.hasnans,b.hasnans,c.hasnans)
print(len(a),len(b))
print(a.count( ),b.count( ))
```

9. ```
import pandas as pd
from pandas import Series
arr = Series([12, 32, 52, -15, 122])
print(arr)
 print('\nValues in this Array   : ',arr.values)
print('Index Values of this Array : ',arr.index)
```

10. ```
import pandas as pd
from pandas import Series
 arr = Series([2, 33, 66, 70, 15], index = ['a', 'e', 'i', 'o', 'u'])
print(arr)
 print('\nValues in this Array     : ',arr.values)
print('Index Values of this Array : ',arr.index)
```

11. ```
df = pd.DataFrame({'one' : pd.Series(np.random.randn(3), index=['a', 'b',
'c']),
'two' : pd.Series(np.random.randn(4), index=['a', 'b', 'c', 'd']),
'three' : pd.Series(np.random.randn(3), index=['b', 'c', 'd'])})
row = df.iloc[1]
column = df['two']
df.sub(row, axis='columns')
df.sub(row, axis=1)
df.sub(column, axis='index')
df.sub(column, axis=0)
df.gt(df2)
df2.ne(df)
(df > 0).all()
(df > 0).any()
(df > 0).any().any().
print(df+df == df*2)
print((df+df).equals(df*2))
print(df.sum(0, skipna=False))
print(df.sum(axis=1, skipna=True))
```

12. ```
data = np.random.randint(0, 7, size=50)
s = pd.Series(data)
s.value_counts()
s5 = pd.Series([1, 1, 3, 3, 3, 5, 5, 7, 7, 7])
print(s5.mode())
```

13. ```
    import pandas as pd
    d = {'one' : pd.Series([1, 2, 3], index=['a', 'b', 'c']),
        'two' : pd.Series([1, 2, 3, 4], index=['a', 'b', 'c', 'd'])}
    df = pd.DataFrame(d)
    print(df.loc['b'])
    ```
14. ```
    import pandas as pd
    data = {'Name':['Tom', 'Jack', 'Steve', 'Ricky'],'Age':[28,34,29,42]}
    df = pd.DataFrame(data)
    print(df)
    ```
15. ```
    import pandas as pd
    from pandas import Series
     f_dict = {'apples': 500, 'kiwi': 20, 'oranges': 100, 'cherries': 6000}
    print('Dictionary Items')
    print(f_dict)
    arr = Series(f_dict)
    print('\nArray Items')
    print(arr)
    ```
16. ```
    import pandas as pd
    from pandas import Series
     f_dict = {'apples': 500, 'kiwi': 20, 'oranges': 100, 'cherries': 6000}
    new_list = ['apples', 'cherries', 'kiwi', 'oranges']
     arr = Series(f_dict, index = new_list)
    print('Array Items')
    print(arr)
    ```
17. ```
    import pandas as pd
    from pandas import Series
     f_dict = {'apples': 500, 'kiwi': 20, 'oranges': 100, 'cherries': 6000}
    new_list = ['apples', 'banana', 'cherries', 'kiwi', 'oranges']
     arr = Series(f_dict, index = new_list)
    print('Array Items')
    print(arr)
    ```
18. ```
    import pandas as pd
    from pandas import Series
     f_dict = {'apples': 500, 'kiwi': 20, 'oranges': 100, 'cherries': 6000}
     arr = Series(f_dict)
    print(arr)
     print('\nAssigning Names')
    arr.name = 'No of Items'
    arr.index.name = 'Fruits'
    print(arr)
    ```
19. ```
    import pandas as pd
    from pandas import Series
    arr = Series([2, 4, -6, 8, -10, 12], index = ['a', 'e', 'i', 'o', 'u', 'z'])
    print(arr)
    print(arr['a'])
    print(arr['u'])
    print(arr[['a', 'o', 'z', 'e']])
    ```
20. ```
    import pandas as pd
    f_dict = {'apples': 500, 'kiwi': 20, 'oranges': 100, 'cherries':6000}
    arr2 = pd.Series(f_dict)
    print(arr2)
    'kiwi' in arr2
    ```

```
    'banana' in arr2
    'oranges' in arr2
```

21. ```
    Import pandas as pd
    from pandas import Series
    dict_items = {'apples': 500, 'kiwi': 20, 'oranges': 100, 'cherries': 6000}
    f_list = ['apples', 'banana', 'cherries', 'kiwi', 'oranges']
    arr = Series(dict_items, index = f_list)
    print(arr)
    print(pd.isnull(arr))
    print(arr.isnull())
    print(pd.notnull(arr))
    print(arr.notnull())
    ```

22. ```
    import pandas as pd
    d = {'one' : pd.Series([1, 2, 3], index=['a', 'b', 'c']),
         'two' : pd.Series([1, 2, 3, 4], index=['a', 'b', 'c', 'd'])}
    df = pd.DataFrame(d)
    df['three']=pd.Series([10,20,30],index=['a','b','c'])
    print df
    df['four']=df['one']+df['three']
    print(df)
    ```

23. ```
    import pandas as pd
    data = {'Name':['Tom', 'Jack', 'Steve', 'Ricky'],'Age':[28,34,29,42]}
    df = pd.DataFrame(data, index=['rank1','rank2','rank3','rank4'])
    print(df)
    ```

24. ```
    import pandas as pd
    data = [{'a': 1, 'b': 2},{'a': 5, 'b': 10, 'c': 20}]
    df = pd.DataFrame(data)
    print(df)
    ```

25. ```
    import pandas as pd
    data = [{'a': 1, 'b': 2},{'a': 5, 'b': 10, 'c': 20}]
    #With two column indices, values same as dictionary keys
    df1 = pd.DataFrame(data, index=['first', 'second'], columns=['a', 'b'])
    #With two column indices with one index with other name
    df2 = pd.DataFrame(data, index=['first', 'second'], columns=['a', 'b1'])
    print(df1)
    print(df2)
    ```

26. ```
    import pandas as pd
    d = {'one' : pd.Series([1, 2, 3], index=['a', 'b', 'c']),
         'two' : pd.Series([1, 2, 3, 4], index=['a', 'b', 'c', 'd'])}
    df = pd.DataFrame(d)
    print(df)
    ```

27. ```
    import pandas as pd
    d = {'one' : pd.Series([1, 2, 3], index=['a', 'b', 'c']),
         'two' : pd.Series([1, 2, 3, 4], index=['a', 'b', 'c', 'd'])}
    df = pd.DataFrame(d)
    print(df ['one'])
    print(df.values)
    ```

28. ```
    import pandas as pd
    d = {'one' : pd.Series([1, 2, 3], index=['a', 'b', 'c']),
         'two' : pd.Series([1, 2, 3, 4], index=['a', 'b', 'c', 'd']),
    ```

```
            'three' : pd.Series([10,20,30], index=['a','b','c'])}
    df = pd.DataFrame(d)
    print ("Our dataframe is:")
    print(df)
    print ("Deleting the first column using DEL function:")
    del df['one']
    print(df)
    df.pop('two')
    print(df)
```

29. ```
    import pandas as pd
    import numpy as np
    d = {'Name':pd.
    Series(['Tom','James','Ricky','Vin','Steve','Smith','Jack']),
        'Age':pd.Series([25,26,25,23,30,29,23]),
        'Rating':pd.Series([4.23,3.24,3.98,2.56,3.20,4.6,3.8])}
    df = pd.DataFrame(d)
    print ("Row axis labels and column axis labels are:")
    print(df.axes
    print(df.empty)
    print(df.ndim)
    print(df.shape)
    print(df.size)
    ```

30. ```
    import pandas as pd
    d = {'one' : pd.Series([1, 2, 3], index=['a', 'b', 'c']),
        'two' : pd.Series([1, 2, 3, 4], index=['a', 'b', 'c', 'd'])}
    df = pd.DataFrame(d)
    print(df[2:4])
    ```

31. ```
    import pandas as pd
    df = pd.DataFrame([[1, 2], [3, 4]], columns = ['a','b'])
    df2 = pd.DataFrame([[5, 6], [7, 8]], columns = ['a','b'])
    df = df.append(df2)
    print(df)
    ```

32. ```
    import pandas as pd
    df = pd.DataFrame([[1, 2], [3, 4]], columns = ['a','b'])
    df2 = pd.DataFrame([[5, 6], [7, 8]], columns = ['a','b'])
    df = df.append(df2)
    df = df.drop(0)
    print(df)
    ```

33. `pd.Series(['foo', 'bar', 'baz']) == pd.Index(['foo', 'bar', 'qux'])`

34. `pd.Series(['foo', 'bar', 'baz']) == np.array(['foo', 'bar', 'qux'])`

35. ```
    s = pd.Series(['a', 'a', 'b', 'b', 'a', 'a', np.nan, 'c', 'd', 'a'])
    s.describe()
    ```

36. ```
    import pandas as pd
    list = [ ['Geeks'], ['For'], ['Geeks'], ['is'],
            [<a>], [<portal>], [<for>], [<geeks>] ]
    df = pd.Series((i[0] for i in list))
    print(df)
    ```

37. ```
    import pandas as pd
    list = [ ['Geeks'], ['For'], ['Geeks'], ['is'],
            ['a'], ['portal'], ['for'], ['geeks'] ]
    df = pd.Series((i[0] for i in list))
    print(df)
    ```
    ```

38. ```
import pandas as pd
import numpy as np
data1 = pd.Series([12,25,37,45])
data2 = pd.Series([10,27,31,40])
print(data1 + data2)
```
39. ```
import pandas as pd
cars = {'Brand': ['Honda Civic','Toyota Corolla','Ford Focus','Audi A4'],
        'Price': [22000,25000,27000,35000]    }
df = pd.DataFrame(cars, columns = ['Brand', 'Price'])
print(df)
```

Find the Error

1. ```
import pandas as pd
s = pd.Series([1,2,3,4,5],index = ['a','b','c','d','e'])
print(s['f'])
```
2. ```
my_list = [[1,2,3,4],
           [5,6,7,8],
           [9,10,11,12],
           [13,14,15,16],
           [17,18,19,20]]
df = pd.DataFrame(my_list)
df = pd.DataFrame(
my_list,
index = ["1->", "2->", "3->", "4->", "5->"],
columns = ["A", "B", "C", "D"]
)
print(df)
```
3. `pd.Series(['foo', 'bar', 'baz']) == pd.Series(['foo', 'bar'])`
4. `pd.Series(['foo', 'bar', 'baz']) == pd.Series(['foo'])`

Answers

Fill in the Blanks

1. "Python Data Analysis Library"
2. NumPy
3. index
4. Two-dimensional array
5. matrix/2-D array
6. row
7. import
8. np.ones
9. np.arrange()
10. Ndim
11. Importing
12. pd.Series()
13. NaN
14. all()
15. get()
16. None, default value
17. map()
18. del, pop()
19. broadcast
20. describe()
21. idxmin(), idxmax()
22. mode()
23. FileNotFound Error
24. df.to_csv()
25. writing

State True or False

1. False
2. True
3. False
4. False
5. False
6. True
7. False
8. True
9. False
10. False
11. True
12. True
13. False
14. False
15. True

Multiple Choice Questions

1. d
2. c
3. a
4. c
5. a
6. c
7. b
8. b
9. a
10. c
11. d
12. b

Give the Output

1. ```
   b    1.0
   c    2.0
   d    NaN
   a    0.0
   dtype: float64
   ```
2. ```
   a    1
   c    3
   d    4
   dtype: int64
   ```
3. ```
   0     10
   2     20
   4     30
   6     40
   8     50
   10    60
   dtype: int32
   ```
4. ```
   t_dict = {'a' : [1,2,3], 'b':
   [4,5], 'c':6, 'd': "Hello World"}
   series_dict = pd.Series(t_dict)
   print(series_dict)
   ```
5. ```
   [[1 1 1]
    [1 1 1]]
   ```
6. ```
   RangeIndex(start=0, stop=4, step=1)
   [2 4 6 8]
   Index(['a', 'b', 'c'],
   dtype='object')
   [11.2 18.6 22.5]
   ```
7. ```
   1 1
   4 3
   32 24
   ```
8. ```
   False False True
   True False False
   4 3
   3 3
   ```
9. ```
   0     12
   1     32
   2     52
   3    -15
   4    122
   dtype: int64
   Values in this Array  : [ 12
   32  52 -15 122]
   Index Values of this Array
   :   RangeIndex(start=0, stop=5,
   step=1)
   ```
10. ```
    a     2
    e    33
    i    66
    o    70
    u    15
    dtype: int64
    Values in this Array   : [ 2 33
    66 70 15]
    Index Values of this Array :
    Index(['a', 'e', 'i', 'o', 'u'],
    dtype='object')
    >>>
    ```
11. ```
         one    two   three
    a    True   True  False
    b    True   True  True
    c    True   True  True
    d    False  True  True
    True
    one           NaN
    two      -1.403811
    three         NaN
    dtype: float64
    a   -1.513989
    b    0.185468
    c   -0.134224
    d   -1.023881
    dtype: float64
    ```
12. ```
    0    3
    1    7
    dtype: int64
    ```
    (Note that the answer may vary.)
13. ```
    one    2.0
    two    2.0
    Name: b, dtype: float64
    ```
14. ```
       Name   Age
    0  Tom    28
    1  Jack   34
    2  Steve  29
    3  Ricky  42
    ```
15. ```
    Dictionary Items
    {'apples': 500, 'kiwi': 20,
    'oranges': 100, 'cherries': 6000}
    Array Items
    apples       500
    kiwi          20
    oranges      100
    ```
    ```

```
    cherries     6000
    dtype: int64
16. Array Items
    apples        500
    cherries     6000
    kiwi           20
    oranges       100
    dtype: int64
17. import pandas as pd
    from pandas import Series
     f_dict = {'apples': 500, 'kiwi':
    20, 'oranges': 100, 'cherries':
    6000}
    new_list = ['apples', 'banana',
    'cherries', 'kiwi', 'oranges']
     arr = Series(f_dict, index = new_
    list)
    print('Array Items')
    print(arr)
18. apples        500
    kiwi           20
    oranges       100
    cherries     6000
    dtype: int64
    Assigning Names
    Fruits
    apples        500
    kiwi           20
    oranges       100
    cherries     6000
    Name: No of Items, dtype: int64
19. a    2
    e    4
    i   -6
    o    8
    u  -10
    z   12
    dtype: int64
    2
    -10
    a    2
    o    8
    z   12
    e    4
    dtype: int64
20. apples        500
    kiwi           20
    oranges       100
    cherries     6000
    dtype: int64
21. apples       500.0
    banana        NaN
    cherries    6000.0
```

```
    kiwi          20.0
    oranges      100.0
    dtype: float64
    apples       False
    banana        True
    cherries     False
    kiwi         False
    oranges      False
    dtype: bool
    apples       False
    banana        True
    cherries     False
    kiwi         False
    oranges      False
    dtype: bool
    apples        True
    banana       False
    cherries      True
    kiwi          True
    oranges       True
    dtype: bool
    apples        True
    banana       False
    cherries      True
    kiwi          True
    oranges       True
    dtype: bool
22.      one   two   three
    a    1.0    1    10.0
    b    2.0    2    20.0
    c    3.0    3    30.0
    d    NaN    4     NaN
         one   two   three   four
    a    1.0    1    10.0   11.0
    b    2.0    2    20.0   22.0
    c    3.0    3    30.0   33.0
    d    NaN    4     NaN    NaN
23.           Name   Age
    rank1     Tom    28
    rank2     Jack   34
    rank3     Steve  29
    rank4     Ricky  42
24.  a    b    c
    0    1    2   NaN
    1    5   10   20.0
25.        a   b
    first   1   2
    second  5  10
           a   b1
    first   1  NaN
    second  5  NaN
26.    one  two
    a   1.0   1
```

```
         b    2.0    2
         c    3.0    3
         d    NaN    4
27.      a    1.0
         b    2.0
         c    3.0
         d    NaN
   Name: one, dtype: float64
   [[ 1.  1.]
    [ 2.  2.]
    [ 3.  3.]
    [nan  4.]]
28.        one    two    three
      a    1.0    1      10.0
      b    2.0    2      20.0
      c    3.0    3      30.0
      d    NaN    4      NaN
   Deleting the first column using DEL function:
           two    three
      a    1      10.0
      b    2      20.0
      c    3      30.0
      d    4      NaN
           three
      a    10.0
      b    20.0
      c    30.0
      d    NaN
29. Row axis labels and column axis labels are:
    [RangeIndex(start=0, stop=7, step=1), Index(['Name', 'Age', 'Rating'], dtype='object')]
    False
    2
    (7, 3)
    21
30.      one    two
      c   3.0    3
      d   NaN    4
31.    a    b
    0  1    2
    1  3    4
    0  5    6
    1  7    8
```

```
32.    a    b
    1  3    4
    1  7    8
33.
    0    True
    1    True
    2    False
    dtype: bool
34. 0    True
    1    True
    2    False
    dtype: bool
35.
    count     9
    unique    4
    top       a
    freq      5
    dtype: object
36. 0       Geeks
    1         For
    2       Geeks
    3          is
    4           a
    5      portal
    6         for
    7       geeks
    dtype: object
37. 0       Geeks
    1         For
    2       Geeks
    3          is
    4           a
    5      portal
    6         for
    7       geeks
    dtype: object
38. 0    22
    1    52
    2    68
    3    85
    dtype: int64
39.       Brand    Price
    0   Honda Civic    22000
    1  Toyota Corolla  25000
    2    Ford Focus    27000
    3       Audi A4    35000
```

Find the Error

1. KeyError
2. NameError: name 'pd' is not defined
3. ValueError: Series lengths must match to compare
4. ValueError: Series lengths must match to compare

More on Python Pandas Module

2

Chapter Objectives

In the last chapter, we have seen the usage of two very important modules – NumPy and Pandas. We have also covered Pandas in detail. The two most widely used data structures of Pandas – Series and Data Frames were described in depth. However, there are a lot more ways in which we can manipulate the data stored in a data frame. So, in this chapter continue with the discussion of the previous chapter and explore some advanced operations that can be performed on a Pandas object. Here, we will cover the following topics:

- Working with data frames – pivoting, sorting, re-indexing and combining data frames
- Plotting histograms
- Quartiles and Quantiles
- Function application
- Aggregation by one and by multiple columns
- Transform function
- Handling missing values
- Importing and exporting between databases and Pandas

2.1 QUICK REVIEW OF PANDAS

Pandas is an open-source Python Library that has functions providing high-performance data manipulation and analysis. Prior to Pandas, Python had very little contribution towards data analysis. But as Pandas evolved, Python came to be used to load, prepare, manipulate, model, and analyze data.

Python with Pandas is used in a wide range of fields including academic and commercial domains including finance, economics, statistics, analytics, etc. Some important features of Pandas include

- Fast and efficient DataFrame object with default and customized indexing
- Ability to read data in objects from different file formats
- Managing missing data
- Reshaping and pivoting of date sets
- Label-based slicing, indexing and sub-setting of large data sets
- Ease of inserting and deleting rows/columns in a data structure
- Support of aggregating and grouping data
- Functionality for high-performance merging and joining of data
- Ability to deal with Time Series data.

Pandas is the fundamental building block for doing practical, real-world data analysis in Python. It has become the most powerful and flexible open-source data analysis/manipulation tool available in any language. The key component in Pandas is the Data Frame.

Typically, data science practitioners often need to perform various data engineering operations such as aggregation, sorting and filtering data. And data frame tends to be the best object for this purpose.

A data frame is a two-dimensional data structure in which data is organized in a tabular fashion using rows and columns. The basic features of data frame are as given below:

- Columns are of different data types.
- Size is mutable.

- Data frame has labelled axes for rows and columns.
- Arithmetic operations can be performed on rows and columns.

2.2 PIVOTING DATA FRAME

The `pivot()` function is used to reshape a given DataFrame object organized by the given index/column values. The syntax of `pivot()` function can be given as,

DataFrame.pivot(self, index=None, columns=None, values=None)

where,
index is an optional argument which specifies the columns that will be used to make a new frame's index. If no column is specified, the existing index is used.
columns is used to specify columns that will be used to make the new frame's columns.
values is an optional argument that specifies column(s) to be used for populating the new frame's values. If nothing is specified, all remaining columns will be used and the result will have hierarchically indexed columns.

The `pivot()` function returns a reshaped DataFrame. However, ValueError will be raised if there are any index or column combinations having multiple values. In other words, ***ValueError is raised if there are any duplicate values in the data frame.***

Example 2.1

```
PIVOTING DATA FRAME
import pandas as pd
# creating a dataframe
df = pd.DataFrame({'NAME': ['Gitisha', 'Sonakshi', 'Meena'], 'DEGREE': ['Masters',
    'Graduate', 'Graduate'],'AGE': [24, 26, 25]})
print("ORIGINAL DATA FRAME:")
print(df)
print("DATA FRAME AFTER USING ONLY AGE AS VALUE:")
df1 = df.pivot('NAME','DEGREE', 'AGE')
print(df1)
print("DATA FRAME AFTER USING AGE AND NAME AS VALUES:")
df1 = df.pivot(index ='NAME', columns ='DEGREE', values =['AGE', 'NAME'])
print(df1)
```

OUTPUT

```
ORIGINAL DATA FRAME:
     NAME      DEGREE    AGE
0    Gitisha   Masters   24
1    Sonakshi  Graduate  26
2    Meena     Graduate  25
DATA FRAME AFTER USING ONLY AGE AS VALUE:
DEGREE     Graduate  Masters
NAME
Gitisha    NaN       24.0
Meena      25.0      NaN
Sonakshi   26.0      NaN
DATA FRAME AFTER USING AGE AND NAME AS VALUES:
           AGE   NAME
DEGREE     Graduate  Masters   Graduate  Masters
NAME
Gitisha    NaN       24        NaN       Gitisha
Meena      25        NaN       Meena     NaN
Sonakshi   26        NaN       Sonakshi  NaN
```

2.3 SORTING A DATAFRAME

To sort data means to arrange data in a specific order. We can sort data either in ascending (small-to-big) order or descending order (big-to-small). Both numerical as well as textual data can be sorted in the specified order. Pandas `sort_values()` function sorts a data frame in Ascending or Descending order of the passed Column. The syntax of this function can be given as,

DataFrame.sort_values(by, axis=0, ascending=True, inplace=False, kind='quicksort', na_position='last')

where,
by specifies column(s) names by which the data frame has to be sorted.
axis specifies rows or columns. axis = 0 indicates 'index' for Rows and axis = 1 indicates 'columns' for Column.
ascending is a Boolean value which sorts data frame in ascending order if True. By default, the values are sorted in ascending order.
inplace is a Boolean value. If its value is True, then the changes are made in the data frame passed to the function.
kind accepts a string that chooses a particular algorithm to sort data frame. It can take the value 'quicksort', 'mergesort' or 'heapsort'. By default, mergesort is used.
na_position takes a string value which can be either 'last' or 'first'. It is used to set the position of Null values. The default of this argument is 'last'.

Note that every parameter has some default value, except the 'by' parameter.
The function returns a sorted Data Frame with the same dimensions as that of the original data frame.

Example 2.2

```
# Sort by Brand in descending order from pandas import DataFrame
Cars = {'Brand': ['Ecosport','Brezza','Nexon','Audi A5'], 'Price': [963000,734000,695
    000,6751000],
    'Year': [2012,2016,2014,2017]
}
df = DataFrame(Cars, columns= ['Brand', 'Price','Year'])
print("ORIGINAL DATA FRAME")
print(df)
# sort by Brand - descending order
df.sort_values(by=['Brand'], inplace=True, ascending=False)
print("SORTED DATA FRAME")
print (df)
```

OUTPUT
```
ORIGINAL DATA FRAME
     Brand    Price    Year
0    Ecosport 963000   2012
1    Brezza   734000   2016
2    Nexon    695000   2014
3    Audi A5  6751000  2017
SORTED DATA FRAME
     Brand    Price    Year
2    Nexon    695000   2014
0    Ecosport 963000   2012
1    Brezza   734000   2016
3    Audi A5  6751000  2017
```

We can sort a data frame not by one but by several columns together. For this, we can specify a list of columns as value in the `by` parameter as given below.

df.sort_values(by=['First Column','Second Column',...], inplace=True)

For example, we can sort both by the 'Year' and the 'Price.' Here, Year will take priority over Price. We will sort by Year and if two records have same value for Year then, the one with lower price will be displayed first (provided sorting is done in ascending order).

Example 2.3

```python
# Sort - multiple columns from pandas import DataFrame
Cars = {'Brand': ['Ecosport','Brezza','Audi Q5','Audi A5'], 'Price': [963000,734000,
    5026000,6751000],
    'Year': [2012,2016,2008,2017]
}
df = DataFrame(Cars, columns= ['Brand', 'Price','Year'])
print("ORIGINAL DATA FRAME")
print(df)
# sort by Year and Price
df.sort_values(by=['Year','Price'], inplace=True)
print("SORTED DATA FRAME")
print(df)
```

OUTPUT

```
ORIGINAL DATA FRAME
    Brand     Price   Year
0   Ecosport  963000  2012
1   Brezza    734000  2016
2   Audi Q5   5026000 2008
3   Audi A5   6751000 2017
SORTED DATA FRAME
    Brand     Price   Year
2   Audi Q5   5026000 2008
0   Ecosport  963000  2012
1   Brezza    734000  2016
3   Audi A5   6751000 2017
```

2.3.1 Sorting by Labels

We can also sort the data frame by using index. The `sort_index()` function sorts a data frame by its row index.

Basically, the term `sort_index()` is a little misleading. Pandas DataFrame allows users to indicate which column acts as the *row index*. If *no* specific column is specified to be the row index, Pandas will create a zero-based row index by default. Once a column is specified as row index, the data frame can be sorted using the `sort_index()` function.

By default, sort_index() function sorts the row labels in ascending order. As an alternative, we can also use the axis argument and set it to 1 and specify the order of sorting. This will sort the data frame by column labels and not column values.

Example 2.4

```python
import pandas as pd
import numpy as np
unsorted_df =
pd.DataFrame(np.random.randn(5,2),index=[1,4,3,2,0],columns=['Z','A'])
sorted_df=unsorted_df.sort_index(axis=1)
print(sorted_df)
```

OUTPUT

```
        A         Z
1   -0.280872   0.239151
4   -0.907434   0.023017
3   -0.402850   0.083142
2    0.551225  -0.645303
0    1.518120  -0.604385
```

PROGRAMMER'S ZONE

1. **Write a program that reads data from the given link into a data frame in Python. Demonstrate sorting of the data frame in different ways.**

```
import pandas as pd
data_url = 'https://raw.githubusercontent.com/jvns/pandas-cookbook/master/data/
    weather_2012.csv'
# read data from url as pandas dataframe
weather = pd.read_csv(data_url)
sort_by_weather = weather.sort_values('Weather')
print("SORTED DATA FRAME")
print(sort_by_weather.head(n=6))
#sort by weather in descending order
sort_by_weather_desc = weather.sort_values('Weather',ascending=False)
print("SORTED DATA FRAME INDESCENDING ORDER")
print(sort_by_weather_desc.head(n=6))
#Sort by Weather and Temp
sort_by_weather_temp = weather.sort_values(['Weather','Temp (C)'])
print("DATA FRAME SORTED BY WEATHER AND TEMP")
print(sort_by_weather_temp.head(n=6))
#Sort by Weather and Temp in different order
sort_by_weather_asc_temp_desc = weather.sort_values(['Weather','Temp (C)'],
    ascending=[True, False])
print("DATA FRAME SORTED BY WEATHER AND TEMP IN DIFFERENT ORDERS")
print(sort_by_weather_asc_temp_desc.head(n=6))
# sort by putting missing values first
sort_na_first = weather.sort_values('Weather',na_position='first')
print("DATA FRAME SORTED BY PUTTING NAs FIRST")
print(sort_na_first.head(n=6))
#sort by index
weather.sort_index(inplace=True)
print(weather.head(n=6))
```

OUTPUT

```
SORTED DATA FRAME
           Date/Time       Temp (C)  ...  Stn Press (kPa)   Weather
7103  2012-10-22 23:00:00       6.4  ...           101.34     Clear
4203  2012-06-24 03:00:00      14.9  ...           101.02     Clear
4204  2012-06-24 04:00:00      14.4  ...           101.04     Clear
4205  2012-06-24 05:00:00      14.0  ...           101.04     Clear
4206  2012-06-24 06:00:00      17.8  ...           101.04     Clear
4207  2012-06-24 07:00:00      20.0  ...           101.03     Clear
[6 rows x 8 columns]
SORTED DATA FRAME INDESCENDING ORDER
           Date/Time       ...                           Weather
4757  2012-07-17 05:00:00  ...         Thunderstorms,Rain,Fog
4761  2012-07-17 09:00:00  ...  Thunderstorms,Rain Showers,Fog
4323  2012-06-29 03:00:00  ...  Thunderstorms,Rain Showers,Fog
5108  2012-07-31 20:00:00  ...  Thunderstorms,Rain Showers,Fog
3580  2012-05-29 04:00:00  ...         Thunderstorms,Rain Showers
4768  2012-07-17 16:00:00  ...         Thunderstorms,Rain Showers
[6 rows x 8 columns]
```

```
DATA FRAME SORTED BY WEATHER AND TEMP
            Date/Time    Temp (C)  ...  Stn Press (kPa)  Weather
344  2012-01-15 08:00:00    -23.3  ...           102.45    Clear
363  2012-01-16 03:00:00    -19.2  ...           103.07    Clear
365  2012-01-16 05:00:00    -19.1  ...           103.02    Clear
364  2012-01-16 04:00:00    -18.7  ...           103.05    Clear
366  2012-01-16 06:00:00    -18.7  ...           103.01    Clear
362  2012-01-16 02:00:00    -18.5  ...           103.08    Clear
[6 rows x 8 columns]
DATA FRAME SORTED BY WEATHER AND TEMP IN DIFFERENT ORDERS
            Date/Time    Temp (C)  ...  Stn Press (kPa)  Weather
5199 2012-08-04 15:00:00     32.8  ...           101.39    Clear
5200 2012-08-04 16:00:00     32.5  ...           101.34    Clear
5201 2012-08-04 17:00:00     32.5  ...           101.32    Clear
5198 2012-08-04 14:00:00     32.0  ...           101.48    Clear
4671 2012-07-13 15:00:00     31.9  ...           101.46    Clear
4118 2012-06-20 14:00:00     31.7  ...           100.83    Clear
[6 rows x 8 columns]
DATA FRAME SORTED BY PUTTING NAs FIRST
            Date/Time    Temp (C)  ...  Stn Press (kPa)  Weather
7103 2012-10-22 23:00:00      6.4  ...           101.34    Clear
4203 2012-06-24 03:00:00     14.9  ...           101.02    Clear
4204 2012-06-24 04:00:00     14.4  ...           101.04    Clear
4205 2012-06-24 05:00:00     14.0  ...           101.04    Clear
4206 2012-06-24 06:00:00     17.8  ...           101.04    Clear
4207 2012-06-24 07:00:00     20.0  ...           101.03    Clear
[6 rows x 8 columns]
            Date/Time    Temp (C)  ...  Stn Press (kPa)              Weather
0    2012-01-01 00:00:00    -1.8  ...           101.24                  Fog
1    2012-01-01 01:00:00    -1.8  ...           101.24                  Fog
2    2012-01-01 02:00:00    -1.8  ...           101.26   Freezing Drizzle,Fog
3    2012-01-01 03:00:00    -1.5  ...           101.27   Freezing Drizzle,Fog
4    2012-01-01 04:00:00    -1.5  ...           101.23                  Fog
5    2012-01-01 05:00:00    -1.4  ...           101.27                  Fog
[6 rows x 8 columns]
```

2.4 COMBINING DATA FRAMES

We can combine two similar data sets. This is especially important where values in one data set are preferred over the other. This situation frequently occurs when one of the two data series representing a particular economic indicator is considered to be of "higher quality". However, the lower-quality series may have a more complete data coverage. So, we can combine two DataFrame objects where missing values in one DataFrame are conditionally filled with like-labelled values from the other DataFrame. The `combine_first()` function is used for implementing this operation.

Example 2.5

```
import numpy as np
import pandas as pd
df1 = pd.DataFrame({'A': [1., np.nan, 3., 5., np.nan], 'B': [np.nan, 2., 3., np.nan,
       6.]}) df2 = pd.DataFrame({'A': [5., 2., 4., np.nan, 3., 7.],
'B': [np.nan, np.nan, 3., 4., 6., 8.]})
print("DATA FRAME 1: ")
print(df1)
```

```
print("DATA FRAME 2: ")
print(df2)
print("COMBINING DATA FRAMES : ")
print(df1.combine_first(df2))
```

OUTPUT

```
DATA FRAME 1:
     A    B
0  1.0  NaN
1  NaN  2.0
2  3.0  3.0
3  5.0  NaN
4  NaN  6.0
DATA FRAME 2:
     A    B
0  5.0  NaN
1  2.0  NaN
2  4.0  3.0
3  NaN  4.0
4  3.0  6.0
5  7.0  8.0
COMBINING DATA FRAMES:
     A    B
0  1.0  NaN
1  2.0  2.0
2  3.0  3.0
3  5.0  4.0
4  3.0  6.0
5  7.0  8.0
```

The `combine_first()` method used in the above code can be replaced with a more general DataFrame method using `combine()`. The `combine()` method takes another DataFrame and a combiner function as an argument to perform its intended task.

2.5 HISTOGRAM

Right from Class 3, we have been studying graphs. In statistics, a histogram represents distribution of numerical data in bins. The count of each bin is represented in the histogram. It is not that only numerical data can be represented; we can even categorize categorical or date data in different bins.

To create histograms, we will be using plotly express module, which can be installed by writing,

`pip install plotly_express==0.4.0`

Plotly Express is a high-level Python visualization library that has very simple syntax for creating even complex charts. You just need to import this module to make richly interactive plots in just a single function call (including faceting, maps, animations, and trendlines).

Plotly Express has built-in data sets which we can use for analysis or creating histograms. The module is totally free and comes with its permissive open-source MIT license. Histograms and other figures created using Plotly can be exported to almost any file format or edited.

The key advantage of this module is that it is easy-to-use, operates on tidy (or clean/standardized) data and produces easy-to-style figures.

Example 2.6

```
# The graph displays count on Y-axis and total_bill on X axis
import plotly_express as px
# use data set tips
df = px.data.tips()
# numerical data total bill is displayed on the X-axis
hist = px.histogram(df, x="total_bill")
hist.show()
```

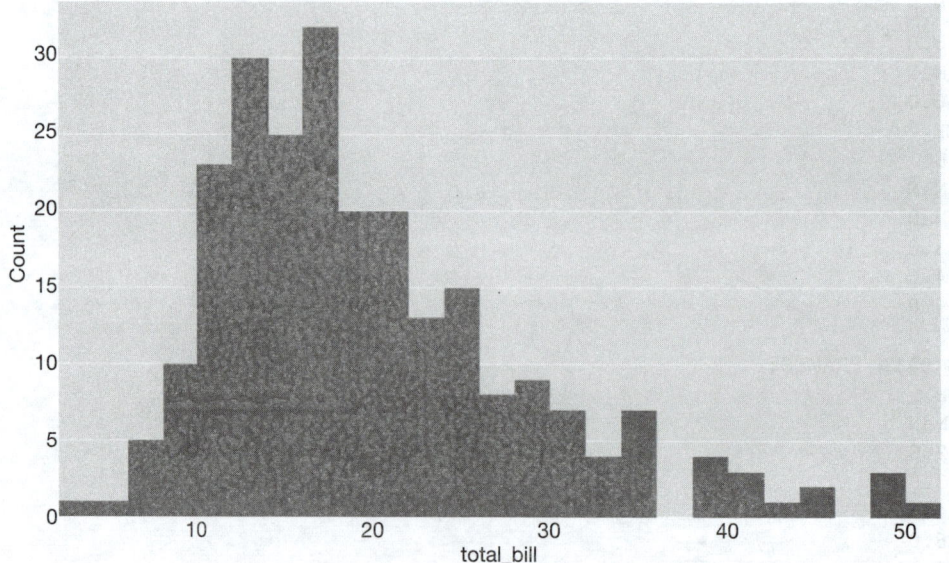

Example 2.7

```
# The graph displays count on Y-axis and days on X axis
import plotly_express as px
# use data set tips
df = px.data.tips()
# categorical data day is displayed on the X-axis
hist = px.histogram(df, x="Day")
hist.show()
```

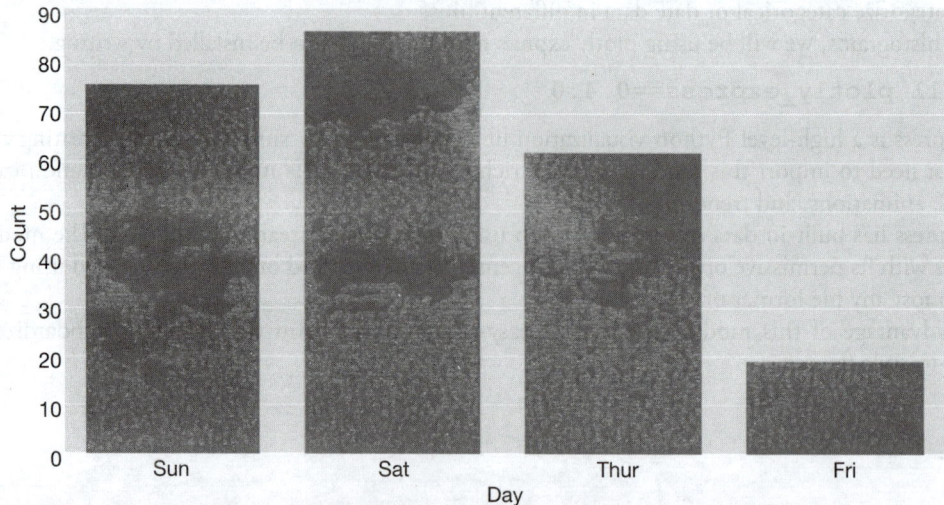

Choosing the Number of Bins

When we draw a histogram, the number of bins is chosen depending on the typical number of samples in a bin. However, we can alter the number of bins as well as the range of values in a particular bin. For example, the code given below categorizes data into 10 bins. The data that will be used has columns like total_bill, tip, sex, smoker, day, time and size.

Example 2.8

```
# Plot graph with specified number of bins
import plotly_express as px
# use data set tips
df = px.data.tips()
hist = px.histogram(df, x="total_bill", nbins=10)
hist.show()
```

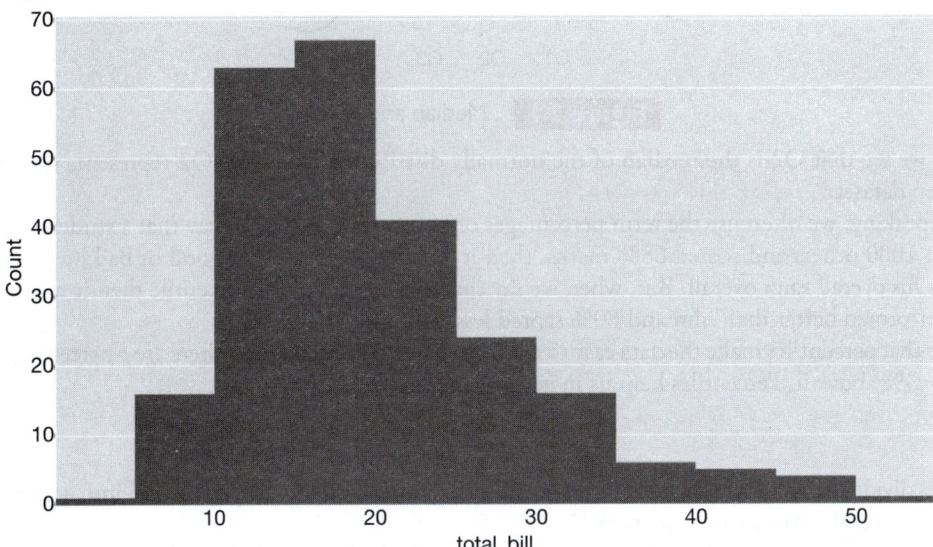

Python allows users to plot several histograms for the different values of one column. Observe how the histogram function is used to plot both total bill and sex on the x-axis.

```
# Plot multiple values of one column
import plotly.express as px
df = px.data.tips()
# plotting histograms for the different values of one column
hist = px.histogram(df, x="total_bill", color="sex")
hist.show()
```

2.6 QUANTILES

As we said earlier, Python is a great language for doing data analysis. We know that Quantile plays a very important role in Statistics when one deals with the Normal Distribution. Quantile is a measure of location and, to evaluate it, `Series.quantile()`, Pandas `dataframe.quantile()` and the `numpy.quantile(arr, q, axis = None)` functions return values at the given quantile over the requested axis. But before going into details of these functions, let us first understand the term quantile.

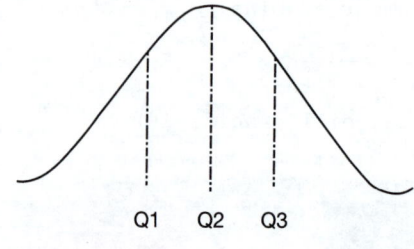

Figure 2.1 Median and IQR

In Fig. 2.1, we see that Q2 is the median of the normally distributed data. Q3–Q2 represents the inter-quantile range of the given dataset.

Practically speaking, we often use the term percentages or percentiles. When we say that a student appeared in an exam along with 1000 others and scored 68% marks, then it is difficult to say how good or bad he performed in the exam, or what is his overall rank overall. But, when we say that a student had 80 percentile then it means 20% of the students have performed better than him and 80% scored less than him.

Thus, we see that percentiles make the data easy to read. pth percentile means that there are p percent of observations below it, $(100 - p)\%$ above it. Percentiles help us in getting an idea on outliers.

Quartiles

While percentiles divide the whole population into 100 groups, quartiles divide the population into 4 groups. Quartiles are values that break up the dataset into quarters:

p = 25: First Quartile or Lower Quartile (LQ). The first quartile is the point below which a quarter of the data lie.

p = 50: Second Quartile or Median. The second quartile is the point below which half of the data lie. We already know this point by the name of median. It is also called the middle quartile.

p = 75: Third Quartile or Upper Quartile (UQ). It is the point below which three-quarters of the data lie.

The `describe()` function computes the 1st, 2nd and 3rd quartiles, but the `quantile()` function can be used to compute any kind of quantile – 0.2, 0.4,0.6, etc. where 0.2 stands for the 20th percentile, 0.4 stands for the 40th percentile, and so on.

Quantile indicates a point in distribution below which, a portion of the data lies. Basically, quantile is a generic term. The measures percentile, quintile, decile and quartiles are all quantiles that divide a distribution into portions. For example,

Percentiles divide the distribution into hundredths.
Quintiles divide the distribution as parts of fifths.
Deciles divide the distribution into parts of tenths.
Quarters divide the distribution into quarters.

The syntax of the `quantile()` function can be given as,

Object_name.quantile(q, axis, numeric_only, interpolation)

where,
q is float or array. Its default value is 0.5 (or 50% quantile). The value of q varies from 0 to 1 as shown in Table I. That is, $0 <= q <= 1$.
axis indicates index or columns. Its value is 0 to specify index or row and 1 for columns. The default value of axis is 0.

numeric_only is a Boolean value. If False, the quantile of datetime and timedelta data will also be computed, else not. Its default value is True. **interpolation** can be 'linear', 'lower', 'higher', 'midpoint', 'nearest'. The default value is linear.

The function returns quantiles (Series or DataFrame). If q is an array, a DataFrame will be returned where the index is q. If q is a float, a Series will be returned where the values are the quantiles. The return value will depend on the value of q. The value of q can be as specified in Table 2.1.

Table 2.1 Value of q and quantile

Value of 'q'	Quantile
0.05	1st quintile
0.1	1st Decile/2nd quintile
0.2	2nd Decile/4th quintile
0.25	1st quarter/5th quintile/ 25th percentile
0.3	3rd Decile/6th quintile/ 30th percentile
0.4	4th Decile/8th quintile/ 40th percentile
0.5	1st half/2nd quarter/5th Decile/10th quintile/50th percentile
0.6	6th Decile/12th quintile/60th percentile
0.7	7th Decile/14th quintile/70th percentile
0.75	3rd quarter/15th quintile/ 75th percentile
0.9	9th Decile/18th quintile/90th percentile
1.0	10th Decile/20th quintile/100th percentile

Example 2.9

```
Import pandas as pd
# Creating the dataframe
df = pd.DataFrame({"A":[1, 2, 3, 4, 5],
                   "B":[6, 7, 8, 9, 10],
                   "C":[9, 8, 7, 6, 5],
                   "D":[1, 2, 6, 3, 4]})
print("Data Frame")
print(df)
print("0.2 Quantile Values of all columns")
print(df.quantile(.2, axis = 0))
print("0.1,0.25,0.5 and 0.75 Quantile Values of all columns")
print(df.quantile([.1, .25, .5, .75], axis = 0))
```

OUTPUT

```
ata Frame
   A   B  C  D
0  1   6  9  1
1  2   7  8  2
2  3   8  7  6
3  4   9  6  3
4  5  10  5  4
```

```
0.2 Quantile Values of all columns
A    1.8
B    6.8
C    5.8
D    1.8
Name: 0.2, dtype: float64
0.1,0.25,0.5 and 0.75 Quantile Values of all columns
        A    B    C    D
0.10   1.4  6.4  5.4  1.4
0.25   2.0  7.0  6.0  2.0
0.50   3.0  8.0  7.0  3.0
0.75   4.0  9.0  8.0  4.0
```

Example 2.10 Demonstrate the use of `numpy.quantile()` function on a one-dimensional array.

```
# numpy.quantile() method
import numpy as np
arr = [45,59,65,75,55,90,87,71,67,49]
print("The array elements are : ", arr)
print("Q1 quantile of arr : ", np.quantile(arr, .25))
print("Q2 quantile of arr : ", np.quantile(arr, .50))
print("Q3 quantile of arr : ", np.quantile(arr, .75))
print("Q4 quantile of arr : ", np.quantile(arr, .1))
```

OUTPUT

```
The array elements are :  [45, 59, 65, 75, 55, 90, 87, 71, 67, 49]
Q1 quantile of arr :  56.0
Q2 quantile of arr :  66.0
Q3 quantile of arr :  74.0
Q4 quantile of arr :  48.6
```

Example 2.11 Demonstrate the use of `numpy.quantile()` function on a two-dimensional array.

```
# numpy.quantile() method
import numpy as np
arr = [[12, 13, 27, 35, 44],
       [18, 9 , 27, 20, 15],
       [20, 3, 54, 41, 60, ]]
print("Array Elements are: : \n", arr)
# quantile of the flattened array
print("50th quantile of arr, axis = None : ", np.quantile(arr, .50))
print("0th quantile of arr, axis = None : ", np.quantile(arr, 0))
# quantile along the axis = 0
print("50th quantile of arr, axis = 0 : ", np.quantile(arr, .50, axis = 0))
print("0th quantile of arr, axis = 0 : ", np.quantile(arr, 0, axis = 0))
# quantile along the axis = 1
print("50th quantile of arr, axis = 1 : ", np.quantile(arr, .50, axis = 1))
print("0th quantile of arr, axis = 1 : ", np.quantile(arr, 0, axis = 1))
```

OUTPUT

```
Array Elements are: :
 [[12, 13, 27, 35, 44], [18, 9, 27, 20, 15], [20, 3, 54, 41, 60]]
50th quantile of arr, axis = None :  20.0
0th quantile of arr, axis = None :  3
50th quantile of arr, axis = 0 :  [18.  9. 27. 35. 44.]
0th quantile of arr, axis = 0 :  [12  3 27 20 15]
50th quantile of arr, axis = 1 :  [27. 18. 41.]
0th quantile of arr, axis = 1 :  [12  9  3]
```

2.7 FUNCTION APPLLICATION

While coding, we often need to apply functions to Pandas objects. For this, Pandas provides `pipe()`, `apply()` and `applymap()` methods to its users. The appropriate method to be used depends on whether the function is expected to operate on an element, row, or column.

The **pipe()** method applies function on a table.
The **apply()** method applies function on a **row** or column.
The **applymap()** method applies function to each element in the Pandas object.

2.7.1 Table-wise Function Application: `pipe()`

`pipe()` function performs the operation for the entire data frame with the help of user-defined or library function. In the example given below, `pipe()` method is used to add 5 to the entire data frame.

Example 2.12

```
# pipe() Method in Pandas
import pandas as pd
import numpy as np
import math
# user defined function
def add(num1,num2):
    return(num1+num2)
# Create a Dictionary of series
Test_marks = {'Marks_Maths':pd.Series([88,90,92,67,73,59]), 'Marks_Science':pd.
    Series([65,67,78,77,89,90])}
df = pd.DataFrame(Test_marks)
print("ORIGINAL MARKS")
print(df)
print("MODIFIED MARKS")
print(df.pipe(add,5))
```

OUTPUT
```
ORIGINAL MARKS
    Marks_Maths  Marks_Science
0            88             65
1            90             67
2            92             78
3            67             77
4            73             89
5            59             90
MODIFIED MARKS
    Marks_Maths  Marks_Science
0            93             70
1            95             72
2            97             83
3            72             82
4            78             94
5            64             95
```

The `pipe()` method is also used for one more thing. Suppose you want to apply a function to a data frame or series, then apply it on another function, so on and so forth. In this scenario, one way would be to perform these operations in a "sandwich" fashion:

`df = func3(func2(func1(df, arg1= 1), arg2= 2), arg3=3)`

However, in this long statement, function calls have become fairly messy and are error-prone. So a better alternative is to use the `pipe()` method. Pipe can therefore be used for function chaining. With `pipe()` the same series of function calls can be written as,

```
df.pipe(func1, arg1=1).
    pipe(func2, arg2=2).
    pipe(func3, arg3=3)
```

This way makes the code become cleaner and it is far easier to track the order in which the functions and their corresponding arguments are applied. For example, in the code given below, we use `pipe()` method to add, divide, subtract and multiply elements of a data frame.

Example 2.13

```
import pandas as pd
# creating a dataframe
def adder(x,a):
    return(x+a)
def div(x,d):
    return(x/d)
def sub_mult(x,sub=2,mult=10):
    return((x-2)*10)
data = {'A': [10,20,30,40,50,60,70,80,90,100], 'B': [15,25,35,45,55,65,75,85,95,105],
    'C': [12,22,32,42,52,62,72,82,92,102]
}
df = pd.DataFrame(data, columns= ['A', 'B', 'C'])
print("ORIGINAL DATA FRAME")
print(df)
df = df.pipe(adder, a=5).pipe(div, d=20).pipe(sub_mult, sub=2, mult=10)
print("MODIFIED DATA FRAME")
print(df)
```

OUTPUT

```
ORIGINAL DATAFRAME
     A    B    C
0   10   15   12
1   20   25   22
2   30   35   32
3   40   45   42
4   50   55   52
5   60   65   62
6   70   75   72
7   80   85   82
8   90   95   92
9  100  105  102
MODIFIED DATA FRAME
      A     B     C
0  -12.5 -10.0 -11.5
1   -7.5  -5.0  -6.5
2   -2.5   0.0  -1.5
3    2.5   5.0   3.5
4    7.5  10.0   8.5
5   12.5  15.0  13.5
6   17.5  20.0  18.5
7   22.5  25.0  23.5
8   27.5  30.0  28.5
9   32.5  35.0  33.5
```

2.7.2 Row- or Column-wise Function Operations: `apply()`

We can apply any function to the axes of a DataFrame object or to a Series object by using the `apply()` method. The `apply()` method takes an optional axis argument. If no value is specified, then *by default, the function will be applied column-wise, taking every column as an array.* In this way, the function passed in the `apply()` method is applied to all the values of the DataFrame or Series.

Example 2.14

```
# apply() Method in Pandas
import pandas as pd
import numpy as np
import math
# user defined function
def reduce(num):
    return(num-2)
#Create a Dictionary of series
Test_marks = {'Marks_Maths':pd.Series([88/90/92/67/73/59]), 'Marks_Science':pd.
    Series([65,67,78/77,89,90])}
df = pd.DataFrame(Test_marks)
print("ORIGINAL MARKS")
print(df)
print("MODIFIED MARKS")
print(df.apply(reduce))
```

OUTPUT

```
ORIGINAL MARKS
   Marks_Maths   Marks_Science
0       88             65
1       90             67
2       92             78
3       67             77
4       73             89
5       59             90
MODIFIED MARKS
   Marks_Maths  Marks_Science
0       86             63
1       88             65
2       90             76
3       65             75
4       71             87
5       57             88
>>>
```

2.7.3 Element-wise Function Application: `applymap()`

To perform element-wise application of a function, the `applymap()` is used. The function performs the specified operation for all the elements of the dataframe. The `applymap()` method takes and returns a single value. Note that this method does not work on a Series.

Example 2.15

```
import pandas as pd
import numpy as np
import math
def abs(x):
    if x>0:
        return x
    else:
        return(-x)
S = pd.Series(10*np.random.randn(5))
print("ORIGINAL VALUES ARE : ")
print(S)
df = pd.DataFrame(S)
df = df.applymap(abs)
print("DATA FRAME WITH ABSOLUTE VALUES IS : ")
print(df)
```

OUTPUT

```
ORIGINAL VALUES ARE :
0    -2.817097
1     6.236797
2    -5.107213
3    14.181766
4    -4.375742
dtype: float64
DATA FRAME WITH ABSOLUTE VALUES:
          0
0   2.817097
1   6.236797
2   5.107213
3  14.181766
4   4.375742
```

2.8 AGGREGATION (GROUP BY)

Aggregation is the process of turning the values of a dataset (or a subset of it) into one single value. Pandas offers a couple of functions that provides SQL-like aggregation functions. These functions can be applied when we group values of one or more columns. In this section, we will read about different ways in which we can perform grouping on Pandas objects.

2.8.1 Group by One Column

Let us compute Mean, Min, and Max values by Group. For this, we will first use the `groupby` function and then pass the aggregation functions to the grouped object as a dictionary within the agg function.

First, we will group by Team with Pandas' `groupby` function. After grouping, we can pass aggregation functions to the grouped object as a dictionary within the `agg()` function. This dictionary will specify the name of the column that is being used as a key for aggregation. We can apply either a single aggregation function or a list of aggregation functions.

Example 2.16

```
import pandas as pd
data = {"Team":[" Bhabha"," Bhabha","Bhabha","Bhabha"," Bhabha"," Bhabha","Bhabha",
    "Aryabhatta","Aryabhatta","Aryabhatta","Aryabhatta","Aryabhatta","Aryabhatta",
    "Aryabhatta"],
    "Status" :["Completed","Completed","Not Completed",'Completed','Not
    Completed", "Completed", "Not Completed", "Completed","Completed","Not
    Completed","Not Completed","Completed", "Not Completed","Completed"], "Score":
    [1,9,5,8,2,7,5,6,4,5,7,8,3,9]}
df = pd.DataFrame(data)
print(df)
# groupping by Team and calculating mean, min and max of Score for each Team
group1 = df.groupby('Team').agg({'Score':['mean','min','max']})
print(group1)
```

OUTPUT

```
     Team         Status         Score
0    Bhabha       Completed      1
1    Bhabha       Completed      9
2    Bhabha       Not Completed  5
3    Bhabha       Completed      8
4    Bhabha       Not Completed  2
5    Bhabha       Completed      7
```

```
6     Bhabha        Not Completed    5
7     Aryabhatta    Completed        6
8     Aryabhatta    Completed        4
9     Aryabhatta    Not Completed    5
10    Aryabhatta    Not Completed    7
11    Aryabhatta    Completed        8
12    Aryabhatta    Not Completed    3
13    Aryabhatta    Completed        9
              Score
              mean        min    max
Team
Aryabhatta    6.000000    3      9
Bhabha        5.285714    1      9
```

In the above code, we have applied multiple aggregation functions to a single column. This is also known as a multiindex. Observe that the grouping column is now the data frame's index.

2.8.2 Grouping by Multiple Columns

We can extend grouping further to work with multiple columns. Therefore, to apply aggregations to multiple columns, we can add additional key:value pairs to the dictionary. Instead of passing a single string value to the `groupby()` function, we will pass a list of column names.

Example 2.17

```
import pandas as pd
data = {"Team":[" Bhabha"," Bhabha","Bhabha","Bhabha"," Bhabha"," Bhabha","Bhabha",
    "Aryabhatta","Aryabhatta","Aryabhatta","Aryabhatta","Aryabhatta","Aryabhatta",
    "Aryabhatta"], "Status":["Completed","Completed"," Not
    Completed","Completed","Not Completed", "Completed","Not Completed",
    "Completed","Completed","NotCompleted","Not Completed","Completed", "Not
    Completed","Completed"], "Score":[1,9,5,8,2,7,5,6,4,5,7,8,3,9]}
df = pd.DataFrame(data)
print(df)
group2 = df.groupby(['Team','Status']).agg({'Score':['mean,' min,'max']})
print(group2)
```

OUTPUT

```
      Team          Status           Score
0     Bhabha        Completed        1
1     Bhabha        Completed        9
2     Bhabha        Not Completed    5
3     Bhabha        Completed        8
4     Bhabha        Not Completed    2
5     Bhabha        Completed        7
6     Bhabha        Not Completed    5
7     Aryabhatta    Completed        6
8     Aryabhatta    Completed        4
9     Aryabhatta    Not Completed    5
10    Aryabhatta    Not Completed    7
11    Aryabhatta    Completed        8
12    Aryabhatta    Not Completed    3
13    Aryabhatta    Completed        9
                               Score
                               mean    min    max
Team          Status
Aryabhatta    Completed        6.75    4      9
              Not Completed    5.00    3      7
Bhabha        Completed        6.25    1      9
              Not Completed    4.00    2      5
```

2.9 TRANSFORM FUNCTION IN PYTHON

The `transform()` function returns a self-produced data frame with transformed values after applying the function specified in its parameter. The resultant data frame has the same length as that of the original data frame passed to it.

Transform functionality is extensively used for feature extraction. The term feature extraction means extracting new features from the existing ones. The time taken by the `transform()` function for feature selection is comparatively less over a large data frame. It also gives a significant advantage over other techniques to do the same operation.

Pandas' pipeline feature allows you to string together Python functions in order to build a pipeline of data processing.

Pandas **DataFrame.transform()** function calls `func` on self-producing a DataFrame with transformed values that have the same axis length as itself. This means that the `transorm()` function will make changes in the original data frame. After applying the changes, the number of rows will still remain the same, only the number of columns may change. The syntax of this is DataFrame.transform(func, axis=0, *args, **kwargs)
where,
func is the function to be used for transforming the data.
axis is 0 or 'index' and 1 or 'columns'. By default it is 0.

The rest of the two arguments will not be used here. From the code given below, let us understand the use of `transform()` function.

Example 2.18

```
# importing pandas as pd
import pandas as pd
# Creating the DataFrame
df = pd.DataFrame({"A":[12, 4, 5, None, 1],
                   "B":[7, 2, 54, 3, None],
                   "C":[20, 16, 11, 3, 8],
                   "D":[14, 3, None, 2, 6]})
# Set the index of the data frame
df.index = ['Row1', 'Row2', 'Row3', 'Row4', 'Row5']
# Print the DataFrame
print(df)
# add 10 to each element of the dataframe
result = df.transform(func = ['sqrt', 'exp'])
# Print the result
print(result)
```

OUTPUT

```
         A     B    C     D
Row1  12.0   7.0   20  14.0
Row2   4.0   2.0   16   3.0
Row3   5.0  54.0   11   NaN
Row4   NaN   3.0    3   2.0
Row5   1.0   NaN    8   6.0
             A                        B    ...           C           D
          sqrt           exp       sqrt    ...         exp        sqrt           exp
Row1  3.464102  162754.791419   2.645751   ...  4.851652e+08    3.741657  1.202604e+06
Row2  2.000000      54.598150   1.414214   ...  8.886111e+06    1.732051  2.008554e+01
Row3  2.236068     148.413159   7.348469   ...  5.987414e+04         NaN           NaN
Row4       NaN            NaN   1.732051   ...  2.008554e+01    1.414214  7.389056e+00
Row5  1.000000       2.718282        NaN   ...  2.980958e+03    2.449490  4.034288e+02

[5 rows x 8 columns]
```

PROGRAMMER'S ZONE

2. **Create a data frame containing 6 rows and 3 columns. Fill it with random values and use the `pipe()` method to scale the value of each element by 10.**

   ```
   import pandas as pd
   import numpy as np
   import math
   # user defined function
   def scale(num):
       return(num*10)
   df = pd.DataFrame(6*np.random.randn(6,3),columns=['A','B','C'])
   df = df.pipe(scale)
   print(df)
   ```

   OUTPUT
   ```
               A          B           C
   0  -14.320374  -41.115159   -33.601141
   1   21.659777   -1.906765    38.518445
   2   -3.252923   45.891514  -103.855270
   3    8.930942  -92.797391    22.087857
   4  -68.109612  -64.390266   -32.272999
   5   77.912319  -49.543111   -14.282236
   ```

3. **Create a data frame containing 5 rows and 3 columns. Fill it with random values and use the `apply()` method to find the mean of values with axis = 1 (or row-wise).**

   ```
   import pandas as pd
   import numpy as np
   import math
   df = pd.DataFrame(6*np.random.randn(5,3),columns=['A','B','C'])
   df = df.apply(np.mean,axis = 1)
   print(df)
   ```

   OUTPUT
   ```
   0    3.684398
   1   -0.375202
   2    2.525387
   3   -3.749754
   4   -3.679718
   dtype: float64
   ```

4. **Read the zoo.csv file (download it from http://46.101.230.157/datacoding101/zoo.csv) and find the following:**
   a. Number of the animals
   b. Sum of the values in the water_need column
   c. Smallest value in the water_need column
   d. Largest value in the water_need column
   e. Mean value of water_need columns
   f. Median value of water_need columns
   g. Mean value of water_need column group by animal

   ```
   import pandas as pd
   import numpy as np
   zoo = pd.read_csv('zoo.csv', delimiter = ',')
   ```

```
print("Data in zoo.csv :")
print(zoo)
num = zoo.animal.count()
print("Number of the animals : ",num)
sum = zoo.water_need.sum()
print("sum of the values in the water_need column = ",
    sum)
min = zoo.water_need.min()
print("Smallest value in the water_need column is : ",
    min)
max = zoo.water_need.max()
print("Largest value in the water_need column is : ",
    max)
mean = zoo.water_need.mean()
print("Mean value of water_need columns is : ", mean)
median_value = zoo.water_need.median()
print("Median value of water_need columns is : ", median_value)
animal_mean = zoo.groupby('animal').mean()[['water_need']]
print("Mean value of water_need column group by animal is : ", animal_mean)
```

> To ignore missing values in a data frame, use the `drop.na()` method of data frame by writing `df.drop.na()`.

OUTPUT

```
Data in zoo.csv :
      animal    uniq_id   water_need
0     elephant  1001      500
1     elephant  1002      600
2     elephant  1003      550
3     tiger     1004      300
4     tiger     1005      320
5     tiger     1006      330
6     tiger     1007      290
7     tiger     1008      310
8     zebra     1009      200
9     zebra     1010      220
10    zebra     1011      240
11    zebra     1012      230
12    zebra     1013      220
13    zebra     1014      100
14    zebra     1015       80
15    lion      1016      420
16    lion      1017      600
17    lion      1018      500
18    lion      1019      390
19    kangaroo  1020      410
20    kangaroo  1021      430
21    kangaroo  1022      410
Number of the animals :  22
Sum of the values in the water_need column =  7650
Smallest value in the water_need column is :  80
Largest value in the water_need column is :  600
Mean value of water_need columns is :  347.72727272727275
Median value of water_need columns is :  325.0
Mean value of water_need column group by animal is :            water_need
animal
elephant    550.000000
kangaroo    416.666667
lion        477.500000
tiger       310.000000
zebra       184.285714
```

5. **Create a data frame storing name, qualification, address and age of students. Find the sum of the Ages group by Qualification. Also compute the mean of ages in each group.**

```
import pandas as pd
import numpy as np
data1 = {'Name':['Jia', 'Aman', 'Jia', 'Parul',
            'Garv', 'Aman', 'Parul', 'Priya'],
    'Age':[23, 22, 24, 32,
        22, 20, 23, 22],
    'Address':['Nagpur', 'Kanpur', 'Allahabad', 'Kannuaj',
            'Jaunpur', 'Kanpur', 'Allahabad', 'Aligarh'],
    'Qualification':['MSc', 'MA', 'MCA', 'PhD',
                'B.Tech', 'B.Com', 'MSc', 'MA']}
df = pd.DataFrame(data1)
print(df)
print(df.groupby(['Qualification']).sum() )
print(df.groupby(['Qualification'], sort = True).mean() )
```

OUTPUT

```
    Name  Age    Address Qualification
0    Jia   23     Nagpur           MSc
1   Aman   22     Kanpur            MA
2    Jia   24  Allahabad           MCA
3  Parul   32    Kannuaj           PhD
4   Garv   22    Jaunpur        B.Tech
5   Aman   20     Kanpur         B.Com
6  Parul   23  Allahabad           MSc
7  Priya   22    Aligarh            MA
                Age
Qualification
B.Com            20
B.Tech           22
MA               44
MCA              24
MSc              46
PhD              32
                Age
Qualification
B.Com            20
B.Tech           22
MA               22
MCA              24
MSc              23
PhD              32
```

> NaN stands for Not a Number.

6. **Write a program that creates a series of the first 11 natural numbers. Use the `transform()` method to find the sqrt and exp of the values in the series.**

```
import numpy as np
import pandas as pd
s = pd.Series(range(11))
print(s)
s = s.transform([np.sqrt, np.exp])
print(s)
```

OUTPUT

```
        sqrt              exp
0   0.000000         1.000000
1   1.000000         2.718282
2   1.414214         7.389056
3   1.732051        20.085537
4   2.000000        54.598150
5   2.236068       148.413159
6   2.449490       403.428793
7   2.645751      1096.633158
8   2.828427      2980.957987
9   3.000000      8103.083928
10  3.162278     22026.465795
```

7. **Write a program to take an object and reindex its axes to be labelled as another object.**

```
import pandas as pd
import numpy as np
df1 = pd.DataFrame(np.random.randn(5,3),columns=['C1','B','C3'])
df2 = pd.DataFrame(np.random.randn(4,3),columns=['C1','C2','C3'])
df1 = df1.reindex_like(df2)
print(df1)
```

OUTPUT

```
         C1   C2        C3
0  -0.453925  NaN  -0.238405
1   0.081728  NaN  -1.057288
2  -1.477602  NaN   1.072387
3   0.320976  NaN  -0.169116
```

> Here, `df1` is altered and reindexed like `df2`. The column names should be matched. Otherwise, NaN will be added for the entire column label.

8. **Write a program to take a data frame and reindex its axes to be labelled as another object. Also fill the NaN using any method of your choice.**

```
import pandas as pd
import numpy as np
df1 = pd.DataFrame(np.random.randn(5,3),columns=['C1','C2','C3'])
df2 = pd.DataFrame(np.random.randn(3,3),columns=['C1','C2','C3'])
df2 = df2.reindex_like(df1,method='nearest')
print(df2)
```

OUTPUT

```
         C1         C2         C3
0   1.861295  -0.017680  -0.435243
1   0.460061  -1.404898   1.683461
2   0.739224   0.053781   1.556290
3   0.739224   0.053781   1.556290
4   0.739224   0.053781   1.556290
```

> The limit argument of the `reindex()` method specifies the maximum count of filling NaN values. For example, we can write, print `df2.reindex_like (df1, method='ffill', limit = 1)`.

2.10 REINDEXING IN PANDAS DATA FRAME

Reindexing, in Pandas, is used to change the index of rows and columns of a data frame. Indexes can be used to reference data structures like Pandas series or Pandas Data Frame. The code given here reindexes the columns and rows in a Pandas Data Frame.

We can reindex a single row or multiple rows by using `reindex()` method. This method takes the new index as well as axis as argument and returns a reindexed data frame.

In Example 2.19, we have re-ordered the rows using `reindex()` and in the second code, we have created new indexes for the data frame. Note that default values in the new index that are not present in the data frame are assigned NaN.

Example 2.19

```
# Reordering indexes
import pandas as pd
import numpy as np
cols =['C1','C2','C3','C4','C5']
index =['R1','R2','R3','R4','R5']
# create a dataframe of random values of array
df = pd.DataFrame(np. random. rand(5,5), columns=cols, index=index)
print(df)
print('Data frame after re-indexing rows:\n',
df.reindexd(['R3', 'R1', 'R2', 'R4', 'R5']))
          C1       C2       C3       C4       C5
R1   0.493102 0.811385 0.008166 0.299422 0.483170
R2   0.998660 0.631610 0.270461 0.457065 0.495796
R3   0.980782 0.734258 0.536033 0.522151 0.930235
R4   0.489830 0.665597 0.138179 0.111670 0.146060
R5   0.801327 0.138832 0.698386 0.935052 0.589710
Data frame after re-indexing rows:
          C1       C2       C3       C4       C5
R3   0.980782 0.734258 0.536033 0.522151 0.930235
R1   0.493102 0.811385 0.008166 0.299422 0.483170
R2   0.998660 0.631610 0.270461 0.457065 0.495796
R4   0.489830 0.665597 0.138179 0.111670 0.146060
R5   0.801327 0.138832 0.698386 0.935052 0.589710
```

Example 2.20

```
# Adding New Indexes
import pandas as pd
import numpy as np
cols =['C1','C2','C3','C4','C5']
index =['R1','R2','R3','R4','R5']
# create a dataframe of random values of array
df = pd.DataFrame(np.random.rand(5,5), columns=cols, index=index)
print(df)
new_index =['R1', 'B', 'R3', 'D','R4']
print('Dataframe after reindexing rows:\n',
df.reindex(new_index))
          C1       C2       C3       C4       C5
R1   0.705821 0.974293 0.749270 0.340964 0.144562
R2   0.734417 0.001402 0.062133 0.607034 0.745289
R3   0.497827 0.422662 0.444784 0.361989 0.966052
R4   0.501082 0.604928 0.253406 0.930383 0.638558
R5   0.728509 0.401761 0.085836 0.993651 0.667026
Dataframe after reindexing rows:
          C1       C2       C3       C4       C5
R1   0.705821 0.974293 0.749270 0.340964 0.144562
B    NaN      NaN      NaN      NaN      NaN
R3   0.497827 0.422662 0.444784 0.361989 0.966052
D    NaN      NaN      NaN      NaN      NaN
R4   0.501082 0.604928 0.253406 0.930383 0.638558
```

```
# Re-indexing columns
import pandas as pd
import numpy as np
cols =['C1','C2','C3','C4','C5']
index =['R1','R2','R3','R4','R5']
# create a dataframe of random values of array
df = pd.DataFrame(np. random. rand(5,5), columns=cols, index=index)
print(df)
print('Data frame after re-indexing rows:\n',
df.reindex(['C3', 'C1', 'C2', 'C4', 'C5'], axis=1))
          C1       C2       C3       C4       C5
R1  0.257785 0.667991 0.706676 0.233302 0.377173
R2  0.056890 0.597683 0.376673 0.139345 0.630611
R3  0.210198 0.795495 0.875716 0.613650 0.805473
R4  0.538860 0.279949 0.578101 0.202765 0.302528
R5  0.624405 0.208100 0.708359 0.679449 0.835302
Data frame after re-indexing rows:
          C3       C1       C2       C4       C5
R1  0.706676 0.257785 0.667991 0.233302 0.377173
R2  0.376673 0.056890 0.597683 0.139345 0.630611
R3  0.875716 0.210198 0.795495 0.613650 0.805473
R4  0.578101 0.538860 0.279949 0.202765 0.302528
R5  0.708359 0.624405 0.208100 0.679449 0.835302
```

Example 2.21

```
# Reindexing columns
import pandas as pd
import numpy as np cols =['C1','C2','C3','C4','C5']
index =['R1','R2','R3','R4','R5']
# create a dataframe of random values of array
df = pd.DataFrame(np.random.rand(5,5), columns=cols, index=index)
print(df)
new_cols = ['A','C2','C3','B','C5']
print('Data frame after re-indexing rows:\n',
df.reindex(new_cols,axis=1))
          C1       C2       C3       C4       C5
R1  0.622108 0.388899 0.058391 0.170691 0.558634
R2  0.144692 0.867697 0.108545 0.908884 0.407697
R3  0.390215 0.689716 0.857022 0.422999 0.226193
R4  0.076215 0.761085 0.986030 0.521373 0.285629
R5  0.540212 0.550815 0.883104 0.176268 0.231696
Data frame after re-indexing rows:
      A       C2       C3       B       C5
R1  NaN 0.388899 0.058391 NaN 0.558634
R2  NaN 0.867697 0.108545 NaN 0.407697
R3  NaN 0.689716 0.857022 NaN 0.226193
R4  NaN 0.761085 0.986030 NaN 0.285629
R5  NaN 0.550815 0.883104 NaN 0.231696
```

We have thus far reindexed the rows. We can also reindex columns using the *axis* keyword. A single column or multiple columns can be reindexed using `reindex()` method and specifying the axis we want to reindex. Default values in the new index that are not present in the dataframe are assigned NaN.

Note that the `reindex()` method also takes an optional parameter method which specifies a filling method with any of the values given below:

- pad/ffill to fill values forward
- bfill/backfill to fill values backward
- nearest to fill from the nearest index values.

2.11 REPLACING THE MISSING VALUES

We can fill missing values in a data frame by passing a value to the keyword fill_value argument of the `reindex()` function. This keyword replaces the NaN values.

Example 2.22

```
# Adding New Indexes and Filling Missing Values
import pandas as pd
import numpy as np cols =['C1','C2','C3','C4','C5']
index =['R1','R2','R3','R4','R5']
# create a dataframe of random values of array
df = pd.DataFrame(np.random.rand(5,5), columns=cols, index=index)
print(df)
new_index =['R1', 'B', 'R3', 'D','R4']
print('Dataframe after reindexing rows:\n',
df.reindex(new_index,fill_value = 'KKK'))
      C1       C2       C3       C4       C5
R1  0.754298 0.677610 0.218998 0.364835 0.023662
R2  0.437800 0.587752 0.859596 0.247670 0.450628
R3  0.650649 0.877077 0.311036 0.550397 0.099493
R4  0.391660 0.018353 0.430367 0.449634 0.785371
R5  0.162567 0.019885 0.149455 0.461566 0.564482
Dataframe after reindexing rows:
      C1        C2        C3        C4        C5
R1  0.754298  0.67761   0.218998  0.364835  0.0236618
B   KKK       KKK       KKK       KKK       KKK
R3  0.650649  0.877077  0.311036  0.550397  0.0994928
D   KKK       KKK       KKK       KKK       KKK
R4  0.39166   0.0183535 0.430367  0.449634  0.785371
```

Example 2.23

```
# Re-indexing columns and filling missing values
import pandas as pd
import numpy as np
cols =['C1','C2','C3','C4','C5']
index =['R1','R2','R3','R4','R5']
# create a dataframe of random values of array
df = pd.DataFrame(np.random.rand(5,5), columns=cols, index=index)
print(df)
new_cols = ['A','C2','C3','B','C5']
print('Data frame after re-indexing rows:\n',
df.reindex(new_cols,axis=1,fill_value = 0.0))
      C1       C2       C3       C4       C5
R1  0.721655 0.994150 0.805925 0.305934 0.274084
R2  0.450128 0.812512 0.897468 0.920742 0.272612
R3  0.029670 0.496479 0.668620 0.688773 0.289656
R4  0.323558 0.429265 0.878404 0.045277 0.607734
R5  0.915661 0.568562 0.143303 0.033207 0.149640
Data frame after re-indexing rows:
     A    C2       C3       B    C5
R1  0.0  0.994150 0.805925 0.0  0.274084
R2  0.0  0.812512 0.897468 0.0  0.272612
R3  0.0  0.496479 0.668620 0.0  0.289656
R4  0.0  0.429265 0.878404 0.0  0.607734
R5  0.0  0.568562 0.143303 0.0  0.149640
```

2.12 ALTERING COLUMN LABELS

Pandas allow users to alter the column labels in two ways – column method and rename method. In this section, we will discuss both of them.

Using the Columns Method

The simplest way to change labels of a data frame already created is to overwrite the column labels by calling the columns method on the data frame object and providing a new list of names to be specified. The code given below demonstrates the use of `column()` method to alter column labels.

Example 2.24

```
import pandas as pd
df = pd.DataFrame([('The Jungle Book','Rudyard Kipling'), ('Malgudi Days'','R.K.Iyer
    Narayanaswami'), ('Godan','Prem Chand')])
print(df)
print('\n')
df.columns = ['title','author']
print(df)
            0                  1
0   The Jungle Book    Rudyard Kipling
1   Malgudi Days       R.K.Iyer Narayanaswami
2   Godan              Prem Chand
        title              author
0   The Jungle Book    Rudyard Kipling
1   Malgudi Days       R.K.Iyer Narayanaswami
2   Godan              Prem Chand
```

Using the Rename Method

The other technique for renaming column labels is to call the rename method on the data frame object. We can pass the list of new labels to the columns parameter of the rename method. That is, to rename the existing data frame rather than creating a copy, we must use the following syntax.

    df.rename(columns={'oldName1': 'newName1', 'oldName2': 'newName2'}, inplace=True)

Example 2.25

```
import pandas as pd
df = pd.DataFrame([('The Jungle Book','Rudyard Kipling'), ('Malgudi Days','R.K.Iyer
    Narayanaswami'), ('Godan','Prem Chand')])
print(df)
print('\n')
df.rename(columns={0: 'TITLE',1 :'AUTHOR'},inplace=True)
print(df)
            0                  1
0   The Jungle Book    Rudyard Kipling
1   Malgudi Days       R.K.Iyer Narayanaswami
2   Godan              Prem Chand
        TITLE              AUTHOR
0   The Jungle Book    Rudyard Kipling
1   Malgudi Days       R.K.Iyer Narayanaswami
2   Godan              Prem Chand
```

Note that since the rename method *renames* existing labels, the data frame must have existing labels. This was not a necessity with columns method. Also, we have set inplace = TRUE. This is important when you have to update the existing data frame rather than return a newly created data frame.

2.13 IMPORTING/EXPORTING DATA BETWEEN MYSQL DATABASE AND PANDAS

Pandas allows users to read data from and write data to several external repositories and formats including MySQL database tables. However, before importing or exporting data to/ from Pandas to MySQL, make sure that you have already imported some important packages like Pandas, mysql-connector-python, pymysql and sqlalchemy. This can be done by simply executing the following commands in Windows Command Prompt.

2.13.1 Exporting Data from Pandas to MySQL

Step 1: Create an SQLAlchemy engine object to connect to the MySQL database server by providing the required details.

Step 2: Using this engine object, connect to the MySQL server by using the `connect()` method.

Step 3: Create a dictionary of Python lists. The list will be taken as data for column and the keys of the dictionary will correspond to column names.

Step 4: Create a data frame by passing the dictionary created in Step 3 as a parameter to the `data.frame()` function of Pandas module.

Step 5: Use the `to_sql()` method on the Pandas dataframe object. Specify the table name and database connection to create a table in MySQL database server and insert data into it with the data from the data frame created in Step 5.

Example 2.26

```
from sqlalchemy import create_engine
import pymysql
import pandas as pd
import mysql.connector as mysql
userDetails = {"UserId":["abc", "def", "ghi", "jkl", "mno", "pqr", "stu"],
               "UserFavItem":["Books", "Clothes", "Watches", "Electonics", "Accessories",
               "Shoes", "Smartphones"],
               "MonthlyOrderFrequency":[5, 1, 2, 2, 7, 6, 1],
               "OrderMode":["Web", "App", "App", "App", "Web", "Web", "App"],
               "InMedicalCare":["No", "No", "No", "No", "Yes", "No", "No"]};
tableName    = "UserDetails"
dataFrame    = pd.DataFrame(data=userDetails)
# create sqlalchemy engine
connection = create_engine("mysql+pymysql://{user}:{pw}@localhost/{db}"
                           .format(user="root", pw="jaimataki", db="mydb"))
'''# Insert whole DataFrame into MySQL
dataFrame.to_sql(tableName, con = connection, if_exists = 'append', chunksize = 1000)
print("DATA WRITTEN SUSSEFULLY")
```

OUTPUT

DATA WRITTEN SUSSEFULLY

In the `to_sql()` function, we pass certain parameters including:
- name of the table into which we want to insert our DataFrame.
- con = connection provides the connection details. The connection is created using the `connect()` method.
- if_exists = 'append' checks whether the specified table already exists or not. If it exists, the new data is appended to the table. Else, a new table with the specified name is created and data is added into it.
- chunksize writes records in batches of a given size at a time. By default, all rows will be written at once.

You may check in MySQL that the table is created and the rows and columns of the table contain data read from the data frame.

2.13.2 Reading/Importing Data from MySQL Database Table into Pandas Data Frame

To read a MySQL table into a Python data frame, we will use the **read_sql()** method of the Pandas module. This function takes the SQL Query and the SQL Connection object to retrieve data from the MySQL database table.

The database connection to MySQL database server is created using **sqlalchemy**. The `create_engine()` method is used to open a connection with the specified database. However, we need to provide the username and password for using MySQL services.

The `read_sql()` method returns a Pandas dataframe object with the default naming scheme. That is, the rows start from zero and get incremented for each row. The names of data frame columns are same as those of column names of the MySQL database table.

Example 2.27

```
from sqlalchemy import create_engine
import pymysql
import pandas as pd
import mysql.connector as mysql
userDetails = {"UserId":["abc", "def", "ghi", "jkl", "mno", "pqr", "stu"],
          "UserFavItem":["Books", "Clothes", "Watches", "Electonics", "Accessories",
          "Shoes", "Smartphones"],
          "MonthlyOrderFrequency":[5, 1, 2, 2, 7, 6, 1],
          "OrderMode":["Web", "App", "App", "App", "Web", "Web", "App"]};
tableName   = "UserDetails"
dataFrame   = pd.DataFrame(data=userDetails)
# create sqlalchemy engine
connection = create_engine("mysql+pymysql://{user}:{pw}@localhost/{db}"
                    .format(user="root", pw="********", db="mydb"))
df = pd.read_sql("SELECT * FROM UserDetails", con = connection)
print(df)
index     UserId    UserFavItem   MonthlyOrderFrequency  OrderMode
0         0         abc           Books                5         Web
1         1         def           Clothes              1         App
2         2         ghi           Watches              2         App
3         3         jkl           Electonics           2         App
4         4         mno           Accessories          7         Web
5         5         pqr           Shoes                6         Web
6         6         stu           Smartphones          1         App
```

Key Terms

Data frame: A two-dimensional data structure in which data is organized in a tabular fashion using rows and columns.

Sorting: Arranging data in a specific order. We can sort data either in ascending (small-to-big) order or descending order (big-to-small).

Quartiles: Values that break up the dataset into quarters.

Aggregation: The process of turning the values of a dataset (or a subset of it) into one single value.

Multi-index: The process of applying multiple aggregation functions to a single column.

Chapter Highlights

- The `pivot()` function is used to reshape a given Data Frame object organized by given index/column values.
- While combining two similar DataFrame objects where one object has missing values, the values are conditionally filled with like-labelled values from the other DataFrame.
- Python supports a large number of methods for computing descriptive statistics and other related operations on Series and DataFrame objects. Aggregation functions like `sum()`, `mean()`, and `quantile()` produce a lower-dimensional result. However, other functions like `cumsum()` and `cumprod()` produce an object of the same size.

- Users can specify the axis by name or integer. The default value of axis is 0, indicating indexes or rows. If axis = 1, the descriptive function is applied on columns.
- DataFrame and NumPy methods like mean, std, and sum, will exclude NAs on Series input by default.
- The `describe()` function computes a variety of summary statistics on a Series or the columns of a DataFrame object.
- The `idxmin()` and `idxmax()` functions can be used with Series and DataFrame objects to compute the index labels with the minimum and maximum corresponding values.
- The `apply()` function can be used for row-wise or column-wise application of a function on a Pandas object.
- In statistics, a histogram represents distribution of numerical data in bins. The count of each bin is represented in the histogram. It is not that only numerical data can be represented; we can even categorize categorical or date data in different bins.
- pth percentile means that there is p percent of observations below it and $(100 - p)\%$ above it. Percentiles help us in getting an idea on outliers.
- `Quantile()` function returns quantiles as Series or DataFrame. If q is an array, a DataFrame will be returned where the index is q. If q is a float, a Series will be returned where the values are the quantiles. The return value will depend on the value of q.
- To compute Mean, Min, and Max values by Group, first use the `groupby` function and then pass the aggregation functions to the grouped object as a dictionary within the `agg` function.
- We perform grouping to work with multiple columns by adding additional key:value pairs to the dictionary.
- The `transform()` function returns a self-produced data frame with transformed values after applying the function specified in its parameter. The resultant data frame has the same length as that of the original data frame passed to it.
- Reindexing, in Pandas, is used to change the index of rows and columns of a data frame.
- Pandas allow users to read data from and write data to several external repositories and formats including MySQL database tables.

Review Questions

1. What is a data frame? How is it created?
2. Explain the use and syntax of `pivot()` function.
3. Define sorting. How can we sort a data frame in Pandas?
4. How can we fill missing values in a data frame or series object? Write a code to demonstrate how missing values can be filled while subtracting two data frame objects.
5. What is a histogram? How does it represent values?
6. What do you understand by the term quartiles?
7. With the help of an example, explain the use of `pipe()` function.
8. What is reindexing? How is it done?
9. What are the two ways of altering column labels in Pandas?
10. Identify the functions to be used for:
    a. providing unique elements from a column by removing duplicates
    b. returning the mean value of all the items in the column
    c. returning the first n rows
    d. returning last n rows
    e. sorting a data frame by its row index
    f. combining two data frames
    g. computing a histogram of a 1D array of values
    h. getting the most frequently occurring value(s) among the values in a Series or DataFrame.
11. Identify the attributes of the data frame object.
    a. Returns the transpose of a data frame by interchanging rows and columns

b. Returns the list of row axis labels and column axis labels
c. Returns the data type of each column
d. Returns a Boolean value stating whether the data frame object is empty or not
e. Returns the number of dimensions of the data frame object
f. Returns a tuple representing the dimensionality of the DataFrame
g. Returns the number of elements in the DataFrame
h. Returns the data values stored in the data frame object as an NDarray.

12. Find the error in the code given below.
```
importing pandas as pd
import pandas as pd
  # creating a DataFrame
df = pd.DataFrame({'A': ['John', 'John', 'Mina'],
      'B': ['Masters', 'Masters', 'Graduate'],
      'C': [27, 23, 21]})
df.pivot('A', 'B', 'C')
```

13. What does it mean when we say that the highest income value is 400,000 but 95th percentile is 20,000 only?
14. Write the steps to import as well as export/import a data frame to/from MySQL.

Programming Exercises

1. Create a data frame storing student's Roll Number, Name, Total Marks and Class. Sort the data frame using Name and Marks.
2. Use pivot operation to reshape the above data frame using Class.
3. Write a program to count the number of null values in a series object.
4. Create a data frame with three columns – Name, Age and Rating
   a. Find the sum of columns.
   b. Find the sum of rows.
   c. Find average age and rating.
   d. Find the standard deviation.
   e. Describe the data frame.
5. Create a data frame with three columns and five rows of random values. Find the row-wise sum using the `apply()` function.
6. Create a data frame recording marks in Physics and Chemistry class tests. Find out at what point or below, 100%(1), 95%(0.95), 50%(0.5) of the scores are lying.
7. Download phon.csv form https://www.kaggle.com/c/titanic/data and write a code to:
   a. print last few rows of dataset
   b. describe the data set
   c. sort values based on Fare and display first 10 rows
   d. set a position for the NaN values in the dataset
   e. count the number of Male and Female passengers
   f. count the number of unique records for Embarked column
   g. see records where "Embarked" column is equal to "C".
   h. display the passengers whose Fare is smaller than 100 and who are female
   i. display the passengers whose fare is more than 500 or older than 70
   j. display the passengers whose cabin is unknown
   k. count of the null values of all columns in a dataframe
   l. ignore the "**Cabin**" column since %70 of that column is **missing**
   m. replace missing values in Age column with its median value.
8. Consider the given table that describes a dataset about a department store. Write the code to know the mean purchase amount of each user.

User_ID	Product_ID	Purchase
1001	P1	100
1001	P2	200
1001	P3	300
1001	P4	500
1002	P2	200
1003	P3	400
1004	P1	200
1004	P2	300
1004	P3	400
1004	P4	500
1005	P1	100
1005	P2	200
1005	P3	300
1005	P4	400
1005	P5	500

User_ID	Product_ID	Purchase	User Mean
1001	P1	100	275
1001	P2	200	275
1001	P3	300	275
1001	P4	500	275
1002	P2	200	200
1003	P3	400	400
1004	P1	200	350
1004	P2	300	350
1004	P3	400	350
1004	P4	500	350
1005	P1	100	300
1005	P2	200	300
1005	P3	300	300
1005	P4	400	300
1005	P5	500	300

9. Create a data frame with any values of your choice. Reindex the data frame rows and fill the missing values with value 100. Reindex the data frame columns and fill the missing values with value 25.
10. Download the gapminder data from the URL: http://bit.ly/2cLzoxH. Print the names of the columns. Rename the column labels using both the ways.
11. Create a data frame with columns country, year and reports. Demonstrate changing the rows and columns.
12. Create a data frame with name, age and marks.
    a. Group the data by a column and return the mean age per group.
    b. Capitalizes all the column headers.
    c. Create a pipeline that applies the mean_age_by_group function and then applies the uppercase column name function

Explain the Instructions

1. `df.sort_values(by=['Year','Brand'], inplace=True)`
2. `data.groupby(['C'])['A'].transform('mean')`
3. ```
   import numpy as np
   unsorted_df = pd.DataFrame(np.random.randn(10,2),index=[1,4,6,2,3,5,9,8,0,7],columns = ['col2','col1'])
   sorted_df=unsorted_df.sort_index()
   print(sorted_df)
   ```
4. ```
   import pandas as pd
   import numpy as np
   unsorted_df = pd.DataFrame(np.random.randn(10,2),index=[1,4,6,2,3,5,9,8,0,7],colu
       mns = ['col2','col1'])
   sorted_df = unsorted_df.sort_index(ascending=False)
   ```

```
    print(sorted_df)
```

5. ```
   import pandas as pd
   import numpy as np
   unsorted_df = pd.DataFrame({'col1':[2,1,1,1],'col2':[1,3,2,4]})
      sorted_df = unsorted_df.sort_values(by='col1')
   print(sorted_df)
   ```

6. ```
   import pandas as pd
   import numpy as np
   unsorted_df = pd.DataFrame({'col1':[2,1,1,1],'col2':[1,3,2,4]})
   sorted_df = unsorted_df.sort_values(by='col1' ,kind='mergesort')
   print(sorted_df)
   ```

7. ```
   pd.DataFrame(np.random.randn(10,2),index=[1,4,6,2,3,5,9,8,0,7],colu
      mns = ['col2','col1'])
   sorted_df = unsorted_df.sort_index(ascending=False)
   print sorted_df
   ```

8. ```
   Income_Data['capital-gain'].quantile([0, 0.1, 0.2, 0.3, 0.4, 0.5, 0.6,
   0.7, 0.8, 0.9, 1])
   bank=pd.read_csv("datasets\\Bank Marketing\\bank_market.csv",encoding =
   "ISO-8859-1")
   bank.shape
   summary_bala=bank["balance"].describe()
   bank['balance'].quantile([0, 0.1, 0.2, 0.3, 0.4, 0.5, 0.6, 0.7, 0.8,
   0.9, 1])
   summary_age=bank['age'].describe()
   print(summary_age)
   bank['age'].quantile([0, 0.1, 0.2, 0.3, 0.4, 0.5, 0.6, 0.7, 0.8, 0.9,
   1])
   ```

9. ```
   import pandas as pds

   # Read a JSON file
   scoreFile = "./scores.json";
   dataFrame = pds.read_json(scoreFile);
   scores = dataFrame["Score"];
   print("Scores as loaded into the pandas.Series instance:");
   print(scores);
   print("First Quartile:%.2f"%scores.quantile(.25));
   print("Second Quartile:%.2f"%scores.quantile(.5));
   print("Third Quartile:%.2f"%scores.quantile(.75));
   print("100th Percentile:%.2f"%scores.quantile(1));
   print("1st Percentile:%.2f"%scores.quantile(.1));
   ```

10. ```
    import pandas as pd
    import numpy as np
    df = pd.DataFrame(np.random.randn(5,3),columns=['col1','col2','col3'])
    df = df.apply(np.mean,axis=1)
    print(df)
    ```

11. ```
    df.rename({'$a':'a',    '$b':'b',    '$c':'c',    '$d':'d',    '$e':'e'},
    axis='columns')
    or
    df.rename({'$a':'a', '$b':'b', '$c':'c', '$d':'d', '$e':'e'}, axis=1)
    ```
    ```

Fill in the Blanks

1. _____ denotes the row labels.
2. To delete a column from the data frame, we can either use the _____ statement or using the _____ method.
3. To access a particular row from the data frame using label or column name, we can use the _____ method.
4. _____ function sorts a data frame in ascending or descending order of passed column.
5. _____ option in aggregation functions specify whether to exclude missing data or not.
6. The default value of axis is _____ indicating _____.
7. The _____ method applies function on Table.
8. _____ is the process of turning the values of a dataset (or a subset of it) into one single value.
9. The process of applying multiple aggregation functions to a single column is known as _____.
10. _____ property of data frame helps to skip missing values.
11. NaN stands for _____.
12. _____ is used to change the index of rows and columns of a data frame.
13. _____ function is used to write a data frame to a SQL Table.
14. The `read_sql()` method returns a _____ object.

State True or False

1. A data frame has columns of different data types.
2. The `drop()` method cannot be used to delete rows from a data frame.
3. We can sort only numerical data and not textual data in Pandas.
4. The `sort_values()` function returns a sorted data frame with same dimensions as that of the original data frame.
5. We can sort a data frame by several columns together.
6. Aggregation functions like `sum()`, `mean()`, and `quantile()` produce a higher-dimensional result.
7. If axis = 1, the descriptive function is applied on indexes or rows.
8. NumPy methods like mean, std, and sum, will exclude NAs on Series input by default.
9. On a mixed-type DataFrame object, `describe()` will restrict the summary to include only numerical columns.
10. The `applymap()` method applies function of a row or column.
11. We can group data by a single column only.
12. The `transform()` function produces a data frame of the same length as that of the original data frame passed to it.
13. Covariance is applied on series data only.

Multiple Choice Questions

1. To access a particular row from the data frame we can even pass an integer location to _____ method.
   a. `loc`   b. `iloc`   c. `pop`   d. `print`
2. _____ is raised if there are any duplicate values in the data frame.
   a. KeyError   b. ValueError   c. IndexError   d. NameError
3. Which argument of the sort function applies changes in the data frame passed to the function?
   a. Kind   b. na_position   c. inplace   d. axis
4. By default, `sort_index()` function sorts on row labels in which order?
   a. ascending   b. descending   c. Both of these.   d. None of these.

5. Which function throws exception when the DataFrame contains character or string data?
   a. sum() b. cumsum() c. cumpod() d. mean()
6. Which function computes a variety of summary statistics on a Series or the columns of a DataFrame object?
   a. stats() b. summarize() c. describe() d. sum()
7. _____ function can be used for function chaining.
   a. pipe() b. apply() c. applymap() d. transform()
8. Which of the following applies a function on a data-frame element-wise?
   a. pipe() b. apply() c. applymap() d. transform()
9. Which function returns a self-produced data frame with transformed values after applying the function specified in its parameter?
   a. pipe() b. apply() c. applymap() d. transform()
10. _____ shows the linear relationship between any two array of values (series).
    a. Correlation b. covariance c. median d. pct_change

Give the Output

1. ```
   import pandas as pd
   import numpy as np
   client_dictionary = {'name': ['Michael', 'Ana', 'Sean'],
   'country': ['UK', 'UK', 'USA'],
   'age': [10, 51, 13],
   'latest date active': ['07-05-2019', '23-12-2019', '03-04-2016']}
   df = pd.DataFrame(client_dictionary)
   df.head()
   df.sort_values(by='name')
   df.sort_values(by='name', ascending=False)
   df.sort_values(by='age')
   #df['latest date active'] = df['latest date active'].astype('datetime64[ns]')
   df.sort_values(by='latest date active')
   df.sort_values(by=['country','name'])
   df.sort_values(by=['country','name'], inplace=True)
   ```

2. ```
   import pandas as pd
   import numpy as np
   unsorted_df = pd.DataFrame(np.random.randn(10,2),index=[1,4,6,2,3,5,9,8,0,7],colu
      mns = ['col2','col1'])
   sorted_df=unsorted_df.sort_index()
   print(sorted_df)
   ```

3. ```
   import pandas as pd
   import numpy as np
   import math
   # user defined function
   def scale(num):
      return(num*10)
   df = pd.Series([1,2,3,4,5,6,7,8,9,10])
   df = df.pipe(scale)
   print(df)
   ```

4. ```
   import pandas as pd
   import numpy as np
   import math
   ```

```
   # user defined function
   def scale(num):
       return(num*10)
   df = pd.DataFrame(6*np.random.randn(6,3),columns=['A','B','C'])
   df = df.apply(scale,axis=1)
   print(df)
```

5. ```
   import pandas as pd
   import numpy as np
   def adder(ele1,ele2):
       return ele1+ele2
   df = pd.DataFrame(np.random.randn(5,3),columns=['col1','col2','col3'])
   df.pipe(adder,2)
   print(df.apply(np.mean))
   ```

6. ```
   import pandas as pd
   import numpy as np
   df = pd.DataFrame(np.random.randn(5,3),columns=['col1','col2','col3'])
   df.apply(np.mean)
   print(df.apply(np.mean))
   ```

7. ```
   data = {"Team": ["Red Sox", "Red Sox", "Red Sox", "Red Sox", "Red Sox", "Red Sox", "Yankees", "Yankees", "Yankees", "Yankees", "Yankees", "Yankees"],
       "Pos": ["Pitcher", "Pitcher", "Pitcher", "Not Pitcher", "Not Pitcher", "Not Pitcher", "Pitcher", "Pitcher", "Pitcher", "Not Pitcher", "Not Pitcher", "Not Pitcher"],
       "Age": [24, 28, 40, 22, 29, 33, 31, 26, 21, 36, 25, 31]}
   df = pd.DataFrame(data)
   grouped_single = df.groupby('Team').agg({'Age': ['mean', 'min', 'max']})
   print(grouped_single)
   grouped_single.columns = ['age_mean', 'age_min', 'age_max']
   grouped_single = grouped_single.reset_index()
   print(grouped_single)
   grouped_multiple = df.groupby(['Team', 'Pos']).agg({'Age': ['mean', 'min', 'max']})
   grouped_multiple.columns = ['age_mean', 'age_min', 'age_max']
   grouped_multiple = grouped_multiple.reset_index()
   print(grouped_multiple)
   ```

8. ```
   import pandas as pd
   import numpy as np
   df = pd.DataFrame([[1, 2, 3],
                      [4, 5, 6],
                      [7, 8, 9],
                      [np.nan, np.nan, np.nan]],
                     columns=['A', 'B', 'C'])
   print(df)
   print(df.agg(['sum', 'min']))
   print(df.agg({'A' : ['sum', 'min'], 'B' : ['min', 'max']}))
   print(df.agg("mean", axis="columns"))
   print(df.agg("mean", axis="rows"))
   ```

9. ```
   import pandas as pd
   import numpy as np
     column=['a','b','c','d','e']
   ```
   ```

```
     index=['A','B','C','D','E']
     df1 = pd.DataFrame(np.random.rand(5,5),
             columns=column, index=index)
       colum=['e','a','b','c','d']
     print(df1.reindex(colum, axis='columns'))
```

10. ```
    import pandas as pd
    import numpy as np
    column =['a', 'b', 'c', 'd', 'e']
    index =['A', 'B', 'C', 'D', 'E']
       df1 = pd.DataFrame(np.random.rand(5, 5),
            columns = column, index = index)
      colum =['a', 'b', 'c', 'g', 'h']
      print(df1.reindex(colum, axis ='columns', fill_value = 1.5))
    print(df1)
    print(df1.reindex(colum, axis ='columns', fill_value ='data missing'))
    print(df1)
    ```

11. ```
    import pandas as pd
    info =pd.DataFrame({"A":[1, 5, 3, 4, 2],
                        "B":[3, 2, 4, 3, 4],
                        "C":[2, 2, 7, 3, 4],
                        "D":[4, 3, 6, 12, 7]})
    info.reindex(columns =["A", "B", "D", "E"])
    info.reindex(columns =["A", "B", "D", "E"], fill_value =37)
    ```

12. ```
    import pandas as pd
    df = pd.DataFrame([[1,2,3,4,5],[6,7,8,9,10],[11,12,13,14,15]],
    index=range(3), columns=list('abcde'))
    print(df)
    df2 = df.rename({'a': 'X', 'b': 'Y'}, axis=1)    # new method
    df2 = df.rename({'a': 'X', 'b': 'Y'}, axis='columns')
    df2 = df.rename(columns={'a': 'X', 'b': 'Y'})    # old method
    print(df2)
    df.rename({'a': 'X', 'b': 'Y'}, axis=1, inplace=True)
    print(df)
    ```

13. ```
    import pandas as pd
    import numpy as np
    N=20
    df = pd.DataFrame({
       'A': pd.date_range(start='2016-01-01',periods=N,freq='D'),
       'x': np.linspace(0,stop=N-1,num=N),
       'y': np.random.rand(N),
       'C': np.random.choice(['Low','Medium','High'],N).tolist(),
       'D': np.random.normal(100, 10, size=(N)).tolist()
    })
    df_reindexed = df.reindex(index=[0,2,5], columns=['A', 'C', 'B'])
    print(df_reindexed)
    ```

14. ```
    import pandas as pd
    import numpy as np
    df1 = pd.DataFrame(np.random.randn(6,3),columns=['col1','col2','col3'])
    print(df1)
    print ("After renaming the rows and columns:")
    print df1.rename(columns={'col1' : 'c1', 'col2' : 'c2'},
    index = {0 : 'apple', 1 : 'banana', 2 : 'durian'})
    ```
    ```

Answers

Explain the Instructions

1. Sort by the columns of 'Year' and 'Brand'
2. Find out mean value of 'A' of each column 'C'
3. Sorting an unsorted data frame
4. Sorting done on the column labels.
5. Col1 values are sorted and the respective col2 value and row index will alter along with col1.
6. Sort data frame by using mergesort algorithm
7. Descending order of index
8. Get the summary of the balance variable by using `.describe()`
   Get relevant percentiles and see their distribution.
   Get the summary of the age variable
9. Prints quantiles of data in the `json` file
10. Creates a data frame filled with random values. Find mean of each column by using `apply()` function
11. Rename column names of a dataframe.

Fill in the Blanks

1. Index
2. `del, pop()`
3. `loc()`
4. `sort_values()`
5. `skipna`
6. 0, indexes or rows.
7. `pipe()`
8. Aggregation
9. multiindex
10. `dropna`
11. Not a Number
12. Reindexing
13. `to_sql`
14. Pandas dataframe

State True or False

1. True
2. False
3. False
4. True
5. True
6. False
7. False
8. True
9. True
10. False
11. False
12. True
13. True

Multiple Choice Questions

1. b
2. b
3. c
4. a
5. c
6. c
7. a
8. c
9. d
10. a

Give the Output

1.
```
      name country  age latest date active
    0  Michael      UK   10        07-05-2019
    1      Ana      UK   51        23-12-2019
    2     Sean     USA   13        03-04-2016
      name country  age latest date active
    1      Ana      UK   51        23-12-2019
    0  Michael      UK   10        07-05-2019
    2     Sean     USA   13        03-04-2016
      name country  age latest date active
    2     Sean     USA   13        03-04-2016
    0  Michael      UK   10        07-05-2019
    1      Ana      UK   51        23-12-2019
      name country  age latest date active
    0  Michael      UK   10        07-05-2019
    2     Sean     USA   13        03-04-2016
    1      Ana      UK   51        23-12-2019
      name country  age latest date active
```

```
   2    Sean      USA    13        03-04-2016
   0    Michael   UK     10        07-05-2019
   1    Ana       UK     51        23-12-2019
        name   country   age   latest date active
   1    Ana       UK     51        23-12-2019
   0    Michael   UK     10        07-05-2019
   2    Sean      USA    13        03-04-2016
None
```

2.
```
        col2      col1
0  -0.362434  -0.815195
1   0.134718  -0.204274
2  -1.205005  -1.041460
3   0.492850   4.333057
4   0.702360   0.254796
5  -1.474636  -0.198478
6   0.107505  -1.006470
7   0.060316  -0.074017
8   0.602565   2.123238
9  -0.129561   0.756998
```

3.
```
0     10
1     20
2     30
3     40
4     50
5     60
6     70
7     80
8     90
9    100
dtype: int64
```

4.
```
          A          B          C
0  24.058581  82.795636  66.822212
1 -56.162128  63.377579 -86.214944
2 -38.962648 -45.365087 -79.845621
3 -21.108311  -5.932410  -9.904205
4 -23.256071 -57.814248 -40.260790
5 -24.519083 -59.828709  46.718290
```

5.
```
col1   -0.368219
col2    0.741642
col3    0.087954
dtype: float64
```

6.
```
col1    0.066034
col2    0.594589
col3   -0.079972
dtype: float64
```

7.
```
              Age
          mean min max
Team
Red Sox   29.333333  22  40
Yankees   28.333333  21  36
     Team    age_mean  age_min  age_max
0  Red Sox  29.333333       22       40
1  Yankees  28.333333       21       36
```

```
      Team          Pos     age_mean   age_min   age_max
0  Red Sox  Not Pitcher     28.000000        22        33
1  Red Sox      Pitcher     30.666667        24        40
2  Yankees  Not Pitcher     30.666667        25        36
3  Yankees      Pitcher     26.000000        21        31
```

8.
```
       A     B     C
0    1.0   2.0   3.0
1    4.0   5.0   6.0
2    7.0   8.0   9.0
3    NaN   NaN   NaN
         A      B      C
sum   12.0   15.0   18.0
min    1.0    2.0    3.0
         A      B
max    NaN    8.0
min    1.0    2.0
sum   12.0    NaN
0    2.0
1    5.0
2    8.0
3    NaN
dtype: float64
A    4.0
B    5.0
C    6.0
dtype: float64
```

9.
```
          e          a          b          c          d
A  0.176115   0.984114   0.917487   0.876535   0.304940
B  0.654958   0.505268   0.740204   0.689726   0.962752
C  0.557356   0.628149   0.295678   0.555936   0.848600
D  0.664569   0.018104   0.371453   0.088043   0.796377
E  0.807926   0.219276   0.881727   0.587020   0.627032
```

10.
```
          a          b          c        g      h
A  0.343524   0.872782   0.948085      1.5    1.5
B  0.179796   0.850623   0.306291      1.5    1.5
C  0.253003   0.045014   0.878181      1.5    1.5
D  0.675426   0.932980   0.401576      1.5    1.5
E  0.939916   0.686038   0.769236      1.5    1.5
          a          b          c          d          e
A  0.343524   0.872782   0.948085   0.049154   0.572482
B  0.179796   0.850623   0.306291   0.870597   0.453902
C  0.253003   0.045014   0.878181   0.821990   0.978511
D  0.675426   0.932980   0.401576   0.927885   0.639104
E  0.939916   0.686038   0.769236   0.665432   0.561583
          a          b          c             g             h
A  0.343524   0.872782   0.948085  data missing  data missing
B  0.179796   0.850623   0.306291  data missing  data missing
C  0.253003   0.045014   0.878181  data missing  data missing
D  0.675426   0.932980   0.401576  data missing  data missing
E  0.939916   0.686038   0.769236  data missing  data missing
          a          b          c          d          e
A  0.343524   0.872782   0.948085   0.049154   0.572482
```

```
     B  0.179796  0.850623  0.306291  0.870597  0.453902
     C  0.253003  0.045014  0.878181  0.821990  0.978511
     D  0.675426  0.932980  0.401576  0.927885  0.639104
     E  0.939916  0.686038  0.769236  0.665432  0.561583
```

11.
```
   A  B   D    E
0  1  3   4  NaN
1  5  2   3  NaN
2  3  4   6  NaN
3  4  3  12  NaN
4  2  4   7  NaN
   A  B   D   E
0  1  3   4  37
1  5  2   3  37
2  3  4   6  37
3  4  3  12  37
4  2  4   7  37
```

12.
```
    a   b   c   d   e
0   1   2   3   4   5
1   6   7   8   9  10
2  11  12  13  14  15
    X   Y   c   d   e
0   1   2   3   4   5
1   6   7   8   9  10
2  11  12  13  14  15
    X   Y   c   d   e
0   1   2   3   4   5
1   6   7   8   9  10
2  11  12  13  14  15
```

13.
```
            A     C    B
0  2016-01-01   Low  NaN
2  2016-01-03   Low  NaN
5  2016-01-06  High  NaN
```

14.
```
       col1      col2      col3
0  0.119605 -0.769871  1.473885
1 -0.996602 -1.370134 -0.238642
2  1.384949  1.460489  1.643380
3  1.355484 -0.442311  0.834330
4 -0.105974  0.655421  0.908107
5 -0.148238 -1.266244  0.976378
After renaming the rows and columns:
              c1        c2      col3
apple   0.119605 -0.769871  1.473885
banana -0.996602 -1.370134 -0.238642
durian  1.384949  1.460489  1.643380
3       1.355484 -0.442311  0.834330
4      -0.105974  0.655421  0.908107
5      -0.148238 -1.266244  0.976378
```

Plotting Graphs   3

Chapter Objectives

In Chapters 1 and 2, we have learnt to organize and analyze data through different ways. We have also learnt how to interpret statistics and use various functions to manipulate and process those data. In this chapter, we will learn how to depict the data using different types of plots. Plots helps us to better understand and deduce the meaning of the underlying data. For this purpose, we will learn to plot:

- Bar chart
- Histogram
- Frequency Plot
- Boxplot
- Scatter Plot

3.1 VISUALIZING DATA THROUGH PLOTS

We study statistics to collect and organize data. This data must be properly organized and presented in such a way that it is easily and clearly interpreted. For this reason, we can either organize data in the form of tables or present it pictorially using bar charts, histograms, frequency plots, scatter plots, boxplots, etc. Visualizing data through charts help users to easily understand and interpret even complex and/or large amount of data in one glance.

In this chapter, we will be using pyplot module which is, in turn, a sub-module of the matplotlib module. So before drawing charts, make sure you have installed the matplotlib module. Matplotlib is the most widely used scientific plotting library in Python. To install matplotlib, use the pip command by writing, pip install matplotlib.

The pyplot module provides an interface for graphing data. It contains over 100 functions and to use them you must import this module by writing, import matplotlib.pyplot as plt where, plt is the standard variable name used. This module allows users to,

- Create a plot
- Visualize data effectively
- Customize the plot with focus on plot legends and text, titles, axes labels and plot layout
- Save the plot for future use
- Show the plot
- Clear the plot area
- Close the plot.

3.2 BAR CHART

A bar chart or bar graph is a chart or graph that presents categorical data with rectangular bars. These bars can be drawn either vertically or horizontally. The height or length of the bars is proportional to the values they represent.

In a bar graph, while one axis of the chart shows the specific categories being compared, the other axis represents a measured value. The main advantage of plotting a bar graph is that it depicts comparisons among discrete categories.

3.2.1 Drawing a Bar Graph in Python

The pyplot module in the Matplotlib provides the `bar()` function that can be used to plot a bar graph. The syntax of this function can be given as,

```
bar(x, height, width, bottom, align)
```

where,

x is a sequence of values representing the x-coordinates of the bars.
height represents the sequence of values representing the height(s) of the bars.
weight is an optional parameter that is either scalar or array-like. It represents the width(s) of the bars. By default, its value is 0.8.
bottom is an optional parameter that is either scalar or array-like. It denotes the y-coordinates of the bars. By default, it is None. It is used when plotting stacked bar graphs.
align can have values 'center' or 'edge'. The default value is 'center'. 'center' is used to center the base of the bar on the x positions. 'edge' aligns the left edges of the bars with the x positions. To align the bars on the right edge, a negative width and align='edge' is used.

Other optional but useful parameters are given below:

color is a scalar or array-like value indicating the colors of the bars.
edgecolor is a scalar or array-like value that specifies the colors of the edges of the bar.
linewidths is a scalar or array-like value denoting the width of the bar edge(s). If its value is zero, then no edges will be drawn.
tick_label is a string or array-like value that specifies the labels of the ticks on the bars. By default, its value is None and it uses default numeric labels.

The code given below plots a bar graph.

Example 3.1

```
import numpy as np
import pandas as pd
from pandas import Series, DataFrame
import matplotlib.pyplot as plt
data = [27,45,36,18,72,81,108,19,9]
x = range(1,10)
plt.bar(x, data)
plt.show()
```

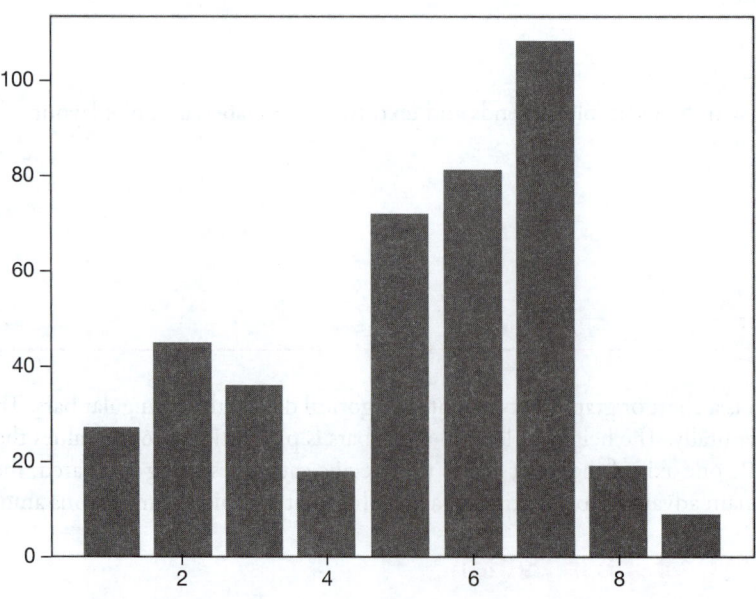

To draw a horizontal bar graph, the barh() function is used.
The syntax of barh() function is matplotlib.pyplot.barh(y, width, height=0.8, align='center')

The bars are positioned at y with the given alignment. Their dimensions are given by width and height.

PROGRAMMER'S ZONE

1. **Write a program that plots a bar graph depicting the number of students who are interested in learning Mathematics, Computers, English, Accountancy and Economics.**

   ```
   import numpy as np
   import pandas as pd
   from pandas import Series, DataFrame
   import matplotlib.pyplot as plt
   fav_subjs = ['Mathematics', 'Computers', 'English', 'Accountancy', 'Economics']
   counts = [10,40,35,29,20]
   plt.bar(fav_subjs,counts)
   plt.show()
   ```

   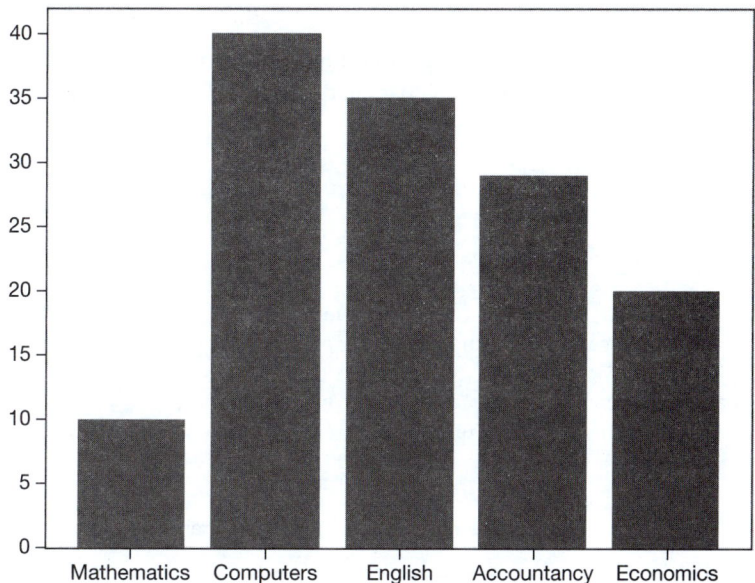

2. **Write a program that draws a horizontal bar graph depicting marks obtained by a student in different subjects.**

   The barh() function is used to plot a horizontal bar graph

   ```
   import numpy as np
   import matplotlib.pyplot as plt
   subjects = ['Mathematics', 'Accounts', 'English',
       'Computers', 'Economics']
   y_pos = np.arange(len(subjects))
   performance = [85,90,100,80,75]
   plt.barh(y_pos, performance, align='center')
   plt.yticks(y_pos, subjects)
   # write some data on x-axis
   plt.xlabel('Marks')
   plt.title('Marks Obtained in Different Subjects')
   plt.show()
   ```

   > The xticks() function takes two parameters – index and label. The function places the Labels on each tick that is generated due to index sequence.

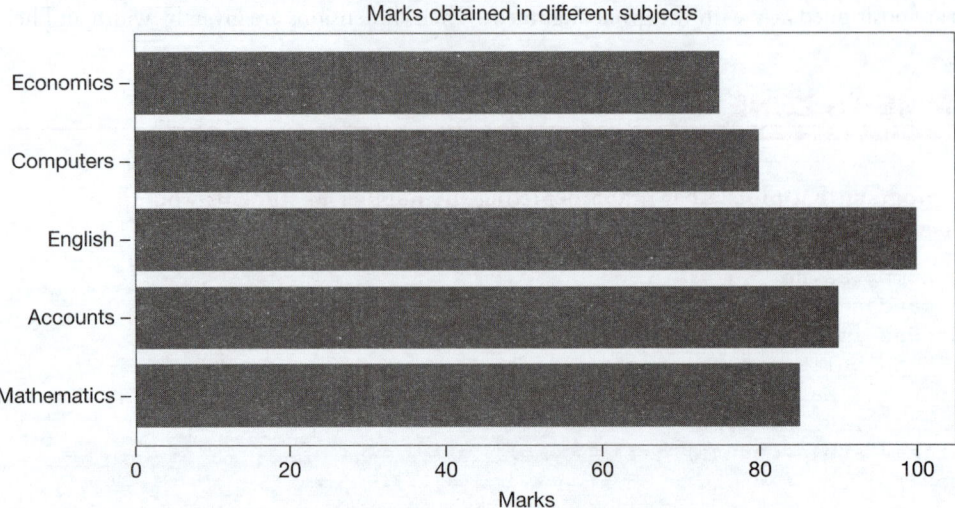

3. **Write a program that plots the marks obtained by two students in four subjects using bar graph.**

   Note that we can plot multiple bar charts by adjusting the thickness and the positions of the bars. In the given code, each bar has a thickness of 0.30 units. Each bar chart is shifted 0.30 units from the previous one.

```
import numpy as np
import matplotlib.pyplot as plt
marks_Jia = (83,79,80,83)
marks_Goransh = (95,84,89,99)
index = np.array([1,2,3,4])
width = 0.30
plt.bar(index, marks_Jia, width, label = 'Marks Obtained by Jia')
plt.bar(index + width, marks_Goransh, width, label = 'Marks Obtained by Goransh')
plt.ylabel('Marks')
plt.title('Comparing Marks of Jia and Goransh')
plt.xticks(index + width / 2, ('Subject1', 'Subject2', 'Subject3', 'Subject4'))
plt.legend(loc='best')
plt.show()
```

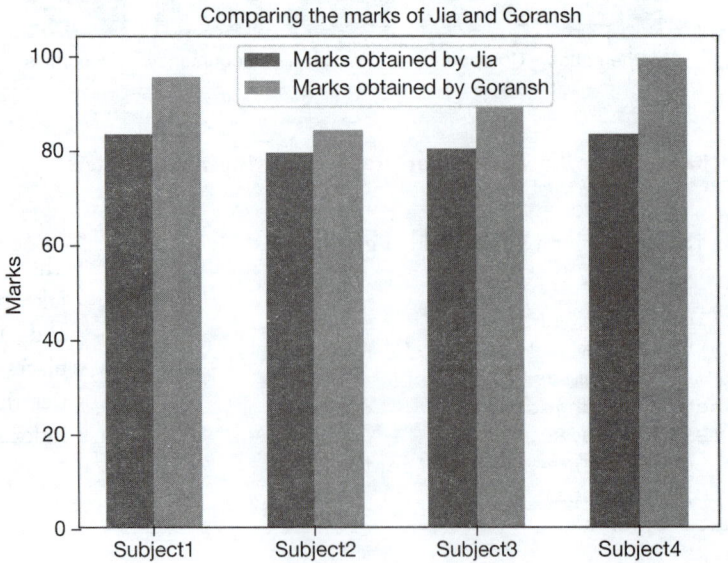

4. **Write a program that creates a stacked bar graph depicting the marks obtained by four students in three tests.**

The stacked bar chart stacks bars that represent different groups on top of each other. The height of the resulting bar shows the combined result of the groups. The `bar()` function allow users to specify a starting value for a bar. In the given code, the first call to `pyplot.bar()` plots the blue bars. The second call to `pyplot.bar()` plots the green bars, with the lower part of the green bars being at the top of the blue bars.

```
import numpy as np
import matplotlib.pyplot as plt
students = ['Reyansh', 'Tanvi', 'Parakh','Ziva']
Test1 = np.array([18,14,12,15])
Test2 = np.array([20,18,16,19])
Test3 = np.array([16,16,13,15])
index = students
plt.bar(index, Test1, width=0.5, label='Test1', color='red', bottom = Test2 +
    Test3)
plt.bar(index, Test2, width=0.5, label='Test2', color='green', bottom = Test3)
plt.bar(index, Test3, width=0.5, label='Test3', color='blue')
plt.xticks(index, students)
plt.ylabel("Marks")
plt.xlabel("Students")
plt.legend(loc="upper right")
plt.title("Marks Obtained in Three Tests")
plt.show()
```

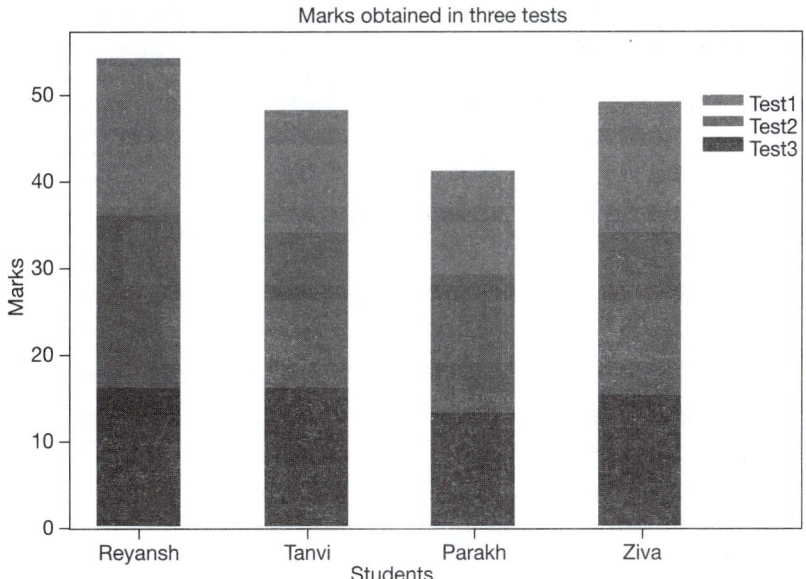

3.2.2 Some Important Miscellaneous Functions

Saving Figure: After plotting the graph, the graph can be saved using the `savefig()` function of pyplot. The syntax of `savefig()` function is,

`plt.savefig(fname, **kwargs),`

where,
fname is the name of the file. We can also specify the destination or path along with the name of the file.
The **kwargs** parameter is optional. It is used to change the orientation, format, face color, quality, dpi, etc.

Changing Font and Font Size: Font size of a plot can be changed with the help of `rc()` function. The `rc()` function is used to customize the rc settings. The syntax of this function can be given as,

```
matplotlib.pyplot.rc('fontname', **font)
```

or

```
matplotlib.pyplot.rc('font', size=sizeInt)
```

where **font** is a user-defined dictionary that specifies the weight, font family, font size, etc. of the text.

Clear Plot: The `clf()` function of the pyplot clears the plot or the entire figure. The syntax of this function is,

```
matplotlib.pyplot.clf()
```

Note that the `clf()` function does not have any argument. Also note that you can use `plt.cla()` to clear the axis and `plt.close()` to close a window that has popped up to display your plot.

Axis Range: The range or limit of the x and y axis can be set by using the `xlim()` and `ylim()` functions of the pyplot, respectively. The syntax for these functions can be given as,

```
matplotlib.pyplot.xlim([starting_point, ending_point])
matplotlib.pyplot.ylim([starting_point, ending_point])
```

Therefore, when we write plt.xlim([0,100]), the points in the x-axis will start at 0 and continue till 100. Similarly, plt.ylim([0,100]) will limit y axis coordinates.

Label Axis: The labels for x- and y-axis can be specified using the `xlabel()` and `ylabel()` functions of pyplot. Syntax of these functions can be given as,

```
matplotlib.pyplot.xlabel(labeltext, labelfontdict, **kwargs)
matplotlib.pyplot.ylabel(labeltext, labelfontdict, **kwargs)
```

where, **labeltext** is a string that specifies the text of the label. The rest are optional parameters and can be ignored for simplicity.

3.3 PLOTTING HISTOGRAMS

Histogram is a graphical representation, which is quite similar to bar graphs. It is a great tool for assessing a probability distribution of a continuous variable that can be easily understood.

Histogram plots the frequency distribution of a numeric array by splitting it to small equal-sized bins. It is an excellent tool for visualizing and understanding the probabilistic distribution of not only numerical data bust also image data.

To construct a histogram, we need to keep in mind three basic steps.

Step 1: Bin the range of values.

Step 2: Divide the entire range of values into a series of intervals.

Step 3: Count how many values fall into each interval.

Remember that the bins are usually specified as consecutive, non-overlapping intervals of a variable.

To plot a histogram, the `hist()` function of matplotlib and pyplot module is used. The syntax of this function is,

plt.hist(data, bins = number of bins)

The function accepts the data and number of bins as arguments. Writing passing bins = 'auto' makes "ideal" number of bins width that generates the most faithful representation of data.

Besides these two parameters, a few additional parameters can also be passed. These optional parameters are,

`range` which specifies the lower and upper range of the bins.
`density` is a Boolean value which if True, will normalize the counts of the first element of the return tuple to form a probability density
`cumulative` is a Boolean value. If True, a histogram is computed where each bin gives the counts in that bin plus all bins for smaller values.
`histtype` specifies the type of histogram to be drawn. Default value is 'bar', which draws a traditional bar-type histogram. If multiple data are given then the bars are arranged side by side. If histtype = 'barstacked', a bar-type histogram where multiple data are stacked on top of each other is drawn. However, if histtype = 'step' an unfilled lineplot is drawn. histtype = 'stepfilled' generates a lineplot that is filled by default.

The code given below draws a simple histogram of 100 random integer data values. A histogram uses its bin edges on the x-axis and the corresponding frequencies on the y-axis.

Example 3.2

```
import numpy as np
import matplotlib.pyplot as plt
from random import seed
from random import randint
# seed random number generator
seed(1)
data = []
# generate some integers
for i in range(100):
    value = randint(0, 100)
    data.append(value)
print(data)
plt.hist(data, bins=25)
plt.show()
```

> The `seed()` function of NumPy module is used to get the same set of random numbers each time the program is executed.

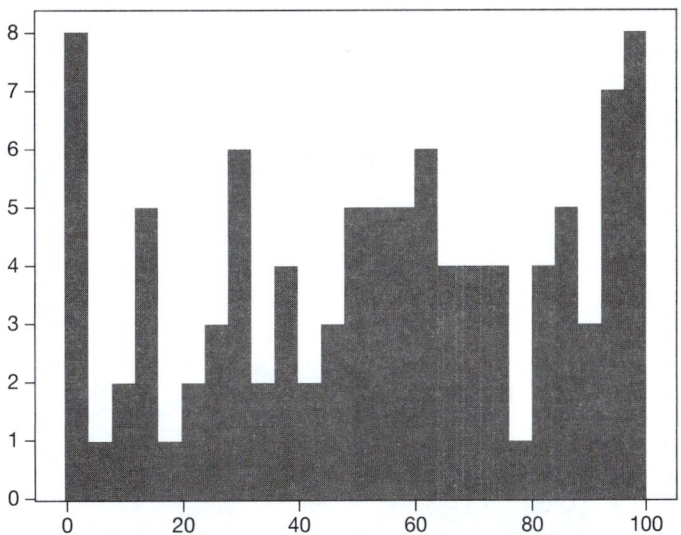

Additional way to determine the number of bins: In the above code, we have specified 25 bins. You can also choose any other number. However, we can also mathematically compute the number of bins by using the following formula:

n = **Range / (Number of intervals)**

where,
n = Number of observations
Range = Maximum value – Minimum value
Number of intervals = $\sqrt{n}$

These formulas can then be used to create the frequency table followed by the histogram. For example, in the above code,

- *n* = number of observations = 100
- Range = Maximum value – Minimum value = 97 – 1 = 96
- Number of intervals = $\sqrt{n} = \sqrt{100} = 10$
- Number of bins = Range / (Number of intervals) = 96/10 = 9.6 or 10

Now we can either write bins = 10 or specify the bins. That is, by writing either,

```
plt.hist(data, bins=10)                    or
plt.hist(data, bins=[0,10,20,30,40,50,60,70,80,90,100])
```

PROGRAMMER'S ZONE

5. **Draw a green-colored histogram plotting 100 random integers with number of bins being optimum.**

   ```
   import numpy as np
   import matplotlib.pyplot as plt
   from random import seed
   from random import randint
   data = []
   # generate some integers
   for i in range(100):
    value = randint(0, 100)
    data.append(value)
   print(data)
   plt.hist(data, bins='auto', color='green',alpha=0.7)
   plt.xlabel('Value')
   plt.ylabel('Frequency')
   plt.title('Plotting Random Integers')
   plt.show()
   ```

   > bins= 'auto' chooses ideal number of bins.

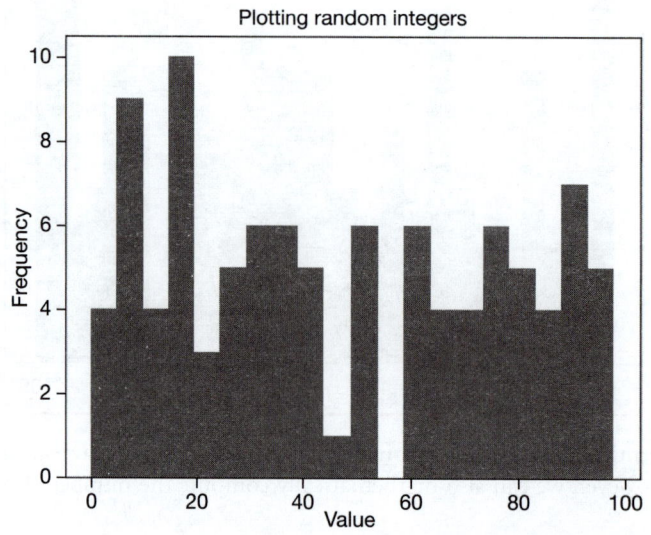

6. **Plot a yellow-colored histogram plotting the number of times 1000 commuters commute every year. Draw grid lines and place suitable labels.**

```
import numpy as np
import matplotlib.pyplot as plt
from random import seed
from random import randint
import pandas as pd
# Generate data on commute times.
commutes = pd.Series(np.random.rand(1000) * 100)
plt.hist(commutes, bins=20, rwidth=0.9, color='yellow')
plt.title('Commute Times for 1,000 Commuters')
plt.xlabel('Counts')
plt.ylabel('Commute Time')
plt.grid(axis='y', alpha=0.75)
plt.show()
```

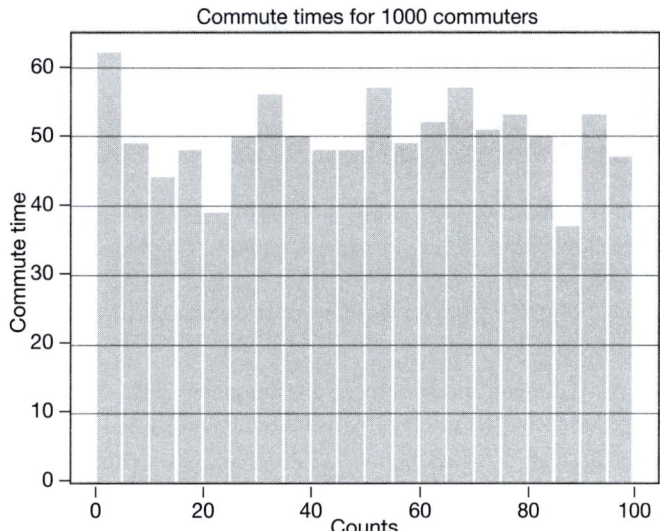

7. **Write a program that plots a stacked histogram of five data sets.**

```
import numpy as np
import matplotlib.pyplot as plt
from random import seed
from random import randint
import pandas as pd
x1 = np.random.normal(0, 10, 1000)
x2 = np.random.normal(4, 10, 1000)
x3 = np.random.normal(-2, 10, 1000)
x4 = np.random.normal(5, 10, 1000)
x5 = np.random.normal(-7, 10, 1000)
colors = ['red','green','blue','orange','olive']
plt.hist([x1,x2,x3,x4,x5],bins = 7, stacked=True, color = colors, alpha = 0.3)
plt.xlabel('Data Values')
plt.ylabel('Counts')
plt.show()
```

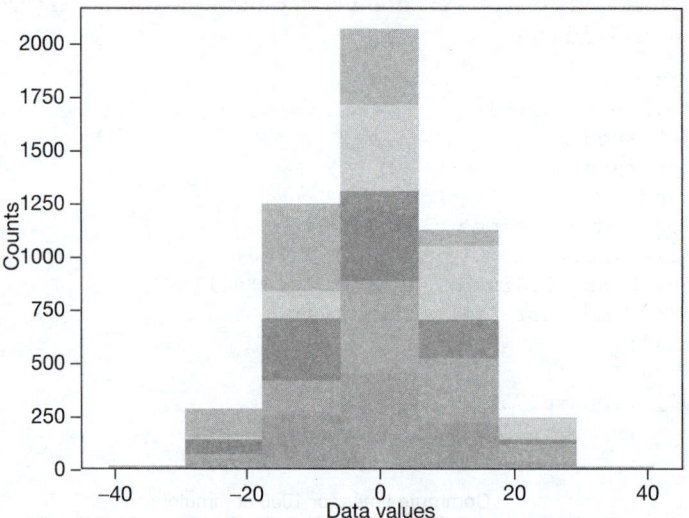

3.4 FREQUENCY POLYGON

A frequency polygon is a graphical form of representation of data. It gives an idea about the shape of the data and the trends that a particular data set follow. It can be used to compare two sets of data and are best for comparing two data sets that have the same sample size.

We usually draw a frequency polygon with a histogram but it can also be drawn without a histogram. The basic steps to draw a frequency polygon are follows:

Step 1: On the horizontal axis (x-axis), mark the class intervals. Frequency will be plotted on the vertical axis (y-axis).
Step 2: Calculate the class_mark for each class interval by using the formula.

```
class_mark = (Upper limit + Lower limit) / 2
```

Step 3: Mark all the class marks on the horizontal axis.
Step 4: Corresponding to each class mark, plot the frequency. The height always depicts the frequency. Note that the frequency is plotted against the class mark and not the upper or lower limit of any class.
Step 5: Join all the plotted points using a line segment. The curve obtained will be kinked. This resulting curve is called the frequency polygon.

The above steps are used to draw a frequency polygon without drawing a histogram. To draw a frequency polygon with a histogram, first draw rectangular bars against the given class intervals. Then, join the midpoints of the bars to obtain the frequency polygon.

Example 3.3 Consider the data set and the corresponding frequency plot given below.

Test Scores	Frequency	Cumulative Frequency
49.5-59.5	5	5
59.5-69.5	10	15
69.5-79.5	30	45
79.5-89.5	40	85
89.5-99.5	15	100

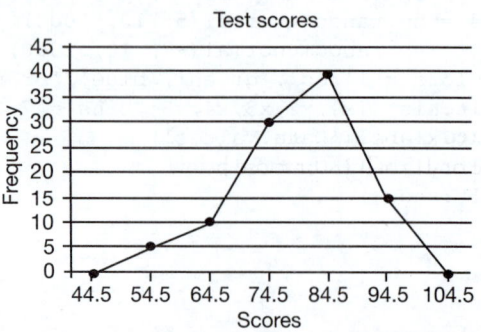

3.5 BOXPLOT

A boxplot or a whisker plot displays the summary of a set of data containing the minimum, first quartile, median, third quartile, and maximum. Recall that quartile is a measure of central tendency that divides a data set in to 4 parts.

In a boxplot, we draw a box from the first quartile to the third quartile. A vertical line goes through the box at the median. The whiskers go from each quartile to the minimum or maximum.

The median (percentile 50%) is drawn with a red line. The box represents Q1 and Q3 (percentiles 25 and 75), and the whiskers give an idea of the range of the data. The position of the whiskers is set by default to

$$1.5 * IQR \ (IQR = Q3 - Q1)$$

from the edges of the box. Outlier points are those past the end of the whiskers.

In a boxplot, the x-axis has the data for which the boxplot has to be drawn and the y-axis denotes the frequency distribution.

3.5.1 Understanding a Boxplot

A boxplot can be very useful when comparing the distribution of data across data sets. In such a case, different boxplots can be drawn for each data in the data set.

Example 3.4 Let us draw a boxplot of the following data which represent the ages of people working on a crucial project.

24, 27, 28, 28, 29, 33, 34, 34, 36, 37

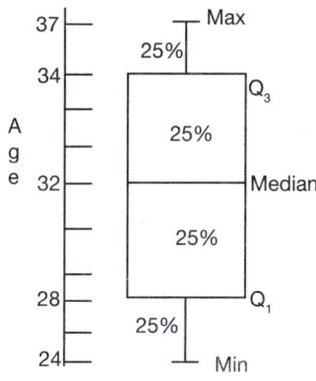

Step 1: Sort the data. Our sample data is already sorted.
Step 2: Find the median. So, here the median is (29 + 33) / 2 = 64 / 2 = 32.
Step 3: Find the quartiles.
The first quartile would be the median of the data points to the *left* of the median. In our data, first quartile is the median of 24, 27, 28, 28, 29. Therefore, the first quartile, Q_1 = 28.
The third quartile would be the median of the data points to the right of the median. In our data, third quartile is the median of 33, 34, 34, 36, 37. Therefore, the third quartile, Q_3 = 34.
Step 4: Find the min and max values. In our data set, min = 24 and max = 37.
Step 5: Label the axis and mark the scales with a five-number summary.
Step 6: Draw a box from Q_1 to Q_3 with a line passing through the median.
Step 7: Draw a whisker from Q_1 to min and another whisker from Q_3 to the max.
Now, once our boxplot graph is ready, let us interpret the information presented by it. The boxplot says that 25% of the people working on the project are below the age of 25 and 75% are above the age of 28.
Similarly, 25% of the people are above the age of 34. Moreover, half of the people are below the age of 32.

> The span from first quartile to the third is called IQR (Inter Quartile Range).

3.5.2 Use of Boxplot Graph

Boxplots are very useful to identify the outliers. John Tukey has provided a precise definition for two types of outliers:

Outliers are either 3 × IQR or more above the third quartile or 3 × IQR or more below the first quartile.
Suspected outliers are slightly more central versions of outliers. They are either 1.5 × IQR or more above the third quartile or 1.5 × IQR or more below the first quartile.

If any outlier is present, then the inner fence on that side of the whisker is taken as 1.5 × IQR from the quartile. All suspected outliers are displayed as unfilled circles and outliers are filled circles. From the figure it is clear that the outer fence is 3 × IQR from the quartile.

Usually, suspected outliers are not uncommon in large normally distributed datasets (for example, those having more than 100 data-points). Outliers are expected in normally distributed datasets with more than about 10 000 data-points.

We should never treat the outliers as bad data points as they often provide useful information. They should never be discarded or removed from the dataset. Rather, they may deserve special consideration as they may be the key to the phenomenon under study or the result of human blunders.

Thus, a boxplot can be used to make the following observations:

- Key values like the mean, median, minimum, maximum, 25th percentile etc.
- Outliers and suspected outliers, if any
- How tightly is the data grouped.

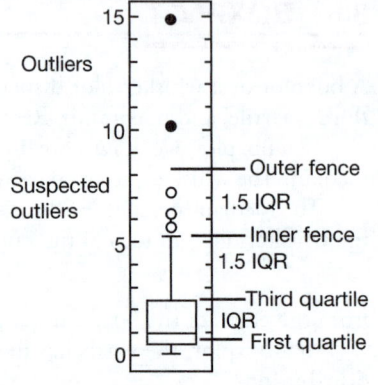

3.5.3 Creating a Boxplot

The `boxplot()` function of the pyplot module is used to draw a boxplot. The syntax of this function can be given as,

`boxplot(x, notch, vert, meanline, showmeans, showbox)`

where,

x is the array or any other sequence of values. It forms the input data.
notch is a Boolean value. If notch = True, a notched boxplot will be drawn, else a rectangular box plot is created
vert is a Boolean value. Its value is True by default. If False, a horizontal boxplot will be drawn
meanline is a Boolean value. If both **meanline** and **showmean** are True then the mean will be rendered as a line spanning the full width of the box.
showbox is a Boolean value which displays the box on the boxplot. If False, the box will not be drawn.
showmeans shows the arithmetic means of the input data values.

To create a boxplot, we first need to generate some random data. In the code given below, we have used the `numpy.random.normal()` function that takes three arguments – mean and standard deviation of the normal distribution, and the number of values to be generated.

Example 3.5

```
import numpy as np
import matplotlib.pyplot as plt
from random import seed
from random import randint
import pandas as pd
x1 = np.random.normal(0, 10, 1000)
x2 = np.random.normal(4, 10, 1000)
x3 = np.random.normal(-2, 10, 1000)
x4 = np.random.normal(5, 10, 1000)
x5 = np.random.normal(-7, 10, 1000)
data=[x1,x2,x3,x4,x5]
plt.boxplot(data)
plt.show()
```

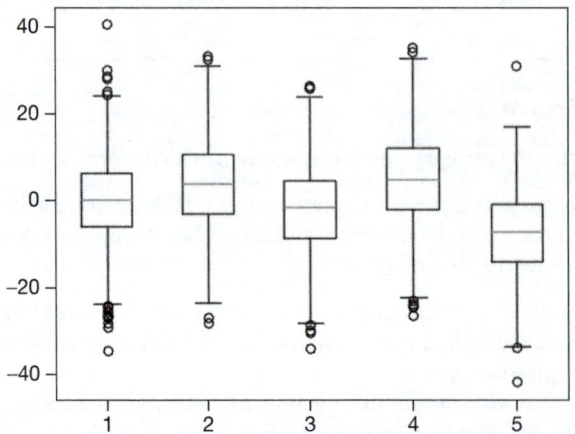

In the above code, we created five arrays to create a single data set. Data is then used to plot the boxplots. To add labels to the boxplots, we can use the labels argument of the `boxplot()` function. We can even pass additional parameters in this function to colour the boxplot. The argument patch_artist=True, fills the boxplot with the default colour. To create notch of the boxplot, we set notch='True'. The code given below uses all these parameters to draw the boxplot.

Example 3.6

```
import numpy as np
import matplotlib.pyplot as plt
from random import seed
from random import randint
import pandas as pd
x1 = np.random.normal(0, 10, 50)
x2 = np.random.normal(4, 10, 50)
x3 = np.random.normal(6, 10, 50)
x4 = np.random.normal(5, 10, 50)
x5 = np.random.normal(3, 10, 50)
data=[x1,x2,x3,x4,x5]
plt.boxplot(data,patch_artist=True, notch = True,
     labels=['Group1','Group2','Group3','Group4','Group5'])
plt.show()
```

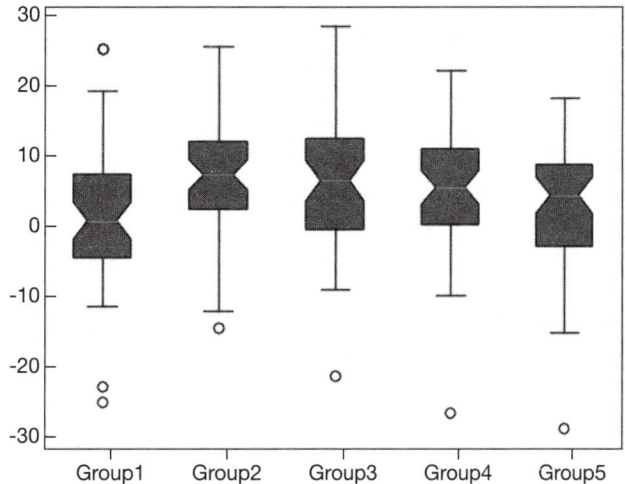

To create a horizontal boxplot, the argument vert is set to 0 by writing vert = 0. Note that while plotting boxplot, we can make use of the `title()`, `xticks()`, `yticks()`, `xlabel()`, `ylabel()`, `xlim()`, `ylim()` and `legend()` functions of the pyplot module.

```
title() function adds title to the plot    legend() adds legend to the plot.
xticks() sets the xticks.                   yticks() sets the yticks.
xlim() sets x limit                         ylim() sets y limit
xlabel() sets x-axis label                  ylabel() sets y-axis label
```

3.6 PIE CHART

We have been drawing and interpreting pie charts in Mathematics. Did you ever notice that a pie chart displays one series of data? It shows the size of items in one data series, proportional to the sum of the items. The area of the whole chart represents 100% or the whole of the data. This means that data points in a pie chart are shown as a percentage of the whole pie. The slices of the pie are called wedges.

The `pie()` function in the Matplotlib library is used to create a pie chart in which the fractional area of each wedge is calculated using the formula, **x/sum(x)**. Since pie charts provide a quick summary, they are commonly used in business presentations like sales, operations, survey results, news articles, and resource usage diagrams like disk and memory.

3.6.1 Plotting a Pie Chart

The Matplotlib library has `pie()` function in the `pyplot` module that is used to create a pie chart representing data stored in an array. The syntax of this function is,

`matplotlib.pyplot.pie(data, explode=None, labels=None, colors=None, autopct=None, shadow=False)`

where,
data is the array of values to be plotted. The fractional area of each slice is calculated as, **data/sum(data)**.
labels is a list containing strings to the labels of each wedge.
color is used to specify the color for each wedge. Usually, a tuple containing the list of colors to be cycled for the wedges of a pie chart is specified under `color`.
autopct is a string that labels wedges with their numerical value.
shadow draws the shadow of each wedge. By default, the value of `shadow` is False and there will be no shadow of the pie chart.

3.6.2 Customizing a Pie Chart

To customize a pie chart, we can use some additional parameters as given below.

startangle specifies the degrees in which the plot has to be rotated in counter-clockwise direction on the x-axis of the pie chart.
shadow is a Boolean value which, if True, makes a shadow below the rim of the pie. **wedgeprop** is used to customize the wedges of the pie. It accepts Python dictionary as parameter with name values pair denoting the wedge properties like linewidth, edgecolor, etc.
explode is a tuple where each element corresponds to a wedge of the pie chart. This means that the length of the tuple should be equal to the number of pies in the pie chart. Based on the numeric value of the elements in the tuple, wedges are exploded to relatively higher or lower distances from the center of the pie chart.

Example 3.7 **The code given below plots a pie chart to show the contribution of each subject's marks in the total marks obtained by a student.**

```
import matplotlib.pyplot as plt
Marks = [80,90,60,85,100]
my_labels = 'Math','Science','English','Social Science','Painting'
plt.pie(Marks,labels=my_labels,autopct='%1.1f%%')
plt.title('Marks Obtained')
plt.axis('equal')
plt.show()
```

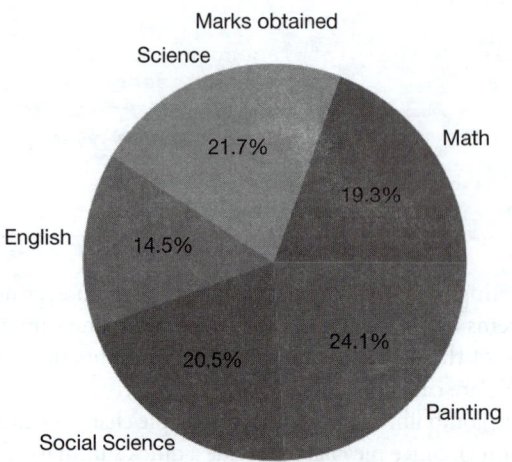

Example 3.8
Plot a pie chart depicting the marks obtained by a student in different subjects. Use colors and explode attribute to customize the chart.

```
import matplotlib.pyplot as plt
Marks = [80,90,60,85,100]
my_labels = 'Math','Science','English','Social Science','Painting'
my_colors = ['lightblue','lightsteelblue','silver','green','yellow']
my_explode = (0, 0.1, 0.2,0.3,0.4)
plt.pie(Marks,labels=my_labels,autopct='%1.1f%%',startangle=15, shadow = True,
    colors=my_colors, explode=my_explode)
plt.title('Marks Obtained')
plt.axis('equal')
plt.show()
```

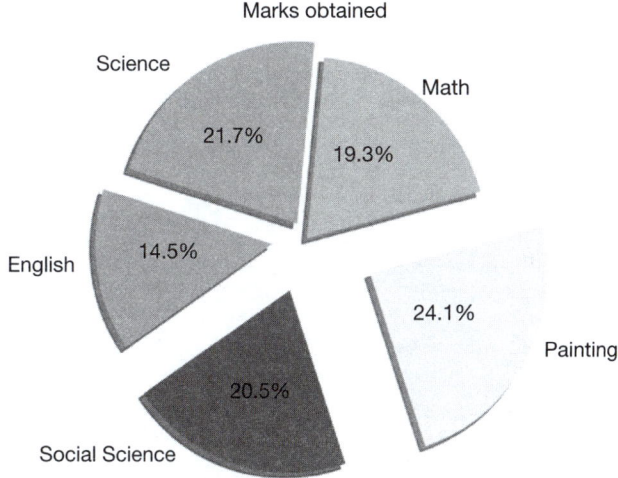

Example 3.9
Plot a pie chart depicting the choice of programming language to be taught at school level. Use colors, shadow and startangle attributes to customize the chart. Also display legends to make the chart readable.

```
import matplotlib.pyplot as plt
labels = ['Python', 'C++', 'Java', 'Ruby']
sizes = [58.4, 30.6, 29.7, 10.3]
colors = ['lightgreen', 'gold', 'lightskyblue', 'lightcoral']
patches, texts = plt.pie(sizes, colors=colors, shadow=True, startangle=90)
plt.legend(patches, labels, loc="best")
plt.axis('equal')
plt.tight_layout()
plt.show()
```

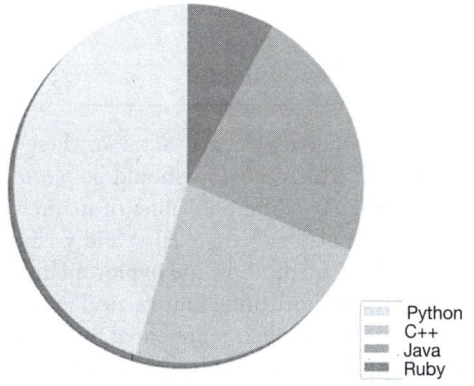

3.7 SCATTER PLOT

A scatter plot is a chart which plots each value in the data set by a dot. A scatter plot is drawn using the `scatter()` function. This function has the capability to render a different size and/or color for each point.

Scatter plot is a type of plot that shows data as a collection of points. To draw a scatter plot, we need two arrays of the same length. The position of a point depends on its two-dimensional value, where each value is a position on either the x- or y-axis. So, one of the arrays species denotes the values of the x-axis, and the other denotes the values of the y-axis.

Scatter Plots are usually used to represent the correlation between two or more variables. It also helps us to identify outliers, if any. For example, the code given below draws a scatter plot to depict the marks obtained by 15 students in a test.

Example 3.10

```
import numpy as np
import matplotlib.pyplot as plt
from random import seed
from random import randint
# seed random number generator
seed(1)
x = []
y = []
# generate some integers
for i in range(20):
    value = randint(0, 100)
    x.append(value)
    value = randint(0, 100)
    y.append(value)
plt.scatter(x, y)
plt.show()
```

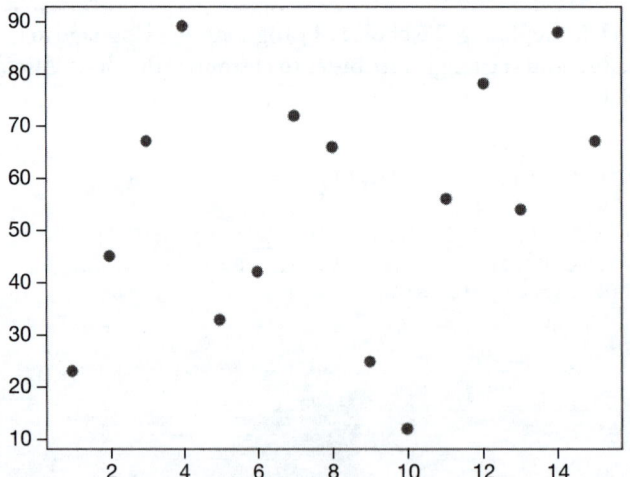

Scatter plot also has some additional optional arguments. Some of these are **marker**, **s**, **face color** and **edge color**. `marker` specifies the style in which the dots should be plotted. `scatter()` function has its own set of short string codes for specifying the style. Try different values of markets (like '^'; (5,1); (5,2); '+'; 'o') to draw interesting scatter plots. As we did before, title of the chart, x label and y label can be specified by using the `plt.title()`, `plt.xlabel()` and `ylabel()` methods of the pyplot module.

Scatter plots are used to plot data points on horizontal and vertical axes in an attempt to show how much one variable is affected by another. Each row in the data table is represented by a marker. The position depends on its values in the columns set on the x- and y-axes. A third variable can be set to correspond to the colour or size of the markers, thus adding yet another dimension to the plot.

PROGRAMMER'S ZONE

8. **Write a program that creates boxplots of class-wise performance. Make use of the additional optional parameters.**

```
import numpy as np
import matplotlib.pyplot as plt
from random import seed
from random import randint
import pandas as pd
x1 = np.random.normal(3, 10, 50)
x2 = np.random.normal(4, 10, 50)
x3 = np.random.normal(6, 10, 50)
x4 = np.random.normal(5, 10, 50)
x5 = np.random.normal(7, 10, 50)
data=[x1,x2,x3,x4,x5]
box = plt.boxplot(data,patch_artist=True,notch = True, vert
    = True, meanline=True,showbox = True, showmeans=True,
    labels=['SecA','SecB','SecC','SecD','SecE'])
plt.title('CLASS PERFORMANCE')
plt.xlabel('CLASS XII')
plt.ylabel('MARKS')
colors = ['cyan', 'lightblue', 'lightgreen', 'tan','yellow']
for patch, color in zip(box['boxes'], colors):
    patch.set_facecolor(color)
plt.show()
```

> The alpha keyword is used to adjust the transparency level.

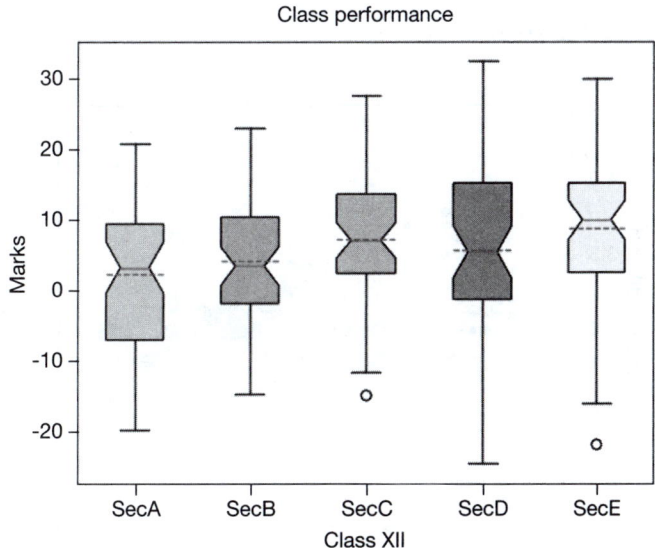

9. **Write a program that draws a scatter plot to represent two data sets of 1000 values. The first array should have the mean value 5.0 and standard deviation of 1.0. The second array should have mean 10.0 and a standard deviation of 2.0:**

```
import numpy
import matplotlib.pyplot as plt
x = numpy.random.normal(5.0, 1.0, 1000)
y = numpy.random.normal(10.0, 2.0, 1000)
plt.scatter(x,y,color = 'red',edgecolor = 'yellow',s=50, alpha = 0.7,marker = 'o')
plt.show()
```

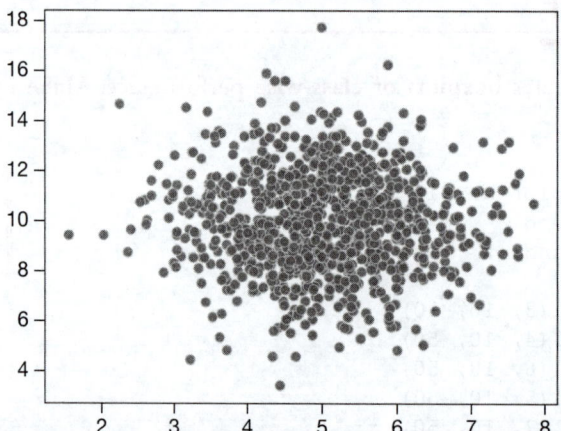

10. **Read the iris dataset. Transpose the data and draw a scatter plot of the first two columns. The (x, y) location of each point should correspond to the sepal length and width; relate the size of the point to the petal width, and the color to the particular species of flower.**

   For this, set the size of dots based on the third column and colour of the dots based on the column target.

   ```
   import numpy
   import matplotlib.pyplot as plt
   from sklearn.datasets import load_iris
   iris = load_iris()
   features = iris.data.T
   plt.scatter(features[0], features[1], alpha=0.2,s=100*features[3], c=iris.target)
   plt.xlabel(iris.feature_names[0])
   plt.ylabel(iris.feature_names[1]);
   plt.show()
   ```

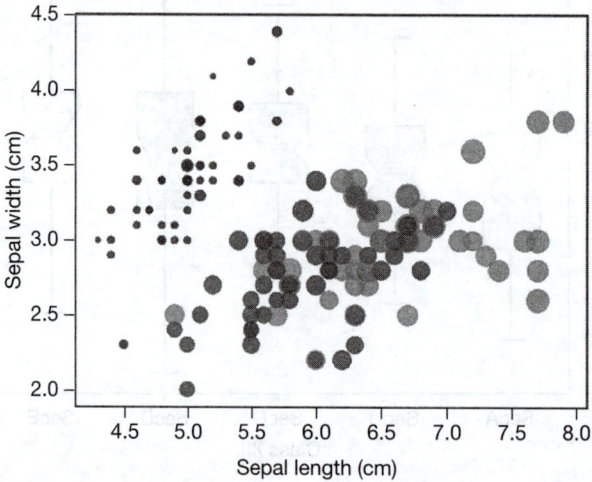

11. **Write a program that plots a scatter plot using two data sets containing random integers.**

   ```
   import numpy as np
   import matplotlib.pyplot as plt
   from random import seed
   from random import randint
   # seed random number generator
   seed(1)
   x = []
   y = []
   # generate some integers
   for i in range(20):
       value = randint(0, 100)
   ```

```
        x.append(value)
        value = randint(0, 100)
        y.append(value)
plt.scatter(x, y, s = 100, color = 'red', alpha = 0.2, marker = r'$\clubsuit$')
plt.show()
```

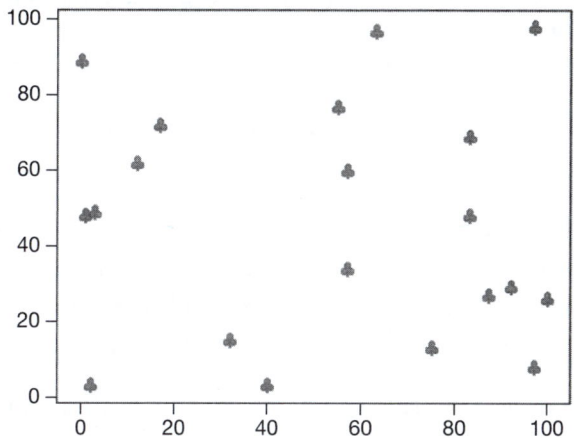

12. Write a Python program to draw a scatter plot comparing two subject marks of Mathematics and Science. Use the marks of 10 students.

```
import matplotlib.pyplot as plt
import pandas as pd
math_marks = [88, 92, 80, 89, 100, 40, 60, 20, 80, 34]
science_marks = [95, 87, 75, 78, 98, 58, 72, 30, 70, 30]
marks_range = [10, 20, 30, 40, 50, 60, 70, 80, 90, 100]
plt.scatter(marks_range, math_marks, label='Marks in Maths', color='red',marker = (5,2))
plt.scatter(marks_range, science_marks, label='Marks in Science', color='olive',
      alpha = 0.2,marker = '^')
plt.title('Scatter Plot')
plt.xlabel('Marks Range')
plt.ylabel('Marks Scored')
plt.legend()
plt.show()
```

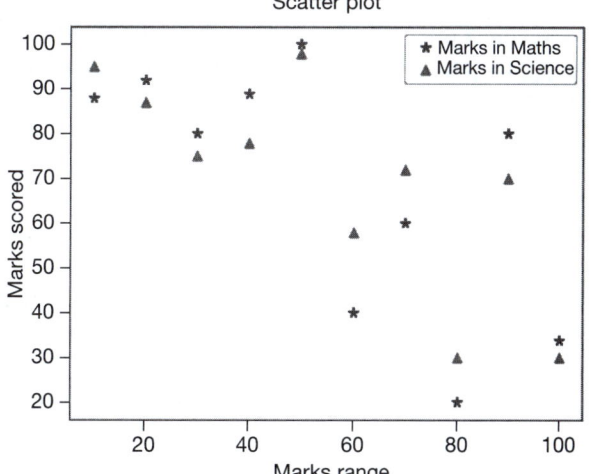

Key Terms

Bar chart: A bar graph is a chart or graph that presents categorical data with rectangular bars.
Stacked bar chart: Stack bars represent different groups on top of each other. The height of the resulting bar shows the combined result of the groups.

Histogram: A graphical representation which is quite similar to a bar graphs. It is a great tool for assessing probability distribution of a continuous variable that can be easily understood.

Frequency polygon: A graphical form of data representation that gives an idea about the shape of the data and the trends that a particular data set follows.

Boxplot: Also known as a whisker plot, it displays a summary of a set of data containing the minimum, first quartile, median, third quartile, and maximum.

Scatter plot: A chart which plots each value in the data set by a dot.

Chapter Highlights

- pyplot module is a sub-module of the matplotlib module.
- Matplotlib is the most widely used scientific plotting library in Python.
- The main advantage of plotting a bar graph is that it depicts comparisons among discrete categories.
- The `bar()` function allows users to specify a starting value for a bar. For example, the first call to `pyplot.bar()` may plot blue bars. The second call to `pyplot.bar()` can plot green bars, with the bottom of the green bars being at the top of the blue bars.
- `plt.cla()` function is used to clear the axis and `plt.close()` to close a window that has popped up to show you your plot.
- Frequency polygons can be used to compare two sets of data and are best suited for comparing two data sets that have the same sample size.
- To draw a frequency polygon with a histogram, first draw rectangular bars against the given class intervals. Then, join the midpoints of the bars to obtain the frequency polygon.
- In a box plot, a vertical line goes through the box at the median. The whiskers go from each quartile to the minimum or maximum.

Review Questions

1. How does plotting graphs help in statistics?
2. What is pyplot? Give its uses.
3. What is a bar chart? How is it useful in interpreting data?
4. Explain the syntax of `hist()` function.
5. How will you calculate the appropriate number of bins when plotting a histogram?
6. How will you plot a frequency polygon without a histogram?
7. How will you plot a frequency polygon with a histogram?
8. What information is revealed by a boxplot?
9. How is a scatter plot drawn?

Programming Exercises

1. Plot a vertical bar graph depicting bronze, silvers and gold medals won by a country in the last Asian Games.
2. Plot a horizontal bar graph depicting bronze, silvers and gold medals by counties in last Asian Games.
3. Plot a vertical bar graph depicting bronze, silvers and gold medals by China and India in last Asian Games.
4. Plot a stacked bar graph depicting bronze, silvers and gold medals by China, India, Japan and Pakistan in last Asian Games.
5. Draw a scatter plot depicting the year of launch and speed of the car.
6. Draw a scatter plot to compare the performance of boys and girls in a class test. From the graph, tell who performed better and whether there were any outliers.
7. Draw a scatter plot representing Unemployment Rate vs. Stock Index Price. These two data sets should be specified using Pandas data frame.
8. Write a Python program to draw a scatter plot for three different groups comparing weights and heights.
9. Plot a stacked histogram showing marks obtained by 10 students in five different subjects.
10. Display a Boxplot representing marks obtained by 10 students in five different subjects.
11. Create a data frame and use its data to draw a pie chart.

Fill in the Blanks

1. pyplot module is a sub-module of the _____ module.
2. Matplotlib is the most widely library in Python for _____.
3. _____ function that can be used to plot a bar graph.
4. The _____ function is used to plot a horizontal bar graph.
5. The range or limit of the x axis can be set by using the _____.
6. To make the number of bin's width ideal, set bins = _____.
7. _____ function is used to get the same set of random numbers each time the program is executed.
8. The formula for calculating class mark is _____.
9. A box is drawn from the first quartile to the _____ quartile.
10. _____ are usually used to represent the correlation between two or more variables.

State True or False

1. A bar graph presents categorical data with rectangular bars.
2. In a bar graph, bars can be drawn only vertically.
3. The `bar()` function is used to draw a stacked bar chart.
4. The labels for x-axis can be specified using the `ylabel()`.
5. Histograms assess probability distribution of a non-continuous variable.
6. Histogram plots the frequency distribution of numeric array by splitting it to small equal-sized bins.
7. Frequency polygon is always drawn along with a histogram.
8. When drawing a frequency plot, frequency is plotted on the x-axis.
9. Frequency is plotted against the class mark and not the upper or lower limit of any class.
10. We can make horizontal boxplot.

Multiple Choice Questions

1. Which function is used to save the plot?
   a. `saveplot()`   b. `savegraph()`   c. `savefig()`   d. `savedraw()`
2. Font size of a plot can be changed with the help of _____ function.
   a. `fs()`   b. `format()`   c. `rc()`   d. `fc()`
3. Which function of the pyplot clears the plot?
   a. `clf()`   b. `clp()`   c. `cla()`   d. `close()`
4. To plot the frequency distribution of a numeric array by splitting it to small equal-sized bins, which function will be used?
   a. `bar()`   b. `barh()`   c. `hist()`   d. `plot()`
5. Default value of histtype in the `hist()` function is _____.
   a. bar   b. barstacked   c. step   d. `stepfilled()`
6. Which of the following plot displays a summary of a set of data containing the minimum, first quartile, median, third quartile, and maximum?
   a. Bar chart   b. Histogram   c. Boxplot   d. Scatter plot
7. In a boxplot, a vertical line goes through the box at the _____.
   a. median   b. first quartile   c. third quartile   d. fourth quartile
8. Which of the following plots is used to identify the outliers?
   a. Bar chart   b. Histogram   c. Boxplot   d. Scatter plot
9. Which plot shows data as a collection of points?
   a. Bar chart   b. Histogram   c. Boxplot   d. Scatter plot
10. IQR is calculated as _____.
    a. Q1 + Q3   b. Q3 – Q1   c. (Q1 – Q3)/2   d. (Q1 + Q3)/2

Fill in the Blanks to Complete the Code

1.  ```
    import matplotlib.pyplot as plt
    _____ = [22,55,62,45,21,22,34,42,42,4,99,102,110,120,121,122,130
    ,111,115,112,80,75,65,54,44,43,42,48]
    plt.hist(population_ages, bins = _____, histtype = _____,
    rwidth=0.8)
    plt.xlabel('_____')
    plt._____('y')
    plt._____('ANALYZING STUDENT PERFORMANCE \n For the Last Semester')
    plt.legend()
    plt._____()
    ```

    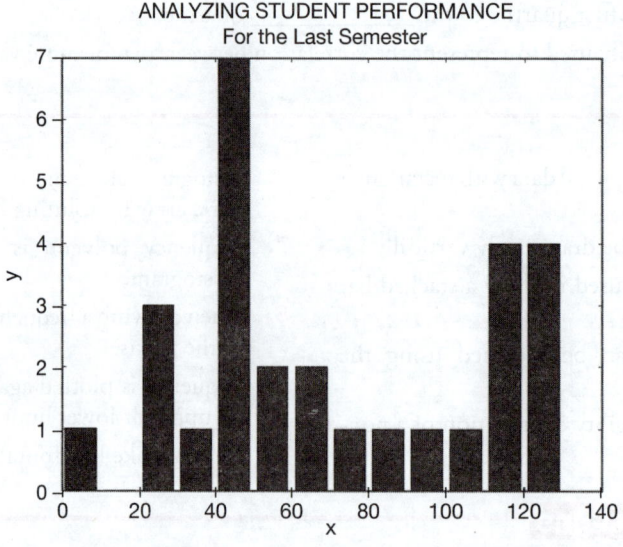

2.  ```
    import matplotlib.pyplot as plt
    plt._____([1,3,5,7,9],[5,2,7,8,2], label="Example one")
    plt.bar([2,4,6,8,10],[8,6,2,5,6], _____ = "Example two",
        color='_____')
    _____.legend()
    plt._____ ('Item')
    plt.ylabel(_____)
    plt.title(_____)
    _____.show()
    ```

    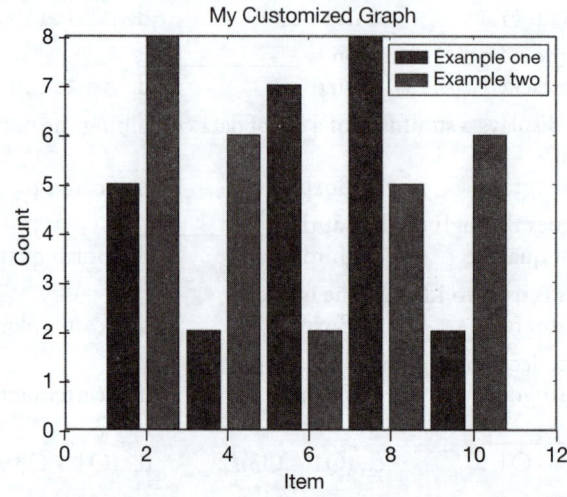

3. ```
import _____ as plt
import numpy _____ np
np._____.seed(1)
x = _____.arange(0.0, 50.0, 2.0)
y = x ** 1.3 + np.random.rand(*x.shape) * 30.0
s = np.random.rand(*x.shape) * 800 + 500
plt.scatter(x, _____, s, _____ = "green",
_____=0.5, _____=r'$\clubsuit$',_____ ="Luck")
plt.xlabel("_____")
plt._____("Gold")
_____.legend(loc='upper left')
plt.show()
```

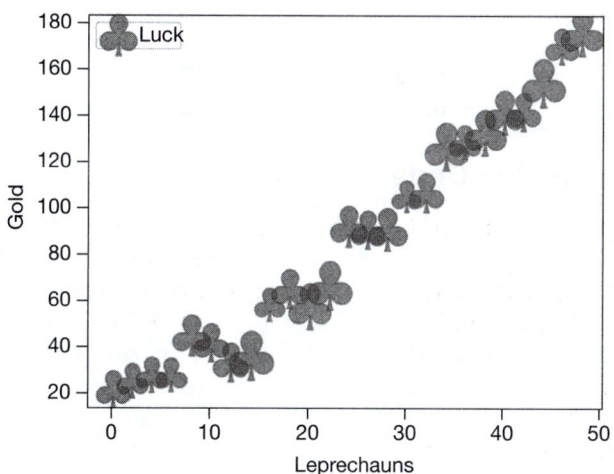

4. ```
import matplotlib.pyplot as _____
import numpy as np
sequence1 = _____.random.random_integers(0,100,100)
_____ = np.random.random_integers(25,75,100)
sequence3 = np._____.random_integers(50,80,100)
plot.boxplot((_____, sequence2, sequence3))
plot.show()
```

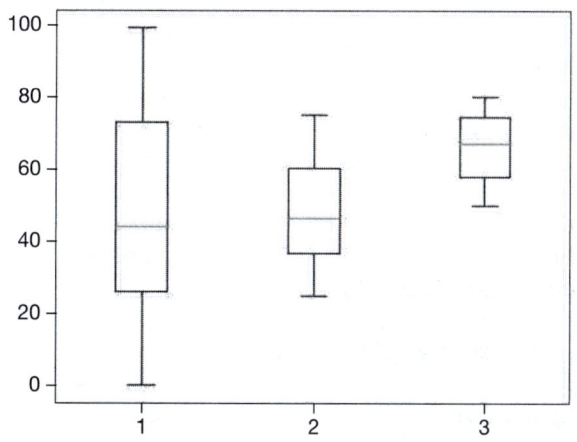

Answers

Fill in the Blanks

1. matplotlib
2. scientific plotting
3. bar()
4. barh()
5. xlim()
6. auto
7. seed()
8. (Upper limit + Lower limit) / 2
9. third
10. Scatter Plots

State True or False

1. True
2. False
3. True
4. False
5. False
6. True
7. False
8. False
9. True
10. True

Multiple Choice Questions

1. a
2. c
3. a
4. c
5. a
6. c
7. a
8. c
9. d
10. b

Fill in the Blanks to Complete the Code

1.
```
import matplotlib.pyplot as plt
population_ages = [22,55,62,45,21,22,34,42,42,4,99,102,110,120,121,122,130,111,115,112,80,75,65,54,44,43,42,48]
bins = [0,10,20,30,40,50,60,70,80,90,100,110,120,130]
plt.hist(population_ages, bins, histtype='bar', rwidth=0.8)
plt.xlabel('x')
plt.ylabel('y')
plt.title('ANALYZING STUDENT PERFORMANCE \n For the Last Semester')
plt.legend()
plt.show()
```

2.
```
import matplotlib.pyplot as plt
plt.bar([1,3,5,7,9],[5,2,7,8,2], label="Example one")
plt.bar([2,4,6,8,10],[8,6,2,5,6], label="Example two", color='g')
plt.legend()
plt.xlabel('Item')
plt.ylabel('Count')
plt.title('My Customized Graph')
plt.show()
```

3.
```
import matplotlib.pyplot as plt
import numpy as np
# Fixing random state for reproducibility
np.random.seed(19680801)
x = np.arange(0.0, 50.0, 2.0)
y = x ** 1.3 + np.random.rand(*x.shape) * 30.0
s = np.random.rand(*x.shape) * 800 + 500
plt.scatter(x, y, s, c="g", alpha=0.5, marker=r'$\clubsuit$', label="Luck")
plt.xlabel("Leprechauns")
plt.ylabel("Gold")
plt.legend(loc='upper left')
plt.show()
```

4.
```
import matplotlib.pyplot as plot
import numpy as np
#Generate the data
sequence1 = np.random.random_integers(0,100,100)
sequence2 = np.random.random_integers(25,75,100)
sequence3 = np.random.random_integers(50,80,100)
plot.boxplot((sequence1, sequence2, sequence3))
plot.show()
```

Structured Query Language (SQL)

4

Chapter Objectives

In class XI, we have already learnt the basic concepts of databases, especially relational databases. We have also read about SQL queries that are executed to store, retrieve and manipulate stored data in databases (MySQL database here). In this chapter, we will quickly recapitulate whatever we have studied so far and then learn some advanced concepts including,

- Clauses like Group By, Having, and Order
- Operations like Union, Intersection, Minus, Cartesian Product and JOIN.
- Concepts of Relational Algebra

4.1 INTRODUCTION TO MYSQL DATABASE

We have used MySQL because it is a fast, easy-to-use RDBMS. It is widely used because of the following reasons:

- MySQL is an open-source software, so users do not have to pay to use it.
- It is a very powerful program that can handle a large subset of the functionality of the most expensive and powerful database packages.
- MySQL uses SQL data language.
- It can be used on a number of operating systems.
- MySQL can be integrated with many languages including PHP, PERL, C, C++, JAVA, etc.
- It performs well with even large data sets having up to 50 million rows or more in a table. The default file size limit for a table is 4 GB. In fact, a database of even 8 million terabytes (TB) is not uncommon these days.
- MySQL can be customized as per user requirements.
- It satisfies ACID property.
- MySQL supports powerful techniques to ensure that only authorized users can access the database.

> MySQL is developed, marketed and supported by a Swedish company MySQL AB.

> The US tech company Sun Microsystems bought MySQL AB in 2008. Later, in 2010 Oracle acquired Sun Microsystems and MySQL has been practically owned by Oracle since then.

4.2 INTRODUCTION TO STRUCTURED QUERY LANGUAGE (SQL)

SQL, pronounced as S-Q-L or sometime See-Qwell, is a database query language. Many people think of it as a database but it is a language that helps users to access and manipulate data stored in a relational database. SQL queries (or statements) can be used to perform operations like retrieving, inserting, updating and deleting data. They can be also used to create tables or modify the structure of existing tables. However, to use SQL queries, you must first install a database, like Oracle, MySQL, MongoDB, PostGres SQL, SQL Server, DB2, etc.

4.2.1 How MySQL Works

MySQL works on client-server model. Computers that install and run RDBMS software are called clients. Whenever they need to access data, they connect to the RDBMS server. That is the "client-server" part.

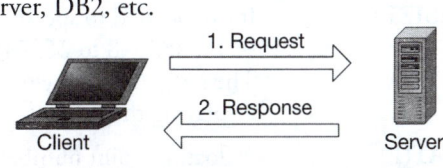

Figure 4.1 Client/server request/response model

Figure 4.1 explains the basic structure of the client-server structure. One or more devices (clients) connect to a server to access data stored in the database server. Every client can make a request from the graphical user interface (GUI) on their screens, and the server responds with the desired output. The basic working of such a client-server model can be understood as,

1. MySQL creates a database for storing and manipulating data.
2. Clients request data using specific SQL statements that are executed on the MySQL.
3. The server application responds with the requested information that is then displayed on the client machine.

> MySQL is written in C and C++.

4.2.2 Uses of SQL

SQL allow users to create queries where a query is a request for data stored in one or more tables in the database. These queries are simple English-like statements. With the help of queries, users can **access, modify, insert and delete data** from table(s) stored in the database.

SQL can also be used to create metadata for describing the data. With SQL, users can **create and drop (delete) tables**.

Users can **create procedures** and functions and set permission on them to restrict their usage.

4.2.3 Types of SQL Queries

The two types of SQL queries that we will be reading about in this section are DDL and DML. While DDL or the Data Definition Language is used to create or modify database objects (like tables, views, indexes, users, etc), the DML or the Data Manipulation Language, on the other hand, is used to manipulate data (like inserting, updating, deleting data). Also refer Table 4.2 that brings out vital differences between `char` and `varchar` data types.

4.3 SQL DATA TYPES

Before we actually start creating tables and inserting records into SQL using DDL and DML, we must first know the permitted data types in SQL. Each column in a table must have a valid name and a data type.

While creating a table, the SQL developer must specify what type of data will be stored in each column. In this chapter, we have used MySQL version 8.0. Some important data types used in MySQL are given in Table 4.1. Also refer Table 4.2 that brings out vital differences between `char` and `varchar` data types.

Table 4.1 Data types in SQL

Data Type	Description
CHAR(SIZE)	A fixed-length string that may have alphabets, digits, and special characters. The size parameter specifies the maximum number of characters. Its value may vary from 0 to 255. By default, its size is 1.
VARCHAR(SIZE)	A variable-length string that may have alphabets, digits, and special characters. The size parameter specifies maximum number of characters. Its value may vary from 0 to 65535.
BOOL	Zero is considered as False, nonzero values are considered as True.
INT(SIZE)	It can be used to specify a signed or unsigned integer. A signed integer is in the range −2147483648 to 2147483647 and an unsigned integer is in the range 0 to 4294967295. The size parameter which can take any value from 0–255, specifies the maximum width for displaying the value.
FLOAT(P)	A floating-point number. MySQL uses the P value to determine whether to use FLOAT or DOUBLE for the resulting data type. If P is from 0 to 24, the data type becomes float and double when P varies from 25 to 53.

Table 4.2 Difference between CHAR and VARCHAR

CHAR Data Type	VARCHAR Data Type
It stands for Character.	It stands for a Variable Character.
Values are stored in fixed lengths and are padded with space characters to match the specified length.	Values are stored in variable length and are not padded with any characters
It can hold a maximum of 255 characters.	It can hold a maximum of 65,535 characters.
It uses static memory allocation.	It uses dynamic memory allocation.
Takes 1 byte per character for storage.	Takes 1 byte per character plus an additional 1 or 2 extra bytes for storing length information.
Used when the length of the variable is known.	Used only when the length of the variable is not known.
It only accepts characters.	It accepts both characters and numbers.
Performs faster than Varchar.	It is slower than Char

4.4 DATE AND TIME TYPES

The MySQL date and time datatypes are as follows:

Date: A date is stored in YYYY-MM-DD format, between 1000-01-01 and 9999-12-31. For example, September 30th, 2021 would be stored as 2021-09-30.

Datetime: A date and time combination in YYYY-MM-DD HH:MM:SS format, between 1000-01-01 00:00:00 and 9999-12-31 23:59:59. For example, 2:20 in the afternoon on September 30th, 2021 would be stored as 2021-09-30 14:20:00.

Timestamp: is a temporal data type that is specified using a combination of both date as well as time. A TIMESTAMP value can be written using 19 characters in the format YYYY-MM-DD HH:MM:SS. Value of a TIMESTAMP ranges from '1970-01-01 00:00:01' UTC to '2038-01-19 03:14:07' UTC.

Time: Stores the time in HH:MM:SS format.

Year(M): Stores a year in a 2-digit or a 4-digit format. If the length is a 2-digit number then it can specify any year from 1970 to 2069 (70 to 69). If the length is a 4-digit number, then YEAR can be from 1901 to 2155. The default length of year is 4.

4.5 OPERATORS IN SQL

An operator is a reserved word or a character in SQL statement that is extensively used in WHERE clause of the query to perform arithmetic or comparison operations. These operators are used to specify conditions in an SQL statement. Just go through the arithmetic, comparison and logical operators given in Tables 4.3, 4.4 and 4.5 respectively. Observe the result when a = 100 and b = 50.

Table 4.3 Arithmetic operators in SQL

Operator	Description	Example	Result
+	Adds values on either side of the operator	a + b	150
−	Subtracts right-hand value from the left-side value	a − b	100
*	Multiplies values on either side of the operand	a*b	5000
/	Divides left-side value with the right-side value	a/b	2
%	Divides left-side value with the right-side value and returns the remainder	a%b	0

Table 4.4 Comparison operators in SQL

Operator	Description	Example	Result
>	Returns True if the left value is greater than the right and False otherwise.	a>b	True
>=	Returns True if the left value is either equal to or greater than the right and False otherwise.	a >= b	True
<	Returns True if the left value is less than the right and False otherwise.	a<b	False
<=	Returns True if the left value is either equal to or less than the right value and False otherwise.	a <= b	False
=	Returns True if the two values on either side are equal and False otherwise.	a=b	False
!= <>	Returns True if the two values on either side are not equal and False otherwise.	a != b a <> b	True True
!<	Returns True if the left value is not less than the right value and False otherwise.	a !< b	True
!>	Returns True if the left value is not greater than the right value and False otherwise.	a !> b	False

Table 4.5 Logical operators in SQL

Operator	Description
ALL	The ALL operator is used to compare a value to all values in another value set.
AND	The AND operator allows the existence of multiple conditions in an SQL statement's WHERE clause.
OR	The OR operator is used to combine multiple conditions in an SQL statement's WHERE clause
ANY	Compares a value to any applicable values in the list as given in the condition.
BETWEEN	Searches for values that are within a set of values provided the minimum value and the maximum value are specified.
IN	Checks for the presence of a value in the list of specified literal values.
LIKE	Searches for similar values using wildcard characters.
NOT	The NOT operator reverses the meaning of the logical operator with which it is used. Eg: NOT EXISTS, NOT BETWEEN, `not in`, etc. This is a negate operator.
IS NULL	Checks if a given value is NULL.
UNIQUE	Ensures there are no duplicate values.

4.6 PERFORMING SIMPLE CALCULATIONS WITH SELECT STATEMENT

We can even use the SQL SELECT statement to perform mathematical calculations. In this special type of SELECT statement, no table is specified in the FROM clause. Let us see a few examples of such SELECT statements.

```
mysql> select 10 + 9;
+--------+
| 10 + 9 |
+--------+
|     19 |
+--------+
1 row in set (0.00 sec)
mysql> select 11*10;
+-------+
| 11*10 |
+-------+
|   110 |
+-------+
1 row in set (0.00 sec)
mysql> select 360/60;
+--------+
| 360/60 |
+--------+
| 6.0000 |
+--------+
1 row in set (0.00 sec)
mysql> select 100 > 50;
+----------+
| 100 > 50 |
+----------+
|        1 |
+----------+
1 row in set (0.00 sec)
mysql> select 90%4;
+------+
| 90%4 |
+------+
|    2 |
+------+
1 row in set (0.00 sec)
```

4.7 SQL NUMERIC FUNCTIONS

Numeric Functions are used to perform operations on numbers and return numbers. Some commonly used numeric functions used in SQL are discussed below.

ABS() returns the absolute value of a number.

```
mysql> SELECT ABS(-98.7);
+------------+
| ABS(-98.7) |
+------------+
|       98.7 |
+------------+
1 row in set (0.01 sec)
```

COS(), **SIN()**, **TAN()**, **COT()** functions return the cosine, sine, tangent and cotangent of the given number respectively.

```
mysql> SELECT TAN(45);
+--------------------+
| TAN(45)            |
+--------------------+
| 1.6197751905438615 |
+--------------------+
1 row in set (0.00 sec)
```

CEIL() returns the smallest integer value that is greater than or equal to a number.

```
mysql> SELECT CEIL(21.345);
+--------------+
| CEIL(21.345) |
+--------------+
|           22 |
+--------------+
1 row in set (0.00 sec)
```

DIV() is used for integer division.

```
mysql> SELECT 100 DIV 20;
+------------+
| 100 DIV 20 |
+------------+
|          5 |
+------------+
1 row in set (0.00 sec)
```

FLOOR() returns the largest integer value that is less than or equal to a number.

```
mysql> SELECT FLOOR(21.345);
+---------------+
| FLOOR(21.345) |
+---------------+
|            21 |
+---------------+
1 row in set (0.00 sec)
```

LEAST() returns the smallest value in the given list.

```
mysql> SELECT LEAST(-10,210,20,-20,30,-30,100,-100);
+---------------------------------------+
| LEAST(-10,210,20,-20,30,-30,100,-100) |
+---------------------------------------+
|                                  -100 |
+---------------------------------------+
1 row in set (0.00 sec)
```

MOD() returns the remainder of *n* divided by *m*.

```
mysql> SELECT 103 MOD 5;
+-----------+
| 103 MOD 5 |
+-----------+
|         3 |
+-----------+
1 row in set (0.00 sec)
```

DEGREES() converts a radian value into degrees.

```
mysql> SELECT DEGREES(1.02);
+-------------------+
| DEGREES(1.02)     |
+-------------------+
| 58.44169510334397 |
+-------------------+
1 row in set (0.00 sec)
```

EXP() returns *e* raised to the power of number.

```
mysql> SELECT EXP(2);
+-------------------+
| EXP(2)            |
+-------------------+
| 7.38905609893065  |
+-------------------+
1 row in set (0.00 sec)
```

GREATEST() returns the greatest value in the given list.

```
mysql> SELECT GREATEST (-10,210,20,-20,30,-30,100,-100);
+------------------------------------------+
| GREATEST(-10,210,20,-20,30,-30,100,-100) |
+------------------------------------------+
|                                      210 |
+------------------------------------------+
1 row in set (0.00 sec)
```

LN(), **LOG10()**, **LOG2()** returns the natural logarithm, base-10 logarithm and base-2 logarithm of a number respectively.

```
mysql> SELECT LOG10(100);
+------------+
| LOG10(100) |
+------------+
|          2 |
+------------+
1 row in set (0.01 sec)
```

PI() returns the value of PI displayed with 6 decimal places.

```
mysql> SELECT PI();
+----------+
| PI()     |
+----------+
| 3.141593 |
+----------+
1 row in set (0.00 sec)
```

POW() returns *m* raised to the *n*th power.

```
mysql> SELECT POW(10,3);
+----------+
| POW(10,3)|
+----------+
|     1000 |
+----------+
1 row in set (0.00 sec)
```

RADIANS() converts a value in degrees to radians.

```
mysql> SELECT RADIANS(360);
+-------------------+
| RADIANS(360)      |
+-------------------+
| 6.283185307179586 |
+-------------------+
1 row in set (0.00 sec)
```

RAND() returns a random number.

```
mysql> SELECT RAND();
+--------------------+
| RAND()             |
+--------------------+
| 0.8558367722256451 |
+--------------------+
1 row in set (0.00 sec)
```

ROUND() returns a number rounded to a certain number of decimal places.

```
mysql> SELECT ROUND(3.14156,2);
+-----------------+
| ROUND(3.14156,2)|
+-----------------+
|            3.14 |
+-----------------+
1 row in set (0.00 sec)
```

SQRT() returns the square root of a number.

```
mysql> SELECT SQRT(144);
+----------+
| SQRT(144)|
+----------+
|       12 |
+----------+
1 row in set (0.00 sec)
```

TRUNCATE() truncates the given number after specified number of places right of the decimal point.

```
mysql> SELECT TRUNCATE(3.141567,3);
+---------------------+
| TRUNCATE(3.141567,3)|
+---------------------+
|               3.141 |
+---------------------+
1 row in set (0.00 sec)
```

4.8 STRING FUNCTIONS

The string functions in MySQL are used to manipulate textual data stored in tables. These functions can also be used along with update commands to change data values stored in tables. Some most frequently used string functions are discussed below:

ASCII() function is used to find the ASCII value of a character.

```
mysql> SELECT ASCII('R');
+-----------+
| ASCII('R')|
+-----------+
|        82 |
+-----------+
1 row in set (0.02 sec)
```

CHAR_LENGTH() function is used to find the length of a string.

```
mysql> SELECT CHAR_LENGTH('GOOD
    MORNING');
+---------------------------+
| CHAR_LENGTH('GOOD MORNING')|
+---------------------------+
|                        12 |
+---------------------------+
1 row in set (0.02 sec)
```

CONCAT() function is used to add two words or strings.

```
mysql> SELECT CONCAT('GOOD','--
    ','MORNING');
+-----------------------------+
| CONCAT('GOOD','--','MORNING') |
+-----------------------------+
| GOOD--MORNING               |
+-----------------------------+
1 row in set (0.05 sec)
```

FIND_IN_SET() function is used to find a symbol from a set of symbols.

```
mysql> SELECT FIND_IN_
    SET('I','M,O,R,N,I,N,G');
+---------------------------------+
| FIND_IN_SET('I','M,O,R,N,I,N,G') |
+---------------------------------+
|                               5 |
+---------------------------------+
1 row in set (0.00 sec)
```

INSTR() function is used to find the occurrence of an alphabet.

```
mysql> SELECT INSTR('GOOD
    MORNING','R');
+--------------------------+
| INSTR('GOOD MORNING','R') |
+--------------------------+
|                        8 |
+--------------------------+
1 row in set (0.02 sec)
```

LCASE() function is used to convert the given string into lower case. You can even use the LOWER() function to do the same work.

```
mysql> SELECT LCASE('GOOD
    MORNING');
+---------------------+
| LCASE('GOOD MORNING') |
+---------------------+
| good morning        |
+---------------------+
1 row in set (0.05 sec)
```

UCASE() function is used to convert the given string into upper case. You can even use the UPPER() function to do the same work.

```
mysql> SELECT UPPER('good
    morning');
+---------------------+
| UPPER('good morning') |
+---------------------+
| GOOD MORNING        |
+---------------------+
1 row in set (0.02 sec)
```

LEFT() function is used to SELECT a sub-string from the left of given size or characters.

```
mysql> SELECT LEFT('GOOD MORNING',7);
+-----------------------+
| LEFT('GOOD MORNING',7) |
+-----------------------+
| GOOD MO               |
+-----------------------+
1 row in set (0.01 sec)
```

LPAD() function makes a string of the specified size by adding the given symbol.

```
mysql> SELECT LPAD('GOOD
    MORNING',20,'*');
+----------------------------+
| LPAD('GOOD MORNING',20,'*') |
+----------------------------+
| ********GOOD MORNING       |
+----------------------------+
1 row in set (0.01 sec)
```

LTRIM() function removes leading white spaces from the given string.

```
mysql> SELECT LTRIM('    GOOD
    MORNING');
+-------------------------+
| LTRIM('    GOOD MORNING') |
+-------------------------+
| GOOD MORNING            |
+-------------------------+
1 row in set (0.00 sec)
```

MID() function displays a sub-string of given length starting from the specified position. The **SUBSTR()** also performs the same task.

```
mysql> SELECT MID('GOOD MORNING
    WORLD',8,4);
+--------------------------------+
| MID('GOOD MORNING WORLD',8,4) |
+--------------------------------+
| RNIN                           |
+--------------------------------+
1 row in set (0.00 sec)
```

REVERSE() function reverses a string.

```
mysql> SELECT REVERSE('GOOD
    MORNING');
+-----------------------+
| REVERSE('GOOD MORNING') |
+-----------------------+
| GNINROM DOOG          |
+-----------------------+
1 row in set (0.00 sec)
```

RPAD() function makes the given string as long as the given size by adding the given symbol on the right.

```
mysql> SELECT RPAD('GOOD
    MORNING',20,'*');
+----------------------------+
| RPAD('GOOD MORNING',20,'*') |
+----------------------------+
| GOOD MORNING********       |
+----------------------------+
1 row in set (0.01 sec)
```

STRCMP() function compares two strings. If both the strings are equal, it returns 0. If the first string is smaller than the second, −1 is returned. Otherwise, the function will return 1.

```
mysql> SELECT STRCMP('GOOD MORNING','GOOD
    EVENING');
+---------------------------------------+
| STRCMP('GOOD MORNING','GOOD EVENING') |
+---------------------------------------+
|                                     1 |
+---------------------------------------+
1 row in set (0.00 sec)
```

REPEAT() function re-writes the given string, the specified number of times.

```
mysql> SELECT REPEAT('BYE',2);
+-----------------+
| REPEAT('BYE',2) |
+-----------------+
| BYEBYE          |
+-----------------+
1 row in set (0.01 sec)
```

RIGHT() function selects a sub-string of given size from the right side of the string.

```
mysql> SELECT RIGHT('GOOD
    MORNING',10);
+-------------------------+
| RIGHT('GOOD MORNING',10) |
+-------------------------+
| OD MORNING              |
+-------------------------+
1 row in set (0.00 sec)
```

RTRIM() function removes white spaces from the end of the given string.

```
mysql> SELECT RTRIM('GOOD MORNING      ');
+---------------------------+
| RTRIM('GOOD MORNING    ') |
+---------------------------+
| GOOD MORNING              |
+---------------------------+
1 row in set (0.00 sec)
```

TRIM() function removes leading and trailing white spaces from the given string.

```
mysql> SELECT TRIM('     GOOD MORNING
    ');
+-------------------------------------+
| TRIM('      GOOD MORNING         ') |
+-------------------------------------+
| GOOD MORNING                        |
+-------------------------------------+
1 row in set (0.01 sec)
```

4.9 RETRIEVING DATA FROM TABLE

The **SELECT** statement in SQL is used to fetch or retrieve data from one or more tables in the database. The results of the SELECT statement is in the form of a table. This resultant table is known as the result-set. The syntax of the SELECT statement can be given as,

`SELECT column1, column2, columnN FROM table_name;`

Here, column1, column2… are the fields of the table from which data has to be fetched. To fetch all the fields from the table, the syntax is

`SELECT * FROM table_name;`

> **Example 4.1** Let us select the entire data from all the fields in the student table. Also, we shall select only the Roll_Number and Marks fields from the student table.

```
mysql> SELECT * FROM STUDENT;
+-------------+----------+--------------+------+-------+-------+
| ROLL_NUMBER | NAME     | PHONE_NUMBER | AGE  | MARKS | CLASS |
+-------------+----------+--------------+------+-------+-------+
|           1 | RAHUL    | 9876543210   |   18 |    89 | 12-D  |
|           2 | SARFARAZ | 9823416790   |   17 |    97 | 11-A  |
|           3 | RIA      | 7825516230   |   16 |    67 | 10-C  |
|           4 | PALAK    | 9999123456   |    9 |    75 | 9-B   |
|           5 | KRISH    | 9807126534   |   14 |    90 | 8-D   |
+-------------+----------+--------------+------+-------+-------+
5 rows in set (0.00 sec)
mysql> SELECT ROLL_NUMBER, MARKS FROM STUDENT;
+-------------+-------+
| ROLL_NUMBER | MARKS |
+-------------+-------+
|           1 |    89 |
|           2 |    97 |
|           3 |    67 |
|           4 |    75 |
|           5 |    90 |
+-------------+-------+
5 rows in set (0.00 sec)
```

4.10 THE WHERE CLAUSE

The WHERE clause is used in the SELECT statement to specify a condition for retrieving data from one or more tables. We use the WHERE clause to filter the records in the table and fetch only those that meet the specified criteria.

In addition to the SELECT statement, the WHERE clause is also used with the UPDATE and DELETE statements. The basic syntax of the SELECT statement with the WHERE clause can be given as,

```
SELECT column1, column2, columnN
FROM table_name
WHERE [condition]
```

We can even use comparison and logical operators in the WHERE clause. Let us see a couple of queries to see how the SELECT statement with WHERE clause actually works.

> **Example 4.2** Display the name and class of the students who have scored less than 90 marks.

`mysql> SELECT NAME, CLASS FROM STUDENT WHERE MARKS < 90;`

```
+-------+-------+
| NAME  | CLASS |
+-------+-------+
| RAHUL | 12-D  |
| RIA   | 10-C  |
| PALAK | 9-B   |
+-------+-------+
3 rows in set (0.00 sec)
```

Example 4.3 Let us now select the phone number, marks and class of a student whose name is SARFARAZ.

```
mysql> SELECT PHONE_NUMBER, MARKS, CLASS FROM STUDENT WHERE NAME = 'SARFARAZ';
+--------------+-------+-------+
| PHONE_NUMBER | MARKS | CLASS |
+--------------+-------+-------+
| 9823416790   |    97 | 11-A  |
+--------------+-------+-------+
1 row in set (0.00 sec)
```

Observe that that all the character and strings should be specified within double quotes ("") but numeric values should be given without any quotes (as shown in the Example 4.3).

4.11 SQL AND AND OR OPERATORS

The SQL AND and OR operators are used to combine multiple conditions to specify a criterion for fetching data from a table. These two operators are called as the conjunctive operators.

As the name implies, the AND operator allows the existence of multiple conditions in an SQL statement's WHERE clause. The basic syntax of using the AND operator can be given as,

```
SELECT column1, column2, columnN
FROM table_name
WHERE [condition1] AND [condition2]...AND [conditionN];
```

We can specify any number of conditions in the WHERE clause using the AND operator. For an action to be taken by the SQL statement, all conditions separated by the AND operator must be TRUE.

Example 4.4 Let us write a query to display the name and class of all the students having marks more than 90 and age >=15.

```
Note that we have inserted an additional row in the table.
mysql> SELECT NAME, CLASS FROM STUDENT WHERE MARKS < 90 AND AGE>=15;
+-------+-------+
| NAME  | CLASS |
+-------+-------+
| RAHUL | 12-D  |
| RIA   | 10-C  |
+-------+-------+
2 rows in set (0.00 sec)
```

The basic syntax of the OR operator with a WHERE clause can be given as,

```
SELECT column1, column2, columnN
FROM table_name
WHERE [condition1] OR [condition2]...OR [conditionN]
```

As per the syntax, *n* number of conditions can be tested using the OR operator. To execute the query, any one of the conditions separated by the OR operator must be TRUE.

Example 4.5 Display the name and class of students scoring more than 90 marks or having age = 18.

```
mysql> SELECT NAME, CLASS FROM STUDENT WHERE MARKS < 90 OR AGE = 18;
+-------+-------+
| NAME  | CLASS |
+-------+-------+
| RAHUL | 12-D  |
| RIA   | 10-C  |
| PALAK | 9-B   |
+-------+-------+
3 rows in set (0.00 sec)
```

Example 4.6 Display the name and class of students who have scored between 75 and 90 (boundaries inclusive).

```
mysql> SELECT NAME, CLASS FROM STUDENT
    -> WHERE MARKS >=75 AND MARKS <=90;
+-------+-------+
| NAME  | CLASS |
+-------+-------+
| RAHUL | 12-D  |
| PALAK | 9-B   |
| KRISH | 8-D   |
+-------+-------+
3 rows in set (0.00 sec)
```

4.12 THE WHERE BETWEEN CLAUSE

The WHERE BETWEEN clause returns values that fall within a given range. This clause is a shorthand for >= AND <=. Note that WHERE BETWEEN operator is inclusive of the starting and ending values. The syntax of this clause can be given as,

```
SELECT column-names
FROM table-name
WHERE column-name BETWEEN value1 AND value2
```

Example 4.7 Display the Name, Class and Marks of students who scored between 75 and 90 (boundaries inclusive) using the WHERE BETWEEN clause.

```
mysql> SELECT NAME, CLASS, MARKS FROM STUDENT
    -> WHERE MARKS BETWEEN 75 AND 90;
+-------+-------+-------+
| NAME  | CLASS | MARKS |
+-------+-------+-------+
| RAHUL | 12-D  |    89 |
| PALAK | 9-B   |    75 |
| KRISH | 8-D   |    90 |
+-------+-------+-------+
3 rows in set (0.01 sec)
```

4.13 THE SQL WHERE IN CLAUSE

The WHERE IN clause returns values that match values in a list or a sub-query. This clause is a shorthand for multiple OR conditions. The general syntax of WHERE IN clause can be given as,

```
SELECT column-names
FROM table-name
WHERE column-name IN (values)
```

Example 4.8 Display the details of all the students who have got marks 89, 67 or 90.

```
mysql> SELECT * FROM STUDENT
    -> WHERE MARKS IN (89, 67, 90);
+-------------+-------+--------------+------+-------+-------+
| ROLL_NUMBER | NAME  | PHONE_NUMBER | AGE  | MARKS | CLASS |
+-------------+-------+--------------+------+-------+-------+
|           1 | RAHUL | 9876543210   |   18 |    89 | 12-D  |
|           3 | RIA   | 7825516230   |   16 |    67 | 10-C  |
|           5 | KRISH | 9807126534   |   14 |    90 | 8-D   |
+-------------+-------+--------------+------+-------+-------+
3 rows in set (0.00 sec)
```

4.14 THE SQL SELECT DISTINCT STATEMENT

The SELECT DISTINCT statement is used to return only distinct (different) values. In other words, this clause eliminates duplicate entries while displaying data from the table. The syntax of DISTINCT clause when used with the SELECT statement can be given as,

> The SQL DISTINCT keyword is used in conjunction with the SELECT statement to eliminate all the duplicate records and fetch only unique records.

```
SELECT DISTINCT column1, column2,.....columnN
FROM table_name
WHERE [condition]
```

table_name specifies name of the table(s) from which data has to be retrieved. We can specify more than one table names also.

The WHERE condition is optional. If present, it specifies the conditions that must be satisfied before retrieving data.

Note that the DISTINCT clause does not ignore NULL values. So, if a table has null values, DISCTINCT clause will include them as well in the result set.

Example 4.9 Consider the table given below.

```
mysql> SELECT * FROM ISSUE;
+--------+--------+-------------+-------+
| RollNO | Name   | Book_Issued | Class |
+--------+--------+-------------+-------+
|    121 | MAHEK  | LAB MANUAL  | XI-A  |
|    253 | NIYON  | PHYSICS     | IX-C  |
|    390 | GIRIJ  | SCIENCE     | X-B   |
|    404 | CHINUK | PHYSICS     | XII-B |
|    507 | fAIZAL | BIOLOGY     | X-D   |
|    611 | NASIMA | MATHS       | VI-A  |
|    729 | KIARA  | SCIENCE     | VII-C |
+--------+--------+-------------+-------+
7 rows in set (0.00 sec)
```

Let us select a value for Book_Issued from the table without using the DISTINCT clause first.

```
mysql> SELECT Book_Issued FROM ISSUE;
```

```
+-------------+
| Book_Issued |
+-------------+
| LAB MANUAL  |
| PHYSICS     |
| SCIENCE     |
| PHYSICS     |
| BIOLOGY     |
| MATHS       |
| SCIENCE     |
+-------------+
7 rows in set (0.00 sec)
```

Now let us use the same query but with DISTICT clause to appreciate the results.

```
mysql> SELECT DISTINCT Book_Issued FROM ISSUE;
+-------------+
| Book_Issued |
+-------------+
| LAB MANUAL  |
| PHYSICS     |
| SCIENCE     |
| BIOLOGY     |
| MATHS       |
+-------------+
5 rows in set (0.00 sec)
```

Did you notice that the first select statement selected all values including duplicates from the Book_Issued column? However, the SELECT statement with DISTINCT clause selected only non-duplicate values. To know how many distinct subject books were issued, we can write

```
mysql> SELECT COUNT(DISTINCT Book_Issued) FROM ISSUE;
+-----------------------------+
| COUNT(DISTINCT Book_Issued) |
+-----------------------------+
|                           5 |
+-----------------------------+
1 row in set (0.00 sec)
```

4.15 ORDER BY CLAUSE

The ORDER BY statement in SQL is used to sort the retrieved data in either ascending or descending order. We can sort the values in the result-set by one or more columns using the ORDER BY clause.

By default, ORDER BY sorts the data in ascending order. To sort in descending order, we can use the keyword DESC. To specifically state ascending as the sorting order, the keyword ASC is used.

The syntax of all ways of using ORDER BY clause with the SELECT statement can be given as,

Sort according to one column: To sort in ascending or descending order we can use the keywords ASC or DESC respectively. The syntax for this can be given as,

```
SELECT expressions
FROM tables
[WHERE conditions]
ORDER BY expression [ ASC | DESC ]
```

where,

Expressions specifies the columns to be retrieved.

Tables is the table from which the records have to be retrieved. At least one table must be listed in the FROM clause.

WHERE condition is optional. If specified, the condition must be satisfied for the records to be selected.
ASC is optional as it is the default sorting order. ASC sorts the result-set in ascending order by *expression*.
DESC is optional. If present, it sorts the result-set in descending order by *expression*.

Sort according to multiple columns: To sort according to multiple columns, separate the names of columns by (,) operator. The syntax can be given as,

```
SELECT * FROM table_name ORDER BY column1 ASC|DESC , column2 ASC|DESC
```

Example 4.10 To sort records of Employee table in ascending order of their salaries, we can write:

```
mysql> SELECT EMPNO, SAL FROM EMPLOYEE ORDER BY SAL;
+-------+-------+
| EmpNo | SAL   |
+-------+-------+
|   456 | NULL  |
|   567 | NULL  |
|   678 | NULL  |
|   123 | 35000 |
|   234 | 50000 |
|   345 | 75000 |
+-------+-------+
6 rows in set (0.05 sec)
```

Correspondingly, to sort records based on ascending order of name and further on descending order of salary, if some employees have the same name, then we can write

```
mysql> SELECT * FROM EMPLOYEE ORDER BY NAME ASC, SAL DESC;
```

4.16 THE WHERE LIKE CLAUSE IN SQL

The WHERE LIKE clause determines if a character string matches a pattern. It is usually used when only a fragment of a text value is known. That is, the SQL LIKE clause is used with the WHERE clause to compare a value to find similar values using wildcard characters. The two wildcard characters that are extensively used with the LIKE clause include % and _.

Here, % represents zero, one or multiple characters. And the underscore represents a single number or character. These two characters can also be used in combinations. The basic syntax of LIKE clause can be given as,

```
SELECT FROM table_name
WHERE column LIKE 'XXXX%'
or
SELECT FROM table_name
WHERE column LIKE '%XXXX%'
or
SELECT FROM table_name
WHERE column LIKE 'XXXX_'
or
SELECT FROM table_name
WHERE column LIKE '_XXXX'
or
SELECT FROM table_name
WHERE column LIKE '_XXXX_'
```

Here, XXXX means any numeric or string value.

Example 4.11 — Let us select details of all the students whose name starts with 'R'.

```
mysql> SELECT * FROM STUDENT WHERE NAME LIKE 'R%';
+-------------+-------+--------------+------+-------+-------+
| ROLL_NUMBER | NAME  | PHONE_NUMBER | AGE  | MARKS | CLASS |
+-------------+-------+--------------+------+-------+-------+
|           1 | RAHUL | 9876543210   |   18 |    89 | 12-D  |
|           3 | RIA   | 7825516230   |   16 |    67 | 10-C  |
+-------------+-------+--------------+------+-------+-------+
2 rows in set (0.03 sec)
```

Example 4.12 — Let us display details of all the students who study in the 'D' section.

```
mysql> SELECT * FROM STUDENT WHERE CLASS LIKE '%D';
+-------------+-------+--------------+------+-------+-------+
| ROLL_NUMBER | NAME  | PHONE_NUMBER | AGE  | MARKS | CLASS |
+-------------+-------+--------------+------+-------+-------+
|           1 | RAHUL | 9876543210   |   18 |    89 | 12-D  |
|           5 | KRISH | 9807126534   |   14 |    90 | 8-D   |
+-------------+-------+--------------+------+-------+-------+
2 rows in set (0.00 sec)
```

Example 4.13 — Display the details of all the students whose phone number starts with a '9' and has a '7' in it.

```
mysql> SELECT * FROM STUDENT WHERE PHONE_NUMBER LIKE '9%7%';
+-------------+----------+--------------+------+-------+-------+
| ROLL_NUMBER | NAME     | PHONE_NUMBER | AGE  | MARKS | CLASS |
+-------------+----------+--------------+------+-------+-------+
|           1 | RAHUL    | 9876543210   |   18 |    89 | 12-D  |
|           2 | SARFARAZ | 9823416790   |   17 |    97 | 11-A  |
|           5 | KRISH    | 9807126534   |   14 |    90 | 8-D   |
+-------------+----------+--------------+------+-------+-------+
3 rows in set (0.00 sec)
```

Example 4.14 — Select details of all the students who are not in class 10, 11 or 12.

```
mysql> SELECT * FROM STUDENT WHERE CLASS LIKE '_-_';
+-------------+-------+--------------+------+-------+-------+
| ROLL_NUMBER | NAME  | PHONE_NUMBER | AGE  | MARKS | CLASS |
+-------------+-------+--------------+------+-------+-------+
|           4 | PALAK | 9999123456   |   15 |    75 | 9-B   |
|           5 | KRISH | 9807126534   |   14 |    90 | 8-D   |
+-------------+-------+--------------+------+-------+-------+
2 rows in set (0.00 sec)
```
Note that here, we want a single digit only after '-'.

Example 4.15 — Display details of all the students who are in class 10, 11 or 12.

```
mysql> SELECT * FROM STUDENT WHERE CLASS LIKE '__-%';
+-------------+----------+--------------+------+-------+-------+
| ROLL_NUMBER | NAME     | PHONE_NUMBER | AGE  | MARKS | CLASS |
+-------------+----------+--------------+------+-------+-------+
|           1 | RAHUL    | 9876543210   |   18 |    89 | 12-D  |
|           2 | SARFARAZ | 9823416790   |   17 |    97 | 11-A  |
|           3 | RIA      | 7825516230   |   16 |    67 | 10-C  |
+-------------+----------+--------------+------+-------+-------+
3 rows in set (0.00 sec)
```

Example 4.16 Display the details of all the students whose name does not have an 'I'.

```
mysql> SELECT * FROM STUDENT
    -> WHERE NAME NOT LIKE '%I%';
+-------------+----------+--------------+------+-------+-------+
| ROLL_NUMBER | NAME     | PHONE_NUMBER | AGE  | MARKS | CLASS |
+-------------+----------+--------------+------+-------+-------+
|           1 | RAHUL    | 9876543210   |   18 |    89 | 12-D  |
|           2 | SARFARAZ | 9823416790   |   17 |    97 | 11-A  |
|           4 | PALAK    | 9999123456   |   15 |    75 | 9-B   |
+-------------+----------+--------------+------+-------+-------+
3 rows in set (0.01 sec)
```

4.17 SQL SELECT MIN, MAX STATEMENT

As the name suggests, the SELECT MIN statement in SQL returns the minimum value for a column. Correspondingly, the SELECT MAX statement returns the maximum value for a column.

The general MIN syntax is:

SELECT MIN(column-name)
FROM table-name

and the general MAX syntax can be given as,

SELECT MIN(column-name)
FROM table-name
mysql> SELECT MIN(MARKS) FROM STUDENT;

Example 4.17 Display the minimum marks obtained by a student.

```
+------------+
| MIN(MARKS) |
+------------+
|         67 |
+------------+
1 row in set (0.04 sec)
```

Example 4.18 Display the maximum marks obtained by a student.

```
Mysql> SELECT MAX(MARKS) FROM STUDENT;
+------------+
| MAX(MARKS) |
+------------+
|         97 |
+------------+
1 row in set (0.04 sec)
```

Example 4.19 Display the details of students scoring maximum marks.

```
mysql> SELECT * FROM STUDENT
    -> WHERE MARKS = (SELECT MAX(MARKS) FROM STUDENT);
+-------------+----------+--------------+------+-------+-------+
| ROLL_NUMBER | NAME     | PHONE_NUMBER | AGE  | MARKS | CLASS |
+-------------+----------+--------------+------+-------+-------+
|           2 | SARFARAZ | 9823416790   |   17 |    97 | 11-A  |
+-------------+----------+--------------+------+-------+-------+
1 row in set (0.00 sec)
```

Example 4.20 Display the maximum marks obtained by students in classes 8 and 9.

```
mysql> SELECT MAX(MARKS) FROM STUDENT WHERE CLASS LIKE '_-_';
+------------+
| MAX(MARKS) |
+------------+
|         90 |
+------------+
1 row in set (0.00 sec)
```

Example 4.21 Display the maximum marks obtained by students in classes 10, 11 and 12.

```
Mysql> SELECT MAX(MARKS) FROM STUDENT WHERE CLASS LIKE '__-_';
+------------+
| MAX(MARKS) |
+------------+
|         97 |
+------------+
1 row in set (0.00 sec)
```

Example 4.22 Display the maximum marks obtained by students having roll number greater than 3.

```
mysql> SELECT MAX(MARKS) FROM STUDENT WHERE ROLL_NUMBER >3;
+------------+
| MAX(MARKS) |
+------------+
|         90 |
+------------+
1 row in set (0.00 sec)
```

4.18 SELECT COUNT, SUM, AVG

The SELECT COUNT statement returns a count of the number of data values. The SELECT SUM returns the sum of the data values. And the SELECT AVG returns the average of the data values.

The general COUNT syntax is:

```
SELECT COUNT(column-name)
FROM table-name
```

Example 4.23 Let us find out the number of rows in our STUDENT table.

```
mysql> SELECT COUNT(ROLL_NUMBER) FROM STUDENT;
+--------------------+
| COUNT(ROLL_NUMBER) |
+--------------------+
|                  5 |
+--------------------+
1 row in set (0.03 sec)
```

The general SUM syntax is:

```
SELECT SUM(column-name)
FROM table-name
```

| Example 4.24 | Let us display the total marks obtained by all the students in the STUDENT table where age is less than or equal to 15. |

```
mysql> SELECT SUM(MARKS) FROM STUDENT
    -> WHERE AGE <= 15;
+------------+
| SUM(MARKS) |
+------------+
|        165 |
+------------+
1 row in set (0.03 sec)
```

The general AVG syntax is:

```
SELECT AVG(column-name)
FROM table-name
```

| Example 4.25 | Find out the average age of students scoring at least 90 marks. |

```
mysql> SELECT AVG(AGE) FROM STUDENT
    -> WHERE MARKS >= 90;
+----------+
| AVG(AGE) |
+----------+
|  15.5000 |
+----------+
1 row in set (0.00 sec)
```

4.19 THE SQL GROUP BY STATEMENT

The GROUP BY statement is used to create a summary of records. The statement groups rows that have the same values (in a column) to create summary rows. For example, we can find the number of students in each class (here we group by class), or average salary of employees in an IT department (here, we can group by department).

Therefore, the GROUP BY clause returns one row for each group, thereby reducing the number of rows in the result set.

The GROUP BY statement is often used with aggregate functions (COUNT, MAX, MIN, SUM, AVG) to group the result-set by one or more columns. The general syntax of GROUP BY statement can be given as,

```
SELECT column_name(s)
FROM table_name
WHERE condition
GROUP BY column_name(s)
ORDER BY column_name(s);
```

4.20 THE HAVING CLAUSE

We have learnt that WHERE clause is a powerful clause that is used for selective selection. But this clause cannot be used with aggregate functions. So, SQL has another clause – HAVING clause that can be used with aggregate functions.

Thus, the HAVING clause allows users to filter the values returned from a grouped query based on the results of aggregation functions. The syntax of HAVING clause can be given as,

```
SELECT expression1, expression2, ... expression_n, aggregate_function
(expression)
FROM tables
[WHERE conditions]
GROUP BY expression1, expression2, ... expression_n
HAVING condition;
```

4.21 COLUMN ALIASES

By default, SELECT statement displays the column heading(s) in the result set as the name of that column in the table. However, we can use a column alias to change the name of the column heading in the result set. The syntax of creating a column alias is,

```
SELECT column_name AS column_alias
FROM table_name.
```

Consider the Employee table given below. And observe how the AS keyword can be used to create a column alias.

```
mysql>  select * from Employee;
+-------+-------+
| EmpNo | Sal   |
+-------+-------+
|   123 | 35000 |
|   234 | 50000 |
|   345 | 75000 |
+-------+-------+
3 rows in set (0.00 sec)
```

```
mysql>  select EmpNo, Sal AS Salary from Employee;
+-------+--------+
| EmpNo | Salary |
+-------+--------+
|   123 |  35000 |
|   234 |  50000 |
|   345 |  75000 |
+-------+--------+
3 rows in set (0.00 sec)
```

Thus, we see that we can use column alias if the original column name does not meet our requirements or clearly defines its purpose. In such a case, column alias can be used to define a meaningful name for the column.

We can also use column alias to give name to a column that is dynamically created by applying an expression to an existing column in the table.

```
mysql> SELECT EmpNo, Sal, Sal + Sal * 0.10 As NEW_SAL FROM EMPLOYEE;
+-------+-------+---------+
| EmpNo | Sal   | NEW_SAL |
+-------+-------+---------+
|   123 | 35000 |   38500 |
|   234 | 50000 |   55000 |
|   345 | 75000 |   82500 |
+-------+-------+---------+
3 rows in set (0.00 sec)
```

From the above discussion, we see that SQL aliases are used to give a table, or a column in a table, a temporary name. They are often used to make column names more readable.

> An alias only exists for the duration of the query.

4.22 SQL JOIN

SQL Join statement is used to combine data or rows from two or more tables based on a common field between them. In this section, we will read about the different types of Joins that can be performed on tables. But before going into the details of these joins, let us consider two tables – STUDENT and STUDENT_COURSE as given below.

STUDENT TABLE

Roll_number	Name	Phone_number	Age	Marks
1	RAHUL	9876543210	18	89
2	SARFARAZ	9823416790	17	97
3	RIA	7825516230	16	67
4	PALAK	9999123456	9	75
5	KRISH	9807126534	14	90
6	NAVYA	9319012783	15	94

STUDENT COURSE TABLE

Course Id	Roll_number
1	2
2	1
3	3
1	4
2	5
6	NULL

The two tables have a relation specified by primary and foreign key – ROLL_NUMBER. The extent of overlapping between the two tables, if any, can be determined by the number of records in first table matches the records in the second table. Depending on what subset of data we would like to select from the two tables, we can use any of the four join types.

Inner Join to select all records from the two tables where the join condition is met.

Left Join to select all records from the first table along with records from the second table for which the join condition is met (if at all).

Right Join to select all records from the second table along with records from the first table for which the join condition is met (if at all).

Full Join to select all records from both the tables regardless of whether the join condition is met or not.

4.22.1 INNER JOIN

The INNER JOIN keyword selects all rows from both the tables if the condition is satisfied. Therefore, the result-set will be created by combining all rows from both the tables where the condition is satisfied or the value of the common field is same, as shown in Fig. 4.2. The syntax for inner join is,

```
SELECT table1.column1,table1.column2,table2.column1,....
FROM table1
INNER JOIN table2
ON table1.matching_column = table2.matching_column;
```

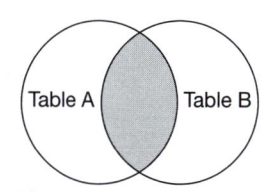

Figure 4.2 Inner join

Note that JOIN is same as INNER JOIN, so whether we write JOIN or INNER JOIN it would not make a difference.

Example 4.26 Write a query that shows the names, marks and courses of students enrolled in different courses.

```
mysql> SELECT STUDENT.ROLL_NUMBER, STUDENT.NAME, STUDENT.MARKS, STUDENT_COURSE.COURSE_
    ID
    -> FROM STUDENT
    -> INNER JOIN STUDENT_COURSE
    -> ON STUDENT.ROLL_NUMBER = STUDENT_COURSE.ROLL_NUMBER;
+-------------+----------+-------+-----------+
| ROLL_NUMBER | NAME     | MARKS | COURSE_ID |
+-------------+----------+-------+-----------+
|           1 | RAHUL    |    89 |         2 |
|           2 | SARFARAZ |    97 |         1 |
|           3 | RIA      |    67 |         3 |
|           4 | PALAK    |    75 |         1 |
|           5 | KRISH    |    90 |         2 |
+-------------+----------+-------+-----------+
5 rows in set (0.01 sec)
```

4.22.2 LEFT JOIN

The LEFT JOIN returns all the rows of the table on the left side of `join` and only the matching rows for the table on the right side of `join`. The rows in the table on the right side that do not match will contain *null in the resultant set*. Refer Fig. 4.3 to understand the concept of Left Join. *The basic syntax of* LEFT JOIN is given below.

```
SELECT table1.column1,table1.column2,table2.column1,....
FROM table1
LEFT JOIN table2
ON table1.matching_column = table2.matching_column;
```

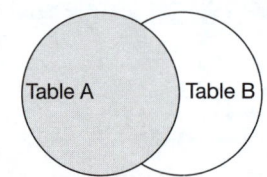

Figure 4.3 Left join

Example 4.27 Write a query that shows the names, marks and courses of all students.

```
mysql> SELECT STUDENT.ROLL_NUMBER, STUDENT.NAME, STUDENT.MARKS, STUDENT_COURSE.COURSE_
    ID
    -> FROM STUDENT
    -> LEFT JOIN STUDENT_COURSE
    -> ON STUDENT.ROLL_NUMBER = STUDENT_COURSE.ROLL_NUMBER;
+-------------+----------+-------+-----------+
| ROLL_NUMBER | NAME     | MARKS | COURSE_ID |
+-------------+----------+-------+-----------+
|           1 | RAHUL    |    89 |         2 |
|           2 | SARFARAZ |    97 |         1 |
|           3 | RIA      |    67 |         3 |
|           4 | PALAK    |    75 |         1 |
|           5 | KRISH    |    90 |         2 |
|           6 | NAVYA    |    94 |      NULL |
+-------------+----------+-------+-----------+
6 rows in set (0.00 sec)
```

4.22.3 RIGHT JOIN

The RIGHT JOIN (as shown in Fig. 4.4) returns all the rows of the table on the right side of the join and only the matching rows for the table on the left side of join. The rows in the table on the left side that do not match will contain *null in the resultant set*. The basic syntax of RIGHT JOIN is given below.

```
SELECT table1.column1,table1.column2,table2.column1,....
FROM table1
RIGHT JOIN table2
ON table1.matching_column = table2.matching_column;
```

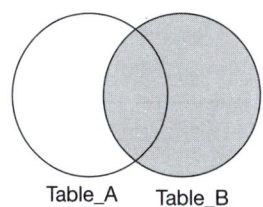

Figure 4.4 Right join

Example 4.28 Write a query that shows the names and marks of students enrolled in all the courses being offered.

```
mysql> SELECT STUDENT.ROLL_NUMBER, STUDENT.NAME, STUDENT.MARKS, STUDENT_COURSE.COURSE_
    ID
    -> FROM STUDENT
    -> RIGHT JOIN STUDENT_COURSE
    -> ON STUDENT.ROLL_NUMBER = STUDENT_COURSE.ROLL_NUMBER;
+-------------+----------+-------+-----------+
| ROLL_NUMBER | NAME     | MARKS | COURSE_ID |
+-------------+----------+-------+-----------+
|           2 | SARFARAZ |    97 |         1 |
|           1 | RAHUL    |    89 |         2 |
|           3 | RIA      |    67 |         3 |
|           4 | PALAK    |    75 |         1 |
|           5 | KRISH    |    90 |         2 |
|        NULL | NULL     |  NULL |         6 |
+-------------+----------+-------+-----------+
6 rows in set (0.00 sec)
```

4.22.4 FULL JOIN

FULL JOIN generates output by combining results of both LEFT JOIN and RIGHT JOIN. The result-set will contain all the rows from both the tables (refer Fig. 4.5). For rows for which there is no matching, the result-set will contain *NULL* values. The general syntax for performing a full join can be given as,

```
SELECT table1.column1,table1.column2,table2.column1,....
FROM table1
FULL JOIN table2
ON table1.matching_column = table2.matching_column;
```

Figure 4.5 Full join

Although MySQL does not support `full join` operation, we can still do it by doing a union of a `left join` with a `right join` as given below.

> SELF JOIN is a join of a table to itself. Each row in a table is joined with itself.
> CROSS JOIN is a type of join in which a join clause is applied between each row of a table and every row of the other table.

```
SELECT STUDENT.ROLL_NUMBER, STUDENT.NAME, STUDENT.MARKS, STUDENT_COURSE.COURSE_ID
  ->   FROM STUDENT
  -> LEFT JOIN STUDENT_COURSE
  ->   ON STUDENT.ROLL_NUMBER = STUDENT_COURSE.ROLL_NUMBER
  -> UNION
  -> SELECT STUDENT.ROLL_NUMBER, STUDENT.NAME, STUDENT.MARKS, STUDENT_COURSE.COURSE_ID
```

```
->    FROM STUDENT
->    RIGHT JOIN STUDENT_COURSE
->    ON STUDENT.ROLL_NUMBER = STUDENT_COURSE.ROLL_NUMBER;
+-------------+----------+--------+------------+
| ROLL_NUMBER | NAME     | MARKS  | COURSE_ID  |
+-------------+----------+--------+------------+
|           1 | RAHUL    |    89  |         2  |
|           2 | SARFARAZ |    97  |         1  |
|           3 | RIA      |    67  |         3  |
|           4 | PALAK    |    75  |         1  |
|           5 | KRISH    |    90  |         2  |
|           6 | NAVYA    |    94  |      NULL  |
|        NULL | NULL     |  NULL  |         6  |
+-------------+----------+--------+------------+
7    rows in set (0.00 sec)
```

Thus, we can conclude that

- JOINS allow us to combine data from more than one table to form the result set.
- JOINS enhance performance of queries.
- INNER JOINS only return rows that meet the given criteria. But OUTER JOINS like the Left Join and Right Join return rows where no matches have been found. The unmatched rows are returned with NULL values.
- The frequently used clause in JOIN operations is "ON". We can even use other clauses like USING, GROUP BY, WHERE, SUB QUERIES, AGGREGATE FUNCTIONS, etc.

4.23 RELATIONAL ALGEBRA IN DBMS

Relational algebra is a **procedural** query language used with relational model. It helps users to retrieve data from a database or perform operations like insert, update or delete data stored in the table. Relational algebra takes a relation (table from which data has to be accessed) as an input and gives a temporary relation holding the data asked for by the user as the output.

Basic/Fundamental Operations

1. Select (σ)
2. Project (Π)
3. Union ($\cup$)
4. Set Difference ($-$)
5. Cartesian product (X)
6. Rename (ρ)

Table: Customer

Customer_ID	Customer_Name	Customer_City
C101	Jack	Bengaluru
C102	Raghav	Mumbai
C103	Chaitanya	Chennai
C104	Govind	Kolkata
C105	Meera	Delhi

Consider the customer table given in Fig. 4.6. We will be using this table to perform all the above-listed operations.

Figure 4.6 Customer table

4.23.1 SELECT Operator

The SELECT operator is denoted by a σ symbol and is used to find the tuples (or rows) in a relation (or table) which satisfy the given condition. Its syntax can be given as,

σ **Condition/Predicate (Relation/Table name)**

Therefore, to select Customer_Id and Customer_Name of a customer from Chennai, we will write

```
σ Customer_City="Chennai" (CUSTOMER)
```

OUTPUT
```
Customer_Id      Customer_Name       Customer_City
-----------------------------------------------------------------
-------------------------         ---------------------
C103             Chaitanya           Chennai
```

4.23.2 PROJECT Operator (∏)

The PROJECT operator, denoted by ∏ symbol, is used to select the desired columns (or attributes) from a table (or relation). It is similar to the `Select` statement in SQL. The syntax of PROJECT operator is,

∏ column_name1, column_name2, ..., column_nameN(table_name)

Points to Remember

- The degree of output relation or the number of columns is equal to the number of attributes specified in the attribute list.
- Projection operator automatically removes all the duplicates while projecting the output relation.
- Cardinality or the number of rows in the original relation and output relation may or may not be same. This is because if there are no duplicates in the original relation, then the cardinality will be same. Otherwise, it will be less (as duplicate rows are present only once in the output relation).
- Projection operator does not obey commutative property, i.e.,

$$\Pi_{<list2>} (\Pi_{<list1>} (R)) \neq \Pi_{<list1>} (\Pi_{<list2>} (R))$$

> If attribute list is a super key on relation R, then there will be same number of tuples in the output relation because there will be no duplicates to filter.

- The terms on either side of the following expression are equivalent because both finally projects columns of list-1

$$\Pi_{<list1>} (\Pi_{<list2>} (R)) = \Pi_{<list1>} (R)$$

In this example, to fetch only customer name and customer ID columns of the table, we can use the project operator as given below.
- While selection operator performs horizontal partitioning of the relation, projection operator performs vertical partitioning of the relation.
- There is only one difference between projection operator of relational algebra and SELECT operation of SQL. While SELECT operation allows duplicates, projection operator does not allow duplicates.

```
∏ Customer_Name, Customer_City (CUSTOMER)
Table: CUSTOMER
---------------
Customer_Id        Customer_Name
----------         --------------
   C101            Jack
   C102            Raghav
   C103            Chaitanya
   C104            Govind
   C105            Meera
```

> Selection operation selects rows based on the specified condition but projection selects all rows for the specified columns.

4.23.3 UNION Operator

The UNION operator, denoted by ∪ symbol, is used to select all the rows (tuples) from two tables (relations). If we have two relations R1 and R2, both having the same columns, then to select all the rows from these relations we can apply the UNION operator.

When doing a union of two tables, the rows that are present in both the tables will only appear once in the result set. This feature ensures there are no duplicates are present in the result-set. The syntax of union operator is,

```
table_name1 ∪ table_name2
```

Remember that before applying the `union` operation, we have to make sure that the two tables have the same number of attributes (columns) and same attribute domain.

Student_Id	Student_Name	Student_Age
S01	Annu	19
S02	Anil	20
S03	Parul	15
S04	Latika	14

Course_Id	Student_Name	Student Id
Cl01	Annu	S01
Cl04	Anil	S02
Cl06	Shyam	S03
Cl09	Parul	S04
C115	Latika	S05

Figure 4.7 Student table with different attributes

Consider the tables T1 and T2 given in Fig. 4.7.

∏ **Student_Name (COURSE)** ∪ ∏ **Student_Name (STUDENT)**

It will give the output,

```
Student_Name
--------------------

Annu
Anil
Shyam
Parul
Latika
```

4.23.4 INTERSECTION Operator

The INTERSECTION operator, denoted by ∩ symbol, is used to select common rows (tuples) from two tables (relations). If we have two relations R1 and R2, both having same columns, the INTERSECTION operator is used to select all those rows that are present in both the relations. The general syntax of using an `intersection` operator can be given as,

table_name1 ∩ table_name2

For example, to see the names of all students from the STUDENT table who have also enrolled in some course, we need to write

```
∏ Student_Name (COURSE) ∩ ∏ Student_Name (STUDENT)
Student_Name
--------------------

Annu
Anil
Shyam
Parul
Latika
```

4.23.5 SET DIFFERENCE Operator

The SET DIFFERENCE operator, denoted by – symbol, is used to select all those tuples (rows) that are present in Relation R1 but **not** present in Relation R2, where R1 and R2 are two relations. The general syntax of using set difference is,

```
table_name1 - table_name2
```

Points to Remember
- The attribute names of both the tables must be same.
- The two relations should be compatible with each other.

For example, to find names of those students that are present in COURSE table but not present in STUDENT table, we will write

```
∏ Student_Name (COURSE) - ∏ Student_Name (STUDENT)
Student_Name
--------------------

Shyam
```

4.23.6 CARTESIAN PRODUCT Operator

The CARTESIAN PRODUCT operator, denoted by X symbol, is used to combine each tuple of the first relation R1 with each tuple of the second relation R2. The general syntax of finding the cartesian product is,

R1 X R2

For example, consider the tables T1 and T2 given in Fig. 4.8. If we write, T1 X T2, then the output will be

Col_A	Col_B
A	100
B	200
C	300

Col_X	Col_Y
X	4
Y	5

Figure 4.8 Table T1 and T2

```
Col_A    Col_B    Col_X    Col_Y
-----    -----    -----    -----
A        100      X        4
A        100      Y        5
B        200      X        4
B        200      Y        5
C        300      X        4
C        300      Y        5
```

From the above output, we can conclude that the number of rows in the output is the cross product of number of rows in each table. In our example, Table 1 has 3 rows and Table 2 has 2 rows, so the output has 3 × 2 = 6 rows.

4.23.7 RENAME Operator

The RENAME operator is used to rename a relation or an attribute of a relation. The syntax of this operation can be given as,

ρ(new_relation_name, old_relation_name)

For example, to rename the CUSTOMER table to CUST_DETAILS, we will write,

```
ρ(CUST_DETAILS, ∏(Customer_Id, Customer_Name)(CUSTOMER))
Table: CUST_DETAILS
-------------------

Customer_Id     Customer_Name
-----------     -------------
   C101            Jack
   C102            Raghav
   C103            Chaitanya
   C104            Govind
   C105            Meera
```

Key Terms

SQL: A database query language.

Clients: Computers that install and run RDBMS software are called clients.

Servers: To access data, clients connect to powerful machines called servers.

Metadata: Data describing data stored in database.

Data Definition Language (DDL): SQL statements used to create or modify database objects (like tables, views, indexes, users, etc).

Data Manipulation Language (DML): SQL statements used to manipulate data (like inserting, updating, deleting data).

Operator: A reserved word or a character in SQL statement that is extensively used in WHERE clause of the query to perform arithmetic or comparison operations.

Database: A collection of related tables.

Conjunctive operators: The SQL AND and OR operators that are used to combine multiple conditions to specify a criterion for fetching data from a table are called as the conjunctive operators.

Foreign key: A field (or collection of fields) in one table that refers to PRIMARY KEY in another table.

Relational algebra: A **procedural** query language used with relational model to retrieve data from database or perform operations like insert, update or delete data stored in the table

Chapter Highlights

- MySQL is an open-source software, so users do not have to pay to use it.
- SQL queries (or statements) can be used to perform operations like retrieving, inserting, updating and deleting data. They can be also used to create tables or modify the structure of existing tables. However, to use SQL queries, you must first install a database such as Oracle, MySQL, MongoDB, PostGres SQL, SQL Server, DB2, etc.
- In MySQL, every client can make a request to a server that responds with the desired output.
- We can use the SQL SELECT statement to perform mathematical calculations.
- Numeric functions are used to perform operations on numbers and return numbers.
- The string functions in MySQL are used to manipulate textual data stored in tables.
- A database is created using the CREATE DATABASE statement.
- To select a particular database and start using it, we need to use database command.
- In SQL, the CREATE TABLE statement is used to create a table.
- A table can be deleted using the DROP TABLE statement. When a table is deleted, all its definition, data, indexes, views, triggers, constraints and permission specifications are removed from the database.
- INSERT INTO statement is used to add new rows of data in a table that exists in the database.
- The SELECT statement in SQL is used to fetch or retrieve data from one or more tables in the database.
- SELECT DISTINCT statement eliminates duplicate entries while displaying data from the table.
- The WHERE clause is used in the SELECT statement to specify a condition for retrieving data from one or more tables.
- The ORDER BY statement in SQL is used to sort the retrieved data in either ascending or descending order.
- The SQL UPDATE statement is used to modify the existing data in a table.
- The DELETE query in SQL is used to delete existing record(s) from a table in the database.
- Column alias is used to change the name of the column heading in the result-set.
- The SQL NULL is both a value as well as a keyword. In simple terms, NULL is a place holder for data that does not exist or whose value is not known.

- PRIMARY KEY constraint helps us to uniquely identify each record in the table. The primary key must contain UNIQUE values, and cannot have NULL values.
- A table can have only one primary key and the primary key may consist of one or more fields.
- To set PRIMARY KEY constraint on an already-created table, the ALTER TABLE command is used.
- Select Operator, denoted by a σ symbol, is used to find the tuples (or rows) in a relation (or table) which satisfy the given condition.
- Project Operator, denoted by ∏ symbol, is used to select the desired columns (or attributes) from a table (or relation). It is similar to the `Select` statement in SQL
- Union Operator, denoted by ∪ symbol, is used to select all the rows (tuples) from two tables.
- Intersection Operator, denoted by ∩ symbol, is used to select common rows (tuples) from two tables (relations).
- Set Difference Operator, denoted by – symbol, is used to select all those tuples (rows) that are present in Relation R1 but **not** present in Relation R2, where R1 and R2 are two relations.
- Cartesian Product Operator, denoted by X symbol, is used to combine each tuple of first relation R1 with each tuple of second relation R2
- Rename Operator, denoted by ρ symbol, is used to rename a relation or an attribute of a relation.

Review Questions

1. What is SQL? Why is it used?
2. MySQL and SQL are the same. Comment on this statement.
3. Explain the working of MySQL.
4. Differentiate between DDL and DML.
5. Why do we need to specify data type? List some data types used in SQL.
6. Differentiate between `char` and `varchar`.
7. How can we create a database in SQL?
8. Write the SQL statements that you will use to:
   a. create a database
   b. see a list of all the databases present in MySQL
   c. change to another database
   d. delete a database
   e. create table
   f. return values that matches values in a list or a sub-query
   g. sort the retrieved data in either ascending or descending order
   h. remove records from a table
   i. return the maximum value for a column
   j. return the minimum value for a column
   k. return a count of the number of data values
   l. return the sum of the data values
   m. return the average of the data values
   n. set PRIMARY KEY constraint on an already-created table
   o. drop a PRIMARY KEY constraint.
9. Differentiate between DROP TABLE and DROP DATABASE statements.
10. Explain the syntax of the SELECT statement.
11. What are conjunctive operators? Explain with the help of an example.
12. With the help of an example, explain how you will use the ORDER BY clause to sort data based on multiple columns.
13. What are column aliases?
14. Explain some operators that are used to handle NULL values in SQL.
15. What does primary key constraint state? How can we enforce such a constraint in SQL?
16. Define relational algebra and list some operations that can be performed by using it.
17. Write the instructions for the following:
    a. The SQL statement creates an index named "idx_lastname" on the "LastName" column in the "Persons" table.

b. Creating an index on the site_name column of websites table.
c. Creating a unique index on the site_name column of websites table.
d. Write the instruction for creating an index on the site_name and server columns of a Website table.

18. Consider the tables given below and write instructions for the following.

CID	First_name	Last_name	Email	Address	City	State	Zipcode
1	Girish	Patel	gpatel@gmail.com	3200 Kirti Nagar	Merrut	UP	22121
2	John	Samuel	John.s@gmail.com	1250 Windsor	Lansdowne	UK	02169
3	Tina	Bhargava	Bhargava.tina@gmail.com	931 Thomas Jefferson Road	Trichy	TN	22902
4	Jamat	Ali	Alij786@gmail.com	11350 Indira Nagar	Bangalore	KA	22960
5	Nick	Jones	nickjones@gmail.com	2050 Jammu Highway	Katra	JK	22902

a. Get a list of those customers who placed an order and the details of the order they placed.
b. Append information about orders to customers table, regardless of whether a customer placed an order or not. **Hint:** Use a left join.
c. Append Orders information with Customer information.
d. Get a list of all orders for which we failed to record information about the customers who placed them.
e. Create a list of all records from both tables, we can use a full join.

Order_id	Order_rate	Amount	CID
1	07/04/1776	234.56	1
2	03/14/1760	78.50	3
3	05/23/1784	124.00	2
4	09/03/1790	65.50	3
5	07/21/1795	25.50	10
6	11/27/1787	14.40	9

19. Consider the given table and write the queries for the following problems: List all orders with product names, quantities and prices.

Product	OrderItem
ID	ID
ProductName	OrderId
SupplierId	ProductId
UnitPrice	UnitPrice
Package	Quantity
IsDiscontinued	

ID	Name	Subject	Age
100	Ashish	Maths	19
200	Rahul	Science	20
300	Naina	Physics	20
400	Sameer	Chemistry	21

20. Consider the given table and write the following queries.
a. Select the name and age of Students.
b. Fetch data for students with age more than 17.
c. Information of male students, of age more than 17

21. Explain the queries:
a. σ topic = "Database" (Tutorials)
b. σ topic = "Database" and author = "guru99"(Tutorials)
c. σ sales > 50000 (Customers)
d. σteacher = "database"(Names)
e. ΠstaffNo, fName, lName, salary(Staff)
f. σsubject = "database"(Books)

g. σsubject = "database" and price = "450"(Books)
h. σsubject = "database" and price = "450" or year > "2010"(Books)
i. ∏subject, author (Books)
j. ∏ author (Books) ∪ ∏ author (Articles)
k. ∏ author (Books) − ∏ author (Articles)
l. σauthor = 'tutorialspoint'(Books X Articles)

Programming Exercises

1. Create a database having two tables with the specified fields, to computerize a library system of a Delhi University College.
   LibraryBooks (Accession number, Title, Author, Department, PurchaseDate, Price)
   IssuedBooks (Accession number, Borrower)
   a) Identify primary and foreign keys. Create the tables and insert at least 5 records in each table.
   b) Delete the record of book titled "Database System Concepts".
   c) Change the Department of the book titled "Discrete Maths" to "CS".
   d) List all books that belong to "CS" department.
   e) List all books that belong to "CS" department and are written by author "Navathe".
   f) List all computer (Department="CS") that have been issued.
   g) List all books which have a price less than 500 or purchased between "01/01/1999" and "01/01/2004".

2. Create a database having three tables to store the details of students of Computer Department in your college.
   Personal information about Student (College roll number, Name of student, Date of birth, Address, Marks (rounded off to whole number) in percentage at 10 + 2, Phone number)
   Paper details (Paper code, Name of the Paper)
   Student's Academic and Attendance details (College roll number, Paper code, Attendance, Marks in home examination).
   a) Identify primary and foreign keys. Create the tables and insert at least 5 records in each table.
   b) Design a query that will return the records (from the second table) along with the name of the student from the first table, for students who have more than 75% attendance and more than 60% marks in Paper 2.
   c) List all students who live in "Delhi" and have marks greater than 60 in paper 1.
   d) Find the total attendance and total marks obtained by each student.
   e) List the name of student who has got the highest marks in Paper 2.

3. Create the following tables and answer the queries given below:
   Customer (CustID, email, Name, Phone, ReferrerID)
   Bicycle (BicycleID, DatePurchased, Color, CustID, ModelNo)
   BicycleModel (ModelNo, Manufacturer, Style)
   Service (StartDate, BicycleID, EndDate)
   a) Identify primary and foreign keys. Create the tables and insert at least 5 records in each table.
   b) List all the customers who have the bicycles manufactured by manufacturer "Honda".
   c) List the bicycles purchased by the customers who have been referred by customer "C1".
   d) List the manufacturer of red-colored bicycles. e) List the models of the bicycles given for service.

4. Create the following tables, enter at least 5 records in each table and answer the following queries:
   EMPLOYEE (Person_Name, Street, City),
   WORKS (Person_Name, Company_Name, Salary),
   COMPANY (Company_Name, City) and
   MANAGERS (Person_Name, Manager_Name).
   a) Identify primary and foreign keys.
   b) Alter table employee, add a column "email" of type `varchar`(20).
   c) Find the names of all managers who work for Samba Bank and NCB Bank.
   d) Find the names, street addresses and cities of residence and salary of all employees who work for "Samba Bank"

and earn more than $10,000.
  e) Find the names of all employees who live in the same city as the company for which they work.
  f) Find the highest salary, lowest salary and average salary paid by each company.
  g) Find the sum of salary and number of employees in each company.
  h) Find the name of the company that pays the highest salary.

5. Create the following tables, enter at least 5 records in each table and answer the following queries:
   Suppliers (SNo, Sname, Status, SCity),
   Parts (PNo, Pname, Colour, Weight, City),
   Project (JNo, Jname, Jcity) and
   Shipment (Sno, Pno, Jno, Quantity).
   a) Identify primary and foreign keys.
   b) Get supplier numbers for suppliers in Paris with status>20.
   c) Get suppliers details for suppliers who supply part P2. Display the supplier list in increasing order of supplier numbers.
   d) Get suppliers' names for suppliers who do not supply part P2.
   e) For each shipment get full shipment details, including total shipment weights.
   f) Get all the shipments where the quantity is in the range 300 to 750, inclusive.
   g) Get part nos. for parts that either weigh more than 16 pounds or are supplied by supplier S2, or both.
   h) Get the names of cities that store more than five red parts.
   i) Get full details of parts supplied by a supplier in Delhi.
   j) Get part numbers for part supplied by a supplier in Allahabad to a project in Chennai.
   k) Get the total number of projects supplied by a supplier (say, S1).
   l) Get the total quantity of a part (say, P1) supplied by a supplier (say, S1).

Fill in the Blanks

1. MySQL works on _____ model.
2. _____ describes data stored in database.
3. _____ Language is used to create or modify database objects (like tables, views, indexes, users, etc).
4. Data type _____ is used to define fixed-length strings.
5. _____ is a reserved word or a character in SQL statement that is extensively used to perform arithmetic or comparison operations.
6. _____ keyword ensures no duplicate values.
7. _____ function displays a sub-string of given length starting from the specified position.
8. _____ statement is used to see a list of all the databases present in MySQL.
9. The DROP DATABASE statement is used to _____ an existing database.
10. In SQL, the _____ statement is used to create a table.
11. Once the table is created, we can use the _____ command to see the description of the newly created table.
12. _____ statement is used to add new rows of data in a table that exists in the database.
13. The _____ statement in SQL is used to fetch or retrieve data from one or more tables in the database.
14. _____ statement eliminates duplicate entries while displaying data from the table.
15. The _____ clause returns values that fall within a given range.
16. The _____ keyword can be used to create a column alias.
17. _____ operator returns true, if the column value is NULL.
18. _____ KEY is a key used to link two tables.
19. The _____ constraint ensures that invalid data is not inserted into the foreign key column.
20. Relational algebra takes a _____ as an input.

21. _____ Operator is used to find the tuples in a relation that satisfy the given condition.
22. A tuple is also known as a _____.
23. A table is also known as a _____.
24. _____ means the number of rows in a relation.
25. _____ Operator is used to select common rows (tuples) from two tables.

State True or False

1. MySQL is a proprietary software.
2. MySQL satisfies ACID property.
3. MySQL is a database query language.
4. The server application responds with the requested information that is displayed on the client machine.
5. DDL is used to manipulate data.
6. `char` performs faster than `varchar`.
7. The ALL keyword is used to compare any applicable value in the list.
8. The `strcmp()` function returns 1, if the first string is smaller than the second.
9. When we delete a database, all the information stored in it is lost.
10. The WHERE clause can be used retrieve data only from a single table.
11. The WHEREIN clause returns values that match values in a list or a sub-query.
12. The ORDER BY clause can be used to sort data according to multiple columns.
13. An underscore represents zero, one or multiple characters.
14. A column alias permanently changes the heading of the column.
15. Equality operator does not work with NULL values.
16. NULL is a data type in SQL.
17. All aggregate functions affect only rows that do not have NULL values.
18. Comparison operations cannot be performed on NULL values.
19. The primary key must contain NULL values.
20. A table can have only one primary key and the primary key may consist of one or more fields.
21. Like SQL, Relational Algebra is a query language.
22. In a project operation, the degree of output relation is not equal to the number of attributes specified in the attribute list.
23. SELECT operator performs vertical partitioning of the relation.
24. While SELECT operator allows duplicates, projection operator does not allow duplicates.
25. UNION operator ensures that there are no duplicate values in the result set.
26. CARTESIAN PRODUCT is used to select all the tuples that are present in Relation R1 but **not** present in Relation R2, where R1 and R2 are two relations.

Multiple Choice Questions

1. We cannot _____ data using SQL statements.
    a. delete   b. update   c. retrieve   d. None of these.
2. Which of the following is not an example of a database?
    a. MySQL   b. SQL   c. PostGres SQL   d. SQL Server
3. Which function returns the smallest integer value that is greater than or equal to a number?
    a. `ceil()`   b. `floor()`   c. `round()`   d. `abs()`

4. Which function is used to remove leading and trailing white spaces from a given string?
   a. TRIM() b. LTRIM() c. RTRIM() d. RPAD()
5. Which clause is used with SELECT statement to filter the records in the table and fetch only those that meet the specified criteria?
   a. ORDER BY b. WHERE c. DISTINCT d. UPDATE
6. Which SQL statement is used to modify the existing data in a table?
   a. ORDER BY b. WHERE c. INSERT INTO d. UPDATE
7. Which clause is used with the WHERE clause to compare a value to find similar values using wildcard characters?
   a. IN b. BETWEEN c. LIKE d. DISTINCT
8. Which operator compares values and gives True even for two NULL values?
   a. IS NULL b. IS NOT NULL c. <=> d. All of these.
9. The SQL NULL is a _____.
   a. value b. keyword c. Both of these. d. None of these.
10. Which function is used for replacing NULL values in MySQL?
    a. IS NULL b. IFNULL() c. IS NOT NULL d. <=>
11. Which command is used to create a FOREIGN KEY constraint on an already existing table?
    a. ALTER TABLE b. CREATE TABLE c. INSERT INTO d. UPDATE TABLE
12. Which operator performs horizontal partitioning of a relation?
    a. SELECT b. PROJECTION c. UNION d. MINUS
13. Which relational algebra operation is used to combine each tuple of first relation R1 with each tuple of second relation R2?
    a. CARTESIAN PRODUCT b. INTERSECTION c. UNION d. MINUS

Give the Output

1. `SELECT 20 + 5 - 10 * 3`
2. `SELECT 100/20 *2 + 8 -4;`
3. `SELECT (50 > 10) AND (50 <= 100);`
4. `SELECT POW(CEIL(ABS(-12.34)),2);`
5. `SELECT LOG10(MOD(110,FLOOR(100.89)));`
6. `SELECT CHAR_LENGTH(CONCAT('PYTHON','PROGRAMMING'));`
7. `SELECT LCASE(RIGHT('PYTHON PROGRAMMING',10));`
8. `SELECT LPAD(LTRIM('          PYTHON PROGRAMMING'),25,'#');`
9. `SELECT REPEAT(MID('PYTHON PROGRAMMING',7,7),3);`
10. `SELECT RPAD(REVERSE('PYTHON'),15,'@');`
11. Consider the tables given below.
    Employee table:

EmpID	EmpFname	EmpLname	Age	EmailID	PhoneNo	Address
1	Vinay	Lal	22	Vinay12@gmail.com	9976673229	Delhi
2	Hemant	Sharma	32	sharmahemant@gmail.com	9827554567	Mumbai
3	Ayush	Prasad	24	Payush@gmail.com	9134555511	Kolkata
4	Hiten	Mishra	25	Hiten_mishra@gmail.com	9899087612	Bengaluru
5	Anitha	Kumar	26	Kumar_a@gmail.com	9512983405	Hyderabad

Project table:

ProjectID	EmpID	ClientID	ProjectName	ProjectStartDate
101	1	5	Project1	2021-01-21
102	2	1	Project2	2020-09-12
103	3	2	Project3	2021-02-10
104	3	4	Project4	2020-04-30
105	5	2	Project5	2020-02-23
106	9	3	Project6	2021-01-19
107	7	1	Project7	2021-02-25
108	8	3	Project8	2020-08-29

Client table:

ClientID	ClientFname	ClientLname	Age	ClientEmailID	PhoneNo	Address	EmpID
1	Kriti	Juneja	30	kjuneja@gmail.com	9465611739	Kolkata	2
2	Alice	John	27	ajohn@gmail.com	9175546568	Kolkata	3
3	Danish	Ali	22	Ali.danish@gmail.com	9577638511	Delhi	9
4	Zubin	Junjunwala	40	Zubin45@gmail.com	9955123422	Hyderabad	3
5	BV	Reddy	32	bvreddy@gmail.com	9643463239	Mumbai	1

Give the output of the following queries.
a. `SELECT Employee.EmpID, Employee.EmpFname, Employee.EmpLname, Projects.ProjectID, Projects.ProjectName`
   `FROM Employee`
   `INNER JOIN Projects ON Employee.EmpID=Projects.EmpID;`
b. `SELECT Employee.EmpFname, Employee.EmpLname, Projects.ProjectID`
   `FROM Employee`
   `FULL JOIN Projects`
   `ON Employee.EmpID = Projects.EmpID;`
c. `SELECT Employee.EmpFname, Employee.EmpLname, Projects.ProjectID, Projects.ProjectName`
   `FROM Employee`
   `LEFT JOIN`
   `ON Employee.EmpID = Projects.EmpID ;`
d. `SELECT Employee.EmpFname, Employee.EmpLname, Projects.ProjectID, Projects.ProjectName`
   `FROM Employee`
   `RIGHT JOIN`
   `ON Employee.EmpID = Projects.EmpID;`

12. Consider the given tables and give the output of:
   a. `A Union B`
   b. `A - B`

Table A		Table B	
Column 1	Column 2	Column 1	Column 2
1	1	1	1
1	2	1	3

Answers

Fill in the Blanks

1. client-server
2. Meta-data
3. Data Definition
4. char
5. Operator
6. UNIQUE
7. MID()
8. SHOW DATABASES
9. remove
10. CREATE TABLE
11. DESC
12. INSERT INTO
13. SELECT
14. SELECT DISTINCT
15. WHERE BETWEEN
16. AS
17. IS NULL
18. FOREIGN
19. FOREIGN KEY
20. relation
21. SELECT
22. row
23. relation
24. Cardinality
25. Intersection

State True or False

1. False
2. False
3. False
4. True
5. False
6. True
7. False
8. False
9. True
10. False
11. True
12. True
13. False
14. False
15. True
16. False
17. True
18. False
19. False
20. True
21. True
22. False
23. False
24. True
25. True
26. False

Multiple Choice Questions

1. d
2. b
3. a
4. a
5. b
6. d
7. c
8. c
9. c
10. b
11. a
12. c
13. a

Give the Output

1. -5
2. 14
3. 1
4. 169
5. 1
6. 17
7. rogramming
8. #######PYTHON
   PROGRAMMING
9. PROGRA PROGRA PROGRA
10. NOHTYP@@@@@@@@

Computer Networks

5

Chapter Objectives

These days, a single computer in isolation is not of much use. To make use of a computer to its full strength, you must connect it with other computer(s). When two or more computers are connected to each other, they communicate with each other to share each other's resources. This is where a computer network comes into picture.

We cannot even imagine our day without the Internet today. This statement, in itself, is sufficient to reveal the importance of a computer's network in today's scenario. In this chapter, we will therefore learn about the following topics in detail:

- Need of a computer network
- Types of computer network
- Network structure
- Network protocols
- Network devices
- Key network technologies
- Static and dynamic websites
- Web servers
- Web hosting services
- Web browsers – Settings, Add-ons and Plug-ins
- HTTP cookies

5.1 INTRODUCTION

A computer communication network or a computer network or a network, as it is simply known as, is a **collection of computers and devices interconnected to facilitate sharing of resources (printer, CD-ROM), information and electronic documents among interconnected devices** (Fig. 5.1). The advantages of interconnecting computing devices include:

File Sharing: It facilitates the sharing and access of files that are stored on a remote computer. Users can sit at their workstation and easily view the files stored on other computers that are connected to the same network, provided they are authorized to do so. This saves the time required to copy a file from one system to another, by using a storage device like pen drive or a CD-ROM.

Figure 5.1 Network-connecting devices

Moreover, users can access or update the information stored in a database, keeping it up-to-date and accurate. Hence, network file sharing is more flexible than using pen drives or optical drives (like CD, DVD or Blu Ray). It allows users to share photos, music files, and documents with other users.

> File sharing allows multiple users to work together on the same project.

Resource Sharing: It facilitates users to share the limited and otherwise expensive resources among a number of computing devices. For example, in your computer lab there may be 30 computers but only one or two have printers. In order to allow every computer to use the printer, there are two options. First, to buy an individual printer for every computer; and second, to connect the already available printers to all the computers in the lab via a network.

Increased Storage Capacity: A number of computers attached to the network enable sharing of files. Files stored on one computer can be easily accessed by another computer. A stand-alone computer may have limited storage capacity but when several computers are connected, the memory of all the computers can be used.

Increased Cost Efficiency: The software available in the market are costly and take time for installation. Computer network is a feasible solution as it allows software to be stored or installed on one computer and then be shared among other computers connected on the same network.

Load Sharing: If one computer is designated to carry out all the jobs, then it is very likely that the computer will slowdown thereby taking hours to complete all the jobs. So, a better option is to transfer extra jobs to another machine (connected on the same network) for execution. This drastically improves the performance of the system.

Facilitate Communications: Using a network, users can communicate efficiently and easily through email and instant messaging thereby allowing users to pass important messages in a speedy manner without wasting paper

5.1.1 Limitations of Computer Network

However, on the downside, there are also a few problems associated with networking:

- If the server fails, the application cannot be accessed
- If the server fails, it can lead to data loss
- The server, if hacked, can lead to misuse of data
- When the number of computers and computing devices exceed the permissible number, the performance and efficiency of the system can decrease considerably.
- Network management is a difficult and tedious job.

5.2 TYPES OF NETWORK

There are different types of computer networks that are widely used, both in homes and business. These networks vary in terms of their scale, scope, design and implementation. In this section we will read about these types of networks which include: LAN, WAN, MAN, CAN and PAN. Of these, LAN and WAN are the original categories of area networks and the others have gradually emerged over many years with advancement in technology.

5.2.1 LAN – Local Area Network

LAN supports communication between two computers or more computers/computing devices in a limited geographical area such as home, school, computer laboratory, office building, or closely positioned group of buildings. Owing to limited scope and cost of operation, LANs (Fig. 5.2) are typically owned, controlled, and managed by a single person or organization.

These days, most of the wired LANs are based on Ethernet technology. In such LANs, computers are connected using cables (like coaxial cables, twisted pair, fiber optic). LANs can also be wireless. Such LANs use radio waves for communication.

LANs are preferred area networks because they have higher data transfer rates, smaller geographic range, and there is no need for leased telecommunication lines.

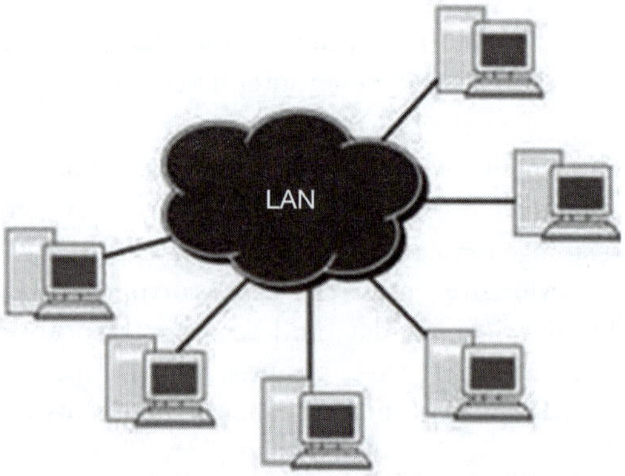

Figure 5.2 Local Area Network

5.2.2 WAN – Wide Area Network

WANs span a large geographic area such as a city, country, or even intercontinental distances, (as shown in Fig. 5.3) using a communication channel that combines many types of media such as telephone lines, cables, and air waves. A WAN often uses transmission facilities provided by common carriers, such as telephone companies. WAN can be created by linking LANs together.

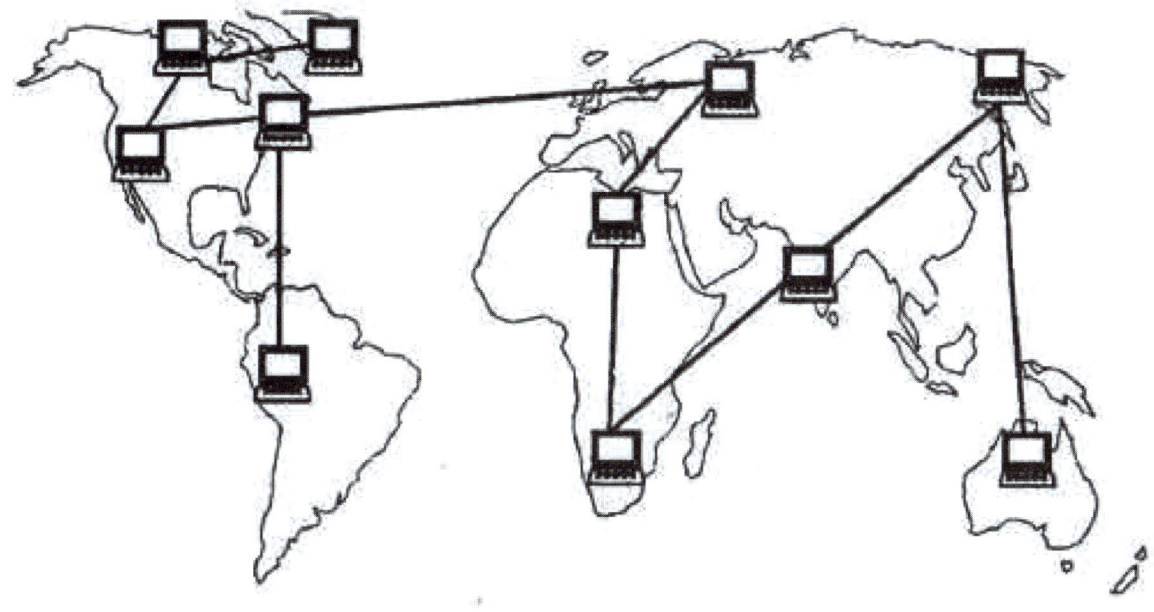

Figure 5.3 Wide Area Network

When individual networks connect together to form a larger network (or a bigger WAN), the resulting network is called an **internetwork**, *generically abbreviated to 'an internet'. Moreover, when WANs from all over the world connect to form a global internet, it is called* **The Internet**. The Internet is therefore, the largest WAN, spanning the Earth.

A WAN is a geographically dispersed collection of LANs. A LAN can be easily connected to a WAN by using a special network device called *router*. WAN and LAN can be easily distinguished from each other in several important ways. Most WANs (like the Internet) are not owned by any one individual or organization. Rather, they exist under collective or distributed ownership and management.

The Internet is a public WAN, but organizations can also form private WAN which is basically two or more LANs connected to each other. For example, a company with offices in Delhi Kolkata, Chennai and Mumbai having a LAN setup at each office can connect their LANs through leased telephone lines, thereby forming a WAN. Table 5.1 highlights the underlying difference between a LAN and a WAN.

Table 5.1 Difference between LAN and WAN

LAN	WAN
• Covers a restricted geographical area • Usually confined to a single or very few buildings • Owned and controlled by a single person or organization • Higher data transmission rate ranging from 10Mbps to 1 Gbps • Lower error rate • Comparatively less cost is involved in its deployment • Devices are physically connected by coaxial or fiber optic cable	• Covers a wider geographical area • Installed nationwide and/or world wide • Owned and controlled collectively • Data transmission rate is comparatively slower • Error rate is higher • High costs involved in its setup • Devices are connected through telephone lines, microwave links or satellite links

5.2.3 MAN – Metropolitan Area Network

MAN is a network that interconnects computers and other devices in a geographic area or region larger than that covered by LAN but smaller than that covered by a WAN. A MAN (Fig. 5.4) may interconnect networks in a city or a campus or a community to form a single larger network (which may then be connected to a WAN). MAN may be formed by interconnecting several LANs by bridging them with backbone lines with the help of fiber optical cables. In areas where cabling is not possible, wireless alternatives like microwave, radio, or infra-red laser links are used to connect two or more LANs.

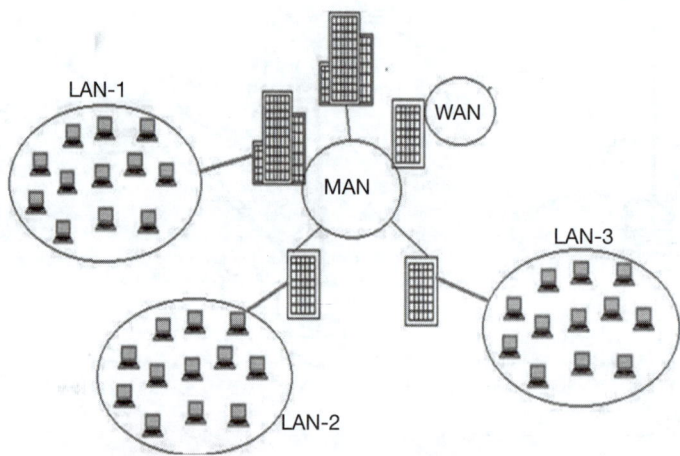

Figure 5.4 Metropolitan Area Network

A MAN can be distinguished from a LAN or WAN in the following ways:

1. The size of the network varies in between that of a LAN and WAN. MAN typically covers an area of between 5 and 50 km range. MANs can cover area as small as a group of buildings to an area the size of a city.
2. MAN (like WAN) is usually not owned by a single individual or an organization. It is generally owned by either a consortium of users or by a network service provider who sells the service to the users.
3. MAN is a high-speed network that allows sharing of regional resources.

Though MAN is not a very widely used area network, it has its own importance for some government bodies and organizations on larger scale.

5.2.4 CAN – Campus Area Network or Corporate Area Network

CAN is a computer network created by interconnecting LANs within a limited geographical area. The network is almost entirely owned by the campus of an enterprise, university, government, military bases, etc (as shown in Fig. 5.5). The size of the area that CAN covers is larger than that of LAN and smaller than that of MAN or WAN.

For example, in case of a university having multiple labs or multiple buildings, it is called the Campus Area Network and in case of an organization with multiple offices or multiple departments in the buildings it is termed as the corporate area network.

These days, CANs are mostly formed using wireless communication mediums rather than cabling and wirings because wireless communication has become more economical than the use of long wires and cables. CANs are economical, beneficial and easy to implement in specific areas of a locality.

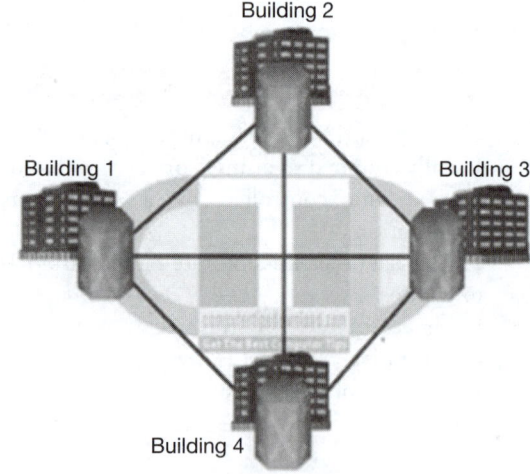

Figure 5.5 Campus Area Network

Therefore, they are widely used by universities and other corporate organizations to work from any block and receive the same speed of data transfer.

5.2.5 PAN – Personal Area Network

PAN is a computer network designed for communication between computer devices like mobile computers, cell phones and PDAs that are close to one person. The scope or the reach of PAN is a few meters (less than 10 meters). PANs are basically used to communicate with the personal devices themselves or for connecting to a higher-level network and the Internet. PANs can either be wired with computer buses such as USB and FireWire or be wireless with network technologies such as Infra-red and Bluetooth. Bluetooth PANs are also called **piconets**.

PANs can be used to transfer files (including email and calendar appointments), digital photos and music. Users can connect their smart TV to the Internet and then download and watch a movie or their favourite serial using PAN.

These days PANs are also used to enable wearable computer devices to communicate with other nearby computers and exchange digital information. Interestingly, even the clothes of a person can be used to transfer the data.

5.3 NETWORK DEVICES

There are three main devices that may be used to connect one computer to another computer. These devices are the hub, switch, and router. To understand which device to use when, we will read about them in detail in this section.

5.3.1 MODEM (MOdulator DEModulator)

A modem is a hardware device that allows a computer to send and receive data over a telephone line or a cable or satellite connection. Earlier, when dial-up connection was used by most Internet users, the modem was used to convert digital data coming from the computer into analog data (in the form of waves) which could be sent the telephone lines. At the receiving end, the modem converted the analog signals coming from telephone lines into digital data that the computer could understand (as shown in Fig. 5.6).

> There are seven layers in the OSI model.

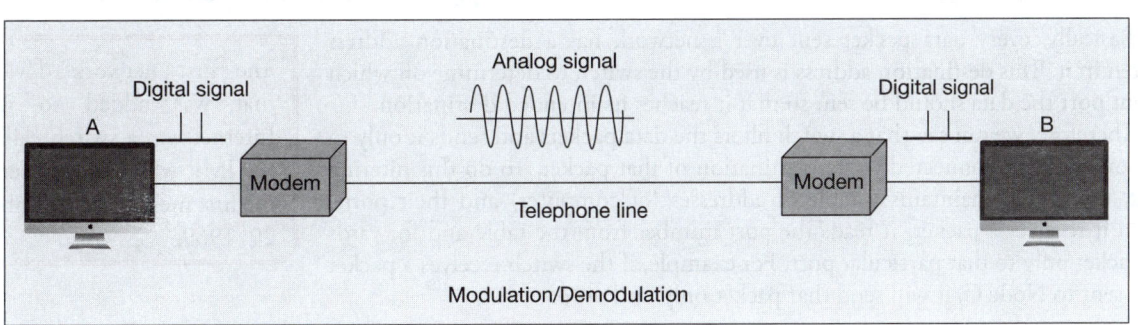

Figure 5.6 MODEM

Therefore, MODEM is the short form of Modulator Demodulator. Modulation is the process of converting digital data (coming from the sending computer) into an analog signal. At the receiving end we have demodulation, which takes an analog signal and turns it back into a digital data that can be read by the receiving computer.

However, these days most people use high-speed broadband connection to access the Internet. In such a scenario, the work of a modem (also known as a broadband modem) has become much simpler as it is no longer required to perform analog-to-digital conversion.

Broadband modems transfer data at a faster speed and do not interfere with phone calls.

Other Types of Modem

Cellular modems establish internet connectivity between a mobile device and a cell phone network.

Cable modems send and receive data over standard cable television lines. Modern cable modems provide an efficient way of transmitting TV, cable Internet, and digital phone signals over the same cable line.

Onboard Modems are the modems which are built onto the computer motherboard. Though onboard modems cannot be removed, they can be disabled easily.

Speed: The speed of a modem is measured in Bits Per Second (bps) or Kilo Bits per Second (kbps). Speed signifies the number of bits that a modem can send or receive in one second. While the speed of the fastest dial-up modem is 56 kbps, the speed of broadband modems is higher.

5.3.2 Switch

A switch is a high-speed network device that is used to connect multiple computers. Switches are usually small, flat boxes with 4 to 8 ports. Through these ports, one can connect computers, modems, and even other switches (refer Fig. 5.7). A high-end switch may have more than 50 ports.

A switch receives incoming data packets and sends them to their destination on a local area network (LAN). A switch operates at the data link layer (Layer 2) or the network layer of the OSI Model.

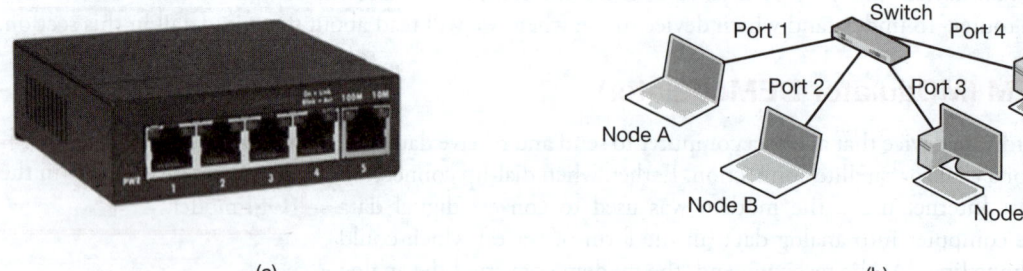

Figure 5.7 (a) Switch; (b) Computers connected through ports on a switch to form a network

Basically, every data packet sent over a network has a destination address written in it. This destination address is used by the switch to determine on which output port the data should be sent so that it reaches its intended destination.

Therefore, we can say that a switch filters the data packets and sends it only to the port which is connected to the destination of that packet. To do this filtering work, the switch maintains a table of addresses (of computer) and their ports. When it receives a packet, it reads the port number from the table and forwards the packet only to that particular port. For example, if the switch receives a packet to be sent to Node C, it will send that packet only on Port 3.

> The first network device that was added to the Internet was a switch called the IMP, which helped send the first message on October 29, 1969.

5.3.3 Repeater

Repeaters are network devices that work at first layer of the OSI Model. Its function is to amplify or regenerate an incoming signal before retransmitting it. This helps a network to cover a larger area. Repeaters are also known as signal boosters.

Need for a Repeater

When an electrical signal is transmitted through a communication channel, it gets attenuated (or distorted). Although the amount of attenuation will depend on the type of communication channel and technology being used, it will always be there. This attenuation poses restrictions to the area covered by the network. To cater to this problem, repeaters are installed at certain intervals.

> Digital repeaters can even reconstruct signals distorted by transmission loss.

Repeaters amplify the attenuated signal and then retransmits it. So, repeaters can also be used to connect two LANs to form a single LAN as shown in Fig. 5.8.

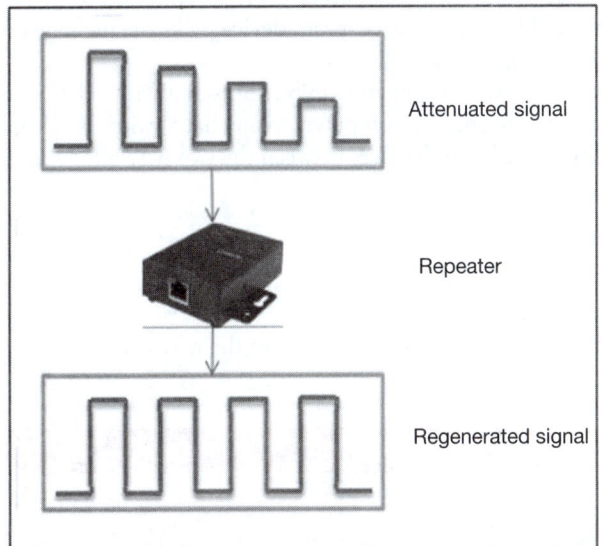
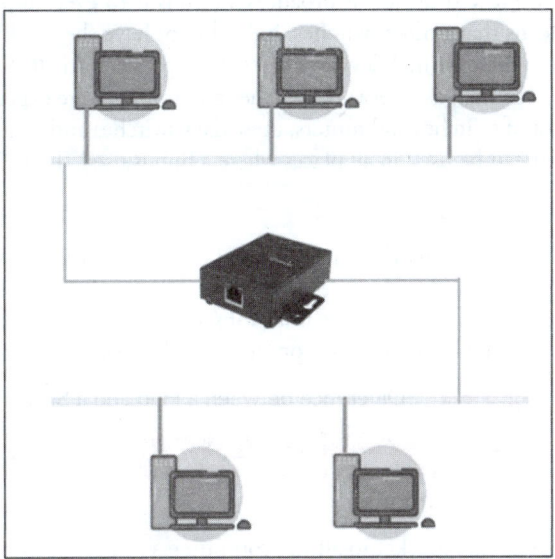

Figure 5.8 (a) Repeater regenerating the input signal; (b) Repeater connecting networks

Types of Repeaters

According to the types of signals regenerated, repeaters can be classified into two categories.
Analog Repeaters that can only amplify only an analog signal.
Digital Repeaters that can reconstruct a distorted signal.
According to the types of networks that they connect, repeaters can also be categorized as wired or wireless.
Wired Repeaters connect wired LANs.
Wireless Repeaters that connect wirelessly are used in wireless LANs and cellular networks.

Advantages of Repeaters

- Repeaters can be easily installed.
- They extend the length or the coverage area of networks.
- They are less expensive as compared to any other network device.
- Repeaters do not have any processing overhead.
- They can regenerate signals from different types of cables.

Disadvantages of Repeaters

- Repeaters cannot connect dissimilar networks.
- They cannot differentiate between actual signal and noise.
- They do nothing to manage traffic on the network.
- Most networks can deploy only a limited number of repeaters.

5.3.4 Hub

A hub, also known as a network hub, is a device that is used to connect computers, printers, servers, or other devices so that they can communicate with each other. Like a switch, a hub has many ports through with multiple devices can be connected to it. A typical hub has 4–24 ports (Fig. 5.9).

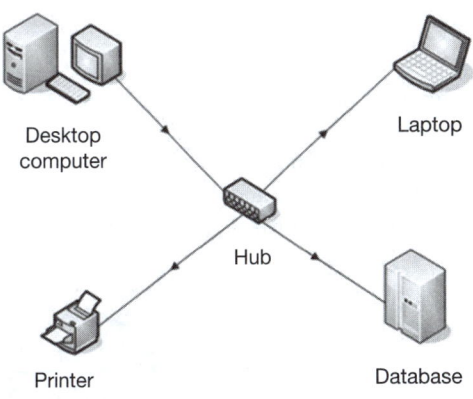

Figure 5.9 Network hub

Every computer on the network is directly connected with the hub. Hubs are usually used for a private or small and simple network (typically LAN) which is not connected to the Internet. When a hub receives a packet of data from a connected device, it broadcasts (sends it to every device) that data packet to all other devices connected to it. This means that unlike switches, hubs do not have the intelligence to filter data. Hence, every device picks the message but only the destined device processes the packet and all the other computers just discard it.

In the past, network switches and routers were expensive. So, most users preferred to buy hubs but with a decline in cost of switches and routers, these days switches and routers are used to connect computers. Note that a switch is a device that can be used in all places where a hub is used. Table 5.2 lists some key differences between the two network devices.

Applications of Hub

- Hubs are used to create small Home Networks.
- Hubs are used to monitor networks.
- Hubs are used in organizations and computer labs to connect computers.
- It enables a computer or any other hardware device to be available to all other devices on the network.

Table 5.2 Difference between a Hub and a Switch

Hub	Switch
Cannot filter traffic.	Filters traffic.
Sends data packet to all the computers connected to it.	Sends data packet only to the computer for which it was intended.
Cheaper than switches.	Costly
Slower performance.	Performance is higher than hub.
Hubs are also known as dumb switches	Switches are also known as smart hubs.
Works at Layer 1 of OSI Model.	Works at Layer 2 of OSI Model.
No data security as everyone receives it.	Data security is ensured as only the intended destination receives the data.

A USB hub is a device that allows multiple devices to connect through a single USB port. It is designed to increase the number of USB devices that can be connected to a computer. For example, if your computer has two USB ports, and you want to connect five USB devices, then you can connect a 4-port USB hub to one of the ports. The hub will create four ports out of one, giving you five total ports. With this hub, you can connect up to 127 devices to a single computer.

5.3.5 Router

Router is a network device that connects multiple computer networks together using either wired or wireless connections. It works at layer 3 of the OSI model and moves data from one network to the other.

A router (as shown in Fig. 5.10) is an intelligent device that routes data to destination computers. It is used to connect two logically and physically different networks, two LANs, two WANs, and a LAN with a WAN. Routers use special software known as routing table that stores the addresses of devices connected to the network.

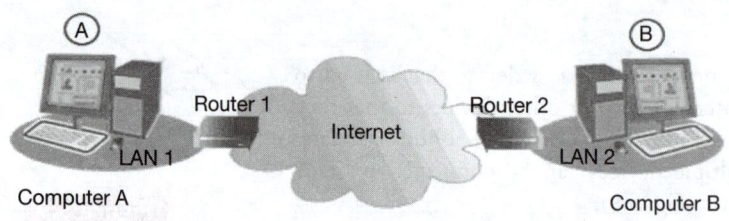

Figure 5.10 Router connecting computers over the Internet

Wireless Routers, also known as Wi-Fi routers or Travel routers, are used by people and families who want to use the functions of a router at other locations besides home. Wireless routers connect to the modem and create a wireless signal in home or office. So, any computer within range can connect to the wireless router and use broadband Internet.

> Routing devices called mobile hotspots share a mobile (cellular) Internet connection with Wi-Fi clients.

How a Router Works

To reach your school from your home, there may be more than one route. But which route do you take depends on factors like shortest distance, traffic on that route, whether that route is safe, etc. as shown in Fig. 5.11. Similarly, when we send data packets for a computer on the Internet, there may be several paths available to reach that computer. But it is the router which evaluates all the routes and forwards the packet on the best possible route.

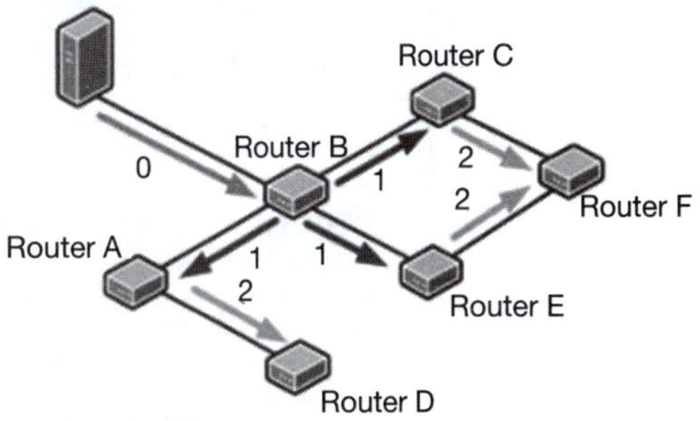

Routers have a small memory that stores an embedded operating system. It maintains a table in its memory (also known as **Routing Table**) that contains information about the available routes and their conditions (like traffic on that route, cost involved, etc). This information is then used to determine the best route for a given packet.

Figure 5.11 Routers find the best path for data delivery

Thus, a router has a lot more capabilities than other network devices (like hub and switch). Note that, if you just want to form a LAN, then you may either use a switch or a hub. But if you want to connect two or more LANs or any other network among themselves or to the Internet, then you must have a router.

There are several companies that make routers include Cisco, Linksys, Juniper, Netgear, Nortel (Bay Networks), Redback, Lucent, 3Com, HP, Dlink, and Belkin, to name a few.

5.3.6 Gateway

Gateway is a device that joins two networks using different protocols (set of rules followed for data transmission). It works on the 7th layer and in fact any layer of the OSI model since a device working at a higher layer supports functionalities for all the lower layers as well. For example, a device at Layer 3 can perform functions for Layers 1, 2 as well as of Layer 3. Similarly, a device at Layer 7 can be used to provide functions for all seven layers in the OSI model.

The most common gateway is a router that connects a home or enterprise network to the internet. When two networks are connected, devices on one network can communicate with the devices on another network.

A gateway can be implemented completely in software, hardware, or in a combination of both (Fig. 5.12).

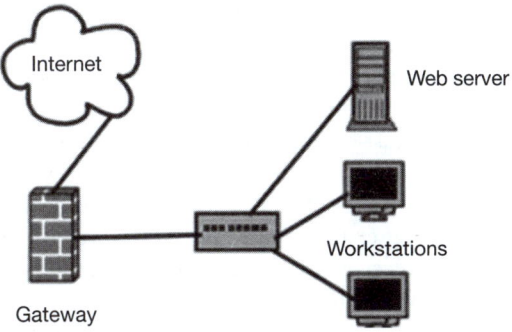

Figure 5.12 (a) Gateway connecting computers over the Internet

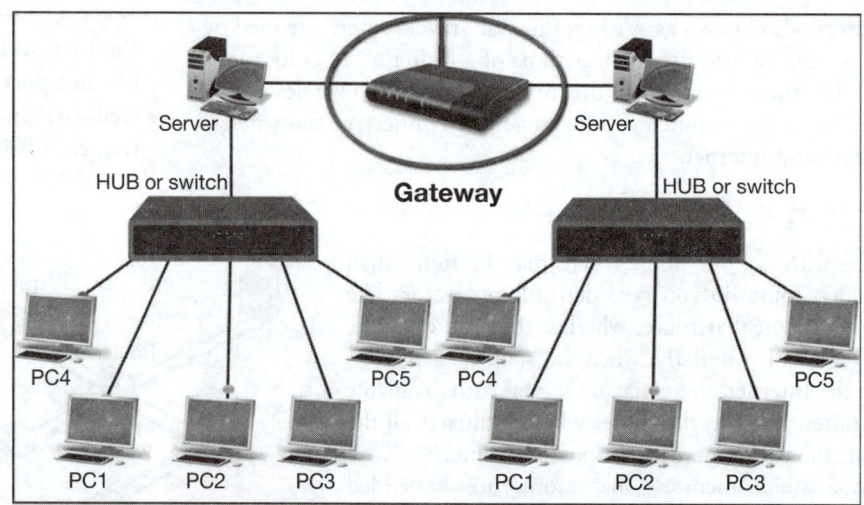

Figure 5.12 (b) Gateway connecting two networks

When to Use a Router and When to Use a Gateway

Routers connect two networks using the same protocol. Gateways connect two networks using different protocols. If two networks that follow the same protocol are to be connected, then a router is enough.

As you see in Fig. 5.12, gateways serve as the entry and exit point of a network. All data that comes inside a network or goes out of the network has to first pass through the gateway.

At your home, whether you have a wired Internet connection or wireless, your modem acts as a gateway for you as it is connected with the router or the gateway device of the ISP which provides you Internet access.

> Like the router, the gateway also decides the best possible path to send data packets.

5.3.7 Wi-Fi Card

You must have observed that whenever you walk around in a public place, your school campus or into a hotel, you ae connected to the internet using a wireless connection. To provide wireless connectivity, Wi-Fi hot spots are scattered throughout the city. These hotspots are usually connected to computers using radio frequencies from a cell phone tower. These computers pick up the radio signal using a wireless Internet card which is also known as the Wi-Fi card. The Wi-Fi card is a small device about the size of a credit card that provides internet capability to laptops, desktops, PDAs and other handheld devices. These days, computers come with one preinstalled wireless card. But for those that did not come with such a card, one can always buy and install it by simply inserting it into a slot (PCI slot, PCI Express slot or USB port) on the side of the computer.

Figure 5.13 Wi-Fi card

The Wi-Fi card (as shown in Fig. 5.13) must be in range of a wireless Internet signal dedicated to the network it is trying to connect. Once connected, the Wi-Fi card acts as both a receiver and transmitter of wireless signal to allow users access the Web with their portable devices. For a wireless network to work, there must be a router which has antennae that enable connectivity. However, the strength of the connectivity totally depends on the quality of radio waves being received at any particular time.

With massive increase in number of Wi-Fi hot spots, the demand for wireless Internet cards has gone up tremendously. Today, everyone wants to share Internet connection and go wireless when moving around the city. Wi-Fi cards are especially very useful in areas where network cables are not available to provide connectivity of various devices.

Computer Networks

5.4 NETWORK TOPOLOGY

A network topology is an arrangement of computers or other computing devices. Topology describes the pattern in which different devices on the network are connected and the way data flows between them. There are different network topologies in use.

5.4.1 Bus Topology

Bus topology is a type of network in which every computer or computing device is connected to single cable as shown in Fig. 5.14. Bus topology is mainly used in cable broadband distribution networks.

Figure 5.14 Bus topology

Advantages of Bus Topology

1. Requires less cost
2. Less cable length required as compared to other network topologies
3. Used in small networks
4. Easy to implement
5. Additional devices can be easily added to the network.

Disadvantages of Bus Topology

1. If there is a fault in the main cable, the entire network fails.
2. Performance of the network decreases with more number of devices.
3. Limited number of devices can be connected to a bus network.
4. Data transmission is usually slower and prone to errors.
5. Data is transmitted only in one direction.

5.4.2 Star Topology

In the star network topology, a central computer, also known as the hub or the server, is directly connected to all other computers or computing devices. In this topology, all data transmission is possible only through the hub (refer Fig. 5.15). For example, if one device has to send data to the other, there is no way for direct data transfer. The sending device sends data to the hub and the hub sends it to the other device.

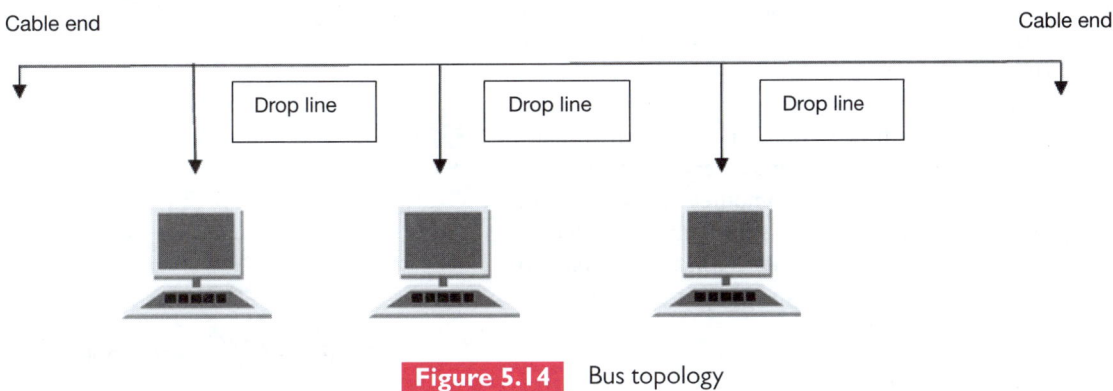

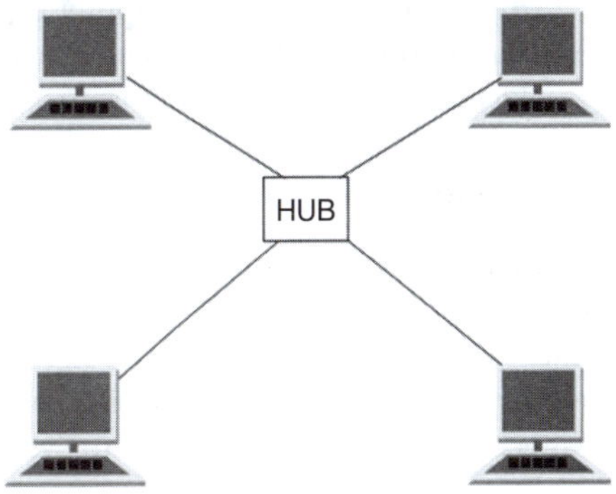

Figure 5.15 Star topology

Advantages of Star Topology

1. Fast performance in a network that has few devices and less data transmission requirements
2. Easy to find and correct errors or failures

3. Easy to set up
4. If a device fails, the network is not affected; it will continue to work smoothly.

Disadvantages of Star Topology

1. Cost of installation is high.
2. If the hub fails, then the entire network fails.
3. Performance of the network depends on the hub's capacity.

5.4.3 Ring Topology

In the ring topology, every computer is connected to two of its neighbours – one on the left and the other on its right, thereby forming a closed loop. The last computer is connected to the first as shown in Fig. 5.16.

In the ring topology, data transfer is unidirectional. This means that data can flow only in one direction (usually clockwise). Data transfer is also slower as every bit of data that is transmitted passes through every computer on the network until it reaches the destination. That is, if Computer 1 has to send data to Computer 4, the Computer 1 will send the data to Computer 2, Computer 2 will send to Computer 3 and finally Computer 3 will send to Computer 4.

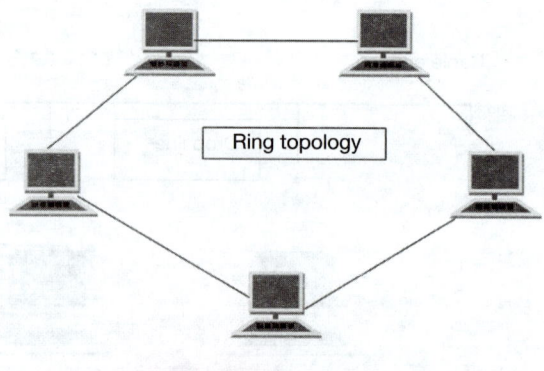

Figure 5.16 Ring topology

Advantages of Ring Topology

1. New devices can be easily added to the network
2. Cheap to install
3. Best suited for networks that do not have a hub
4. More reliable than star topology as the communication does not depend on a single hub
5. Easy to install
6. Can span over larger distances
7. Every node has equal chance to transmit data

Disadvantages of Ring Topology

1. Finding and correcting errors in the network is difficult.
2. Adding or removing a computer disturbs the entire network.
3. If one computer fails, the entire network is affected.
4. Delay in data transmission is directly related to number of devices connected on the network.

5.4.4 Mesh Topology

The mesh network topology links all computers or computing devices (nodes) directly to all other devices on the network (refer Fig. 5.17). Mesh topology creates multiple paths between two devices and provides connectivity even if one or more devices fail. The Internet is a partial mesh network in which every device is directly or indirectly connected to every other device.

Advantages of Mesh Topology

1. Data transmission is very fast as every connection between two devices carries its own data.
2. If one computer fails, the entire network is not affected.

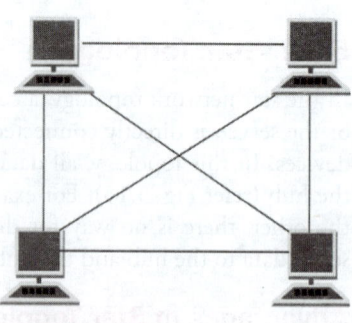

Figure 5.17 Mesh topology

3. Easy to find and correct errors.
4. Provides data security as data is transferred only through the dedicated connection between two devices leaving no scope for any other device to intercept the data.

Disadvantages of Mesh Topology

1. Difficult to install
2. Lot of cables are required, so cabling cost is more
3. It is the most expensive network as, for n nodes, $n \times (n-1)/2$ physical links (cables) are required

5.4.5 Tree Topology

A tree topology is also known as a hierarchical topology because all the computers are connected by forming a hierarchy as shown in Fig. 5.18. This topology has at least three levels to the hierarchy.

The easiest way to understand a tree topology is to visualize it as a *star of stars* network where star topologies are themselves connected in a star configuration. The tree topology is usually used to connect computers in a WAN.

Advantages of Tree Topology

1. New devices can be easily added to the network
2. Easy to manage and maintain the network
3. Finding and correcting faults in the network is easy.

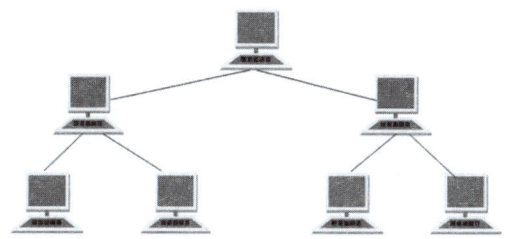

Figure 5.18 Tree topology

Disadvantages of Tree Topology

1. Lot of cabling required; this also increases the cost of the network
2. Difficult to manage when number of devices increases beyond a limit
3. If the central hub fails, the entire network fails.

5.4.6 Hybrid Topology

Hybrid topology is a combination of two or more topologies. For example, in your school if the computers in one lab are connected using bus topology and in the other lab, they are connected using star topology (refer Fig. 5.19), then when we connect the two topologies, a hybrid topology will be formed.

Since hybrid topology is a mixture of two or more topologies, it reaps the advantages of the individual topologies.

Advantages of Hybrid Topology

1. Detecting and correcting errors is easy
2. More effective than other topologies
3. New devices can be easily added
4. More flexible than other topologies.

Disadvantages of Hybrid Topology

1. Complex in design
2. Expensive

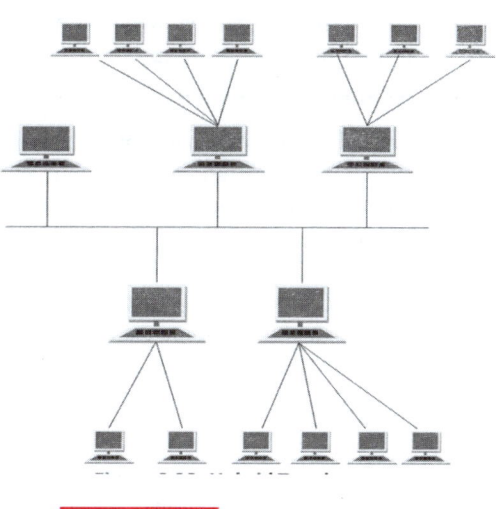

Figure 5.19 Hybrid topology

5.5 INTERNET

The Internet is a global network that connects billions of computers all over the world. It is a network of networks. The Internet links computers in different organizations, academic institutions, government offices, and home to share information among a large group of users.

Each computer on the Internet is called a **host**. To connect to the Internet, the user must gain access through a commercial Internet service provider (**ISP**). The Internet, sometimes known as the Net, allows the users to perform the following functions:

- Connect computers to share a huge pool of information
- Exchange emails
- Converse with other users. This conversation can be text-based, voice-based, video-based, or a combination of all of them.
- Surf websites using a Web browser. The most popular browsers are Microsoft Edge, Opera, Google Chrome, and Mozilla Firefox.

An additional feature of the Internet is that it lacks a central controlling authority. Although there are different governing boards that work to establish policies and standards, the Internet is bound by few rules and answers no single organization. We often interchange the terms WWW and Internet. But the two terminologies are not synonymous. Figure 5.20 clearly illustrates the difference between the two terms.

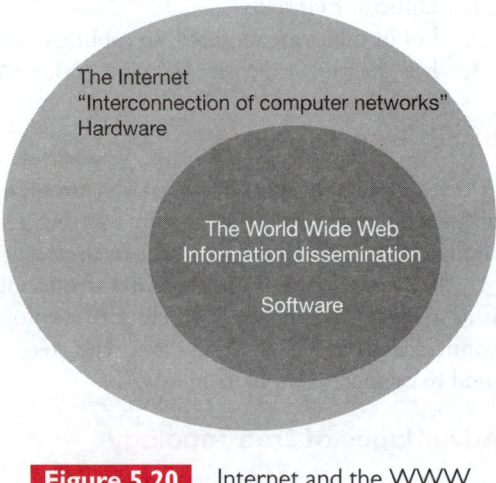

Figure 5.20 Internet and the WWW

5.6 UNIFORM RESOURCE LOCATOR OR UNIVERSAL RESOURCE LOCATOR

A uniform resource locator (URL) specifies the unique address for a file that is accessible on the Internet. It is provided by the user in the address bar. For example, when you type www.google.com, after pressing the Enter key, there is a long sequence of characters in the address bar. This is the URL. This means that to access any page on the Internet, we need to provide its URL.

The file on the Internet that we want to access can be a Web page, an audio file, video file, or image with extensions such as .htm, .php, .mp4, .avi, .jpg, .bmp, .gif, .asp, .cgi, .xml, etc. The syntax for a URL is as follows:

Protocol://domain-name/path

where **Protocol** specifies the name of the protocol to be used to access the file resource. Commonly used protocols are http, https, ftp, telnet, news, gopher, mailto, etc. These fields specify how to connect.

domain name identifies the name of the website. This means that the domain field identifies where to connect.

path is a hierarchical description that indicates the location of the file. It indicates to the web server what to connect.

For example, when we just write **http://www.google.com**, http is the protocol, www.google.com is the domain name, and by default, the home page which is saved as index.htm is displayed to the user. Refer to Fig. 5.21 which shows another sample URL.

Figure 5.21 Components of URL

If we provide the URL as **http://www.example.com/Student/ABC.TXT**, then http is used to fetch the file ABC.TXT from Student directory stored in the computer on which the website www.example.com is hosted.

There are basically two types of URLs as shown in Fig. 5.22. While an absolute URL specifies the complete URL containing all three fields (protocol, domain, and path), relative URLs, on the other hand, contain only one field which is the domain name.

Many a time, you must have observed a complex URL as the one given here, especially when you log in to your email account or search for a string on google.

http://www.google.com/cgi-bin/search.cgi?q=computer%20fundamentals

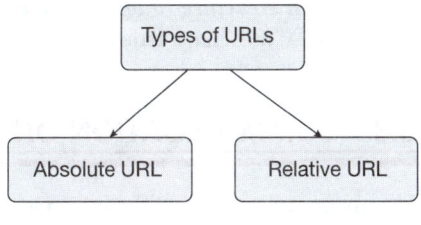

Figure 5.22 Types of URL

Although it seems complex, it is actually very simple to interpret. In the query, http is in the protocol, www.google.com is the domain, and search.cgi is a file in the cgi-bin directory.

Anything following the question mark (?) in a URL is a pair of variable(s) and its value(s). In the URL, q=computer%20fundamentals means that q is a variable name, and computer%20fundamentals is the value of q. Since blank spaces are not allowed in a URL, blank space has been written as %20. Spaces can also be written as a **+**(plus) sign. In the query, the user is trying to search computer fundamentals on Google.

> A domain name is not the same as URL because it is just a small part of the entire URL.

These values are sent by the user's computer to Google's server. Google will find relevant pages and will display the result on the user's screen. Similarly, when we log in to our email account, we supply two values to the server—username and password. In such a situation, multiple variables are separated with an ampersand (&) sign as shown here:

http://www.gmail.com/config/passwd.cgi?u=erree&p=s2ejmd3

In the URL, there are two different variables—u with value erree and p with value s2ejmd3.

5.7 WORLD WIDE WEB

The technical definition of the World Wide Web (WWW) can be given as 'all the resources and users on the Internet that are using the hypertext transfer protocol (HTTP)'. On the Web, all the documents are formatted in a special markup language called Hypertext Markup Language (HTML) that supports links to other documents, graphics, audio, and/or video files. This feature enables users to jump from one document to another, simply by clicking on hot spots.

You must have noted that when you position your cursor on a hotspot, also known as hyperlink, the cursor changes to a hand-shaped figure. When you click on the hyperlink, you are taken to another part of the information. Sometimes, there are buttons, images, or portions of images that can be clicked.

In simple terminology, the WWW is a part of the Internet that allows easy navigation through the use of Graphical User Interfaces (GUIs) and hypertext links between different addresses. The WWW that is simply referred to as Web was created in 1989 by Tim Berners-Lee. The Web can be perceived as the user part of the Internet. Novice or professional users make use of the Web to communicate and access information for business and recreational purposes. Application programs called Web browsers make it easy to access the Web. Some popular Web browsers are Mozilla Firefox, Opera, Google Chrome and Microsoft Edge (refer Fig. 5.23).

Figure 5.23 Popular Web browsers

Many a time, we think that the Internet and the WWW are the same, but this notion is not correct. *The Internet and the Web work together. While the Internet provides the underlying structure, the Web on the other hand, utilizes that structure to offer content, documents, multimedia, etc.* For example, the Internet is like the highway, and the WWW is like a truck that uses the highway to get from one place to another.

5.8 COMMUNICATION ON THE INTERNET

We can communicate on the Internet through emails, chats, Internet (Web) conferencing, etc.

5.8.1 Electronic Mail

Electronic mail, e-mail or email is a piece of information that is exchanged between two users over networks (or even the Internet). An email message may contain text, files, images, or other attachments and can be sent to one or more individuals. The success of email can be estimated by the fact that the first email was sent by Ray Tomlinson in 1971 and in 1996, more electronic mails were exchanged than postal mail.

To send and receive email messages, a user must have a valid email address. The majority of Internet Service Providers provide a free email account to customers but there are several companies (like Gmail, Yahoo) that provide free webmail accounts. Some key benefits of using email include

- Quick, as recipients get it instantly
- Secure, as you are sure that once the email is sent, the intended person will receive it
- Inexpensive, as it is free of cost
- An email can be used to send text messages, pictures, files or other important documents
- One email can be sent to multiple receivers simultaneously
- Messages can be sent 24 × 7, that means at any time of the day
- Sending email is a paperless exchange of information. It saves trees and thus, helps in conserving Nature.

5.8.1.1 Email Addressing

Email addresses use a standard formula. It has two parts that are separated by the @ symbol. The first part of the address identifies the user and the second part consists of the webmail or the ISP that has provided the email facility.

In the first part you can have your real name/nick name or any characters of your choice but for the second part, you do not have an option. For example, gauri_mathew@gmail.com is a valid email address. Here, the part preceding @ symbol identifies the person having the email address and the second part succeeding @ identifies the webmail, that is, gmail in this case.

> The second part of the email address denotes the domain name.

Many people have more than one email address. They keep one for personal use and share it with their friends and families. They share the other for professional use. Many organizations provide their own email service to the employees. Therefore, you must have seen that in the second part, the name of the company is there. For example, an employee working at Google may an email address as abc@google.com.

Rules to Form a Valid E-Mail Address: To form a valid email address, you must keep in mind the following points while specifying the username (or the first) part of the email address.

- The username cannot be longer than 64 characters.
- The domain name cannot be longer than 254 characters.
- Uppercase and lowercase letters can be used.
- Digits 0 to 9 can be used.
- The email address must contain exactly one @ sign.
- Space and special characters: ( ) , : ; < > \ [ ] are allowed. But as a good practice, you must not use them.
- The username and e-mail addresses, as a whole, cannot begin or end with a dot sign (.) also known as a period.
- The username cannot have two or more consecutive periods.

5.8.1.2 Mailbox: Inbox and Outbox

Every email address or account has a mailbox. Mailbox is the container which stores all the emails that are sent and received using that email account. For this, it has a few folders like Sent, Receive, Junk, Spam or Delete.

- **Inbox:** Inbox is the folder in which all the incoming emails (emails that are received) are stored and can be accessed. All the email messages received are displayed in a tabular form and sorted according to the date.
- **Outbox:** Outbox is the folder in which all the emails sent are stored temporarily when it is not fully sent. This means that Outbox keeps the email which is pending to be delivered and not sent because of any reason like non-availability of Internet connection, etc.
- **Draft:** It is the folder in which email messages that are composed (or written) but not sent or queued to be sent, are stored. For example, you may write an email to a friend but not send it because of some reason (like you may not have finished writing it) will be saved for future use in the Drafts folder.
- **Junk:** It is the folder in which all fake and spam kinds of email messages are stored. Such messages may contain mails that contain virus, malware, spyware or malicious programs that are capable of stealing data. The email client application analyzes all the received email messages and then sorts out which to put in Inbox and which to junk.
- **Sent Items:** It is the folder that stores all the email messages that were successfully delivered.
- **Deleted Items:** It is the folder that stores all the email messages that have been deleted so that you can reuse, send, forward or print them if the need arises.

To better understand these folders, let us put this way. Outbox and Drafts are the folders where outgoing email messages are *temporarily* stored. While you are writing a message, it is automatically saved in drafts. When you click the Send button, two things can happen. Either the message is delivered successfully to the receiver or it is not delivered. In the former case, the message is stored in Sent and in the latter case, the message is shifted to the Outbox folder.

5.8.2 Chatting

Internet chatting is a very popular service of the Internet that allows two or more online users to come together to talk using an instant messenger. Chatting helps users to stay connected with their concerned people in business or family, who may live many miles apart. Though chatting can be fun and entertaining, users must take protective measures to avoid internet stalkers and predators.

However, to chat with users on the Internet, every user must have an account with a username and password to enter the website. Chatting involves the exchange of typed-in messages between a group of users who take part from anywhere on the Internet. The chatting program also enables the users to arrange a private chat between two parties who met initially in a group chat.

These days, even the business organizations are using chatting services to host online business meetings, or to answer any queries of customers or provide them online support and assistance.

Whether a business chat or a personal chat, it can be ongoing or scheduled for a particular time and duration. Most chats are focused on a particular topic of interest and some involve guest experts or celebrities to talk to other online people who want to join the chat.

5.8.3 Internet Conferencing

The evolution of the internet has changed the way in which business houses arrange conferences among the concerned parties. These days, organizations are increasingly switching to Internet conferencing to reduce the extra costs involved in travelling and making telephone calls, thereby resulting in better time management and enhanced productivity.

Internet conferencing is quite similar to traditional teleconferencing. However, during an Internet conference call, the participants will sit at their respective offices while being connected to each other through the Internet. This is shown in Fig. 5.24. Many Internet conferencing software allows unlimited number of users to participate in Web meetings.

Figure 5.24 Internet conferencing

Today, there are a number of software available on the Internet that can be easily downloaded to host a conference call at little or no cost. To start an Internet conference call, the users need a computer with an Internet connection, related software, a webcam and a microphone (to see and hear what the remote or distant participants are saying). During the conference, users can share information, files, video, and audio clips.

Internet conferencing has taken virtual meetings (because users are not present at the same place) to a new level. This Internet service is increasingly being used to collaborate with various teams in a company, to deliver presentations, to host small-scale or large-scale seminars, to connect with technical support, and so on. The advantages of Internet conferencing are multiple and aid small and established business alike.

5.9 VOICE OVER INTERNET PROTOCOL (VOIP)

VoIP is a technology that allows users to make voice calls using a broadband Internet connection instead of a regular (or analog) phone line. Users can talk to anyone having Internet connection or at least a telephone number, be it local, long distance, or an international number.

> VoIP (voice over IP) is the transmission of voice and multimedia content over Internet Protocol (IP) networks.

5.9.1 How VoIP / Internet Voice Works

VoIP services converts our (analog) voice into a digital signal that can be sent over the Internet. However, if a user is calling another person's regular phone number, the signal is converted to a regular telephone signal before it reaches the destination.

VoIP allows users to make a call directly from their computer, a special VoIP phone, or a traditional phone connected to a special adapter. Moreover, wireless hot spots in airports, parks, cafes, etc., allow them to connect to the Internet and use VoIP service wirelessly.

5.9.2 What Kind of Equipment Do I Need?

To use VoIP services, we need to have the following components (refer Fig. 5.25).

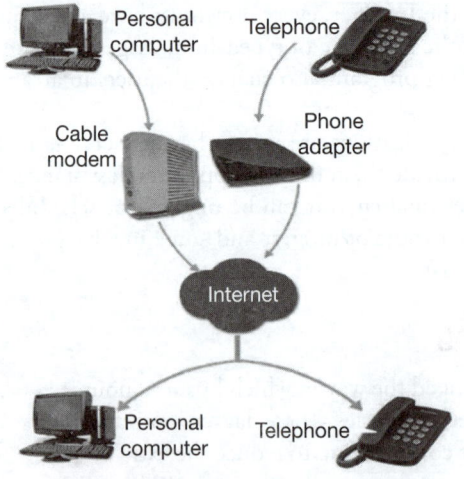

Figure 5.25 Components of VoIP setup

A broadband high-speed **Internet connection** is required.

A **computer** (or even a smartphone), **adaptor**, or **specialized phone** for making calls. When using computer, some software and an inexpensive microphone is also required. Special VoIP phones plug directly into the broadband connection and operate like a traditional telephone. When using a traditional telephone with a VoIP adapter, you just need to dial the number. The service provider may also provide a dial tone.

Once we have the required set-up, we can make a local or long-distance call using our equipment. The increasing usage of VoIP can be easily understood from the graph given in Fig. 5.26, which shows the market size of VoIP applications from the year 2014 to 2024. (*Sources:* Statista estimates; grand view research.)

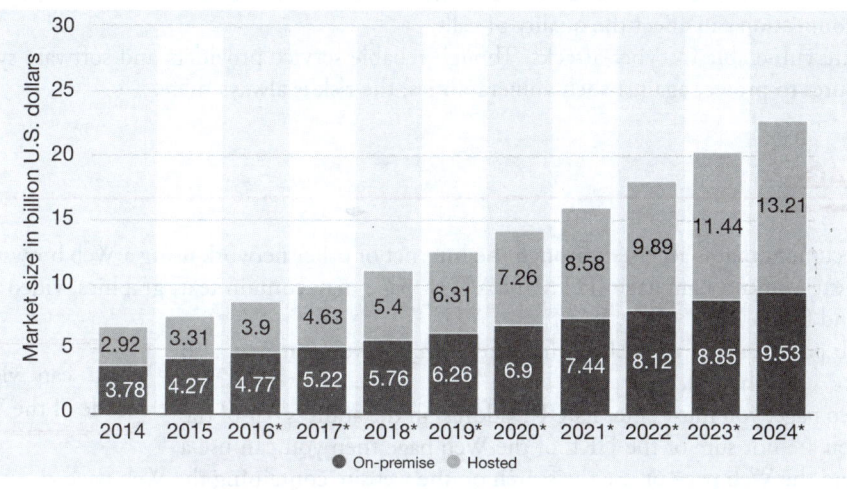

Figure 5.26 Market size of VoIP applications

5.9.3 Advantages of VoIP

Users can access features and services that are not available with a traditional phone, or are available but only for an additional fee.

Users do not need to pay for both broadband connection and a traditional telephone line.

VoIP applications integrate voice, video and text chat. Apple's FaceTime, Zoom, Google Meet and WhatsApp are all examples of VoIP applications.

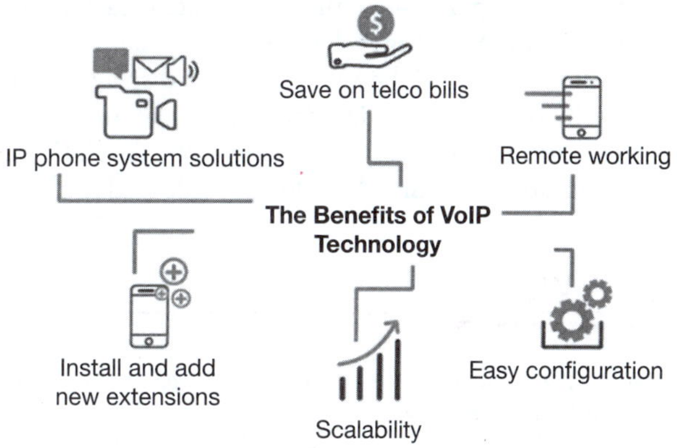

- VoIP applications allow users to place a conference call involving more than one user simultaneously. This makes VoIP systems much more scalable.
- Services that are usually charged by telecommunication companies like call forwarding, caller ID or automatic redialling, are offered for free using VoIP technology.
- A VoIP system provides significant cost savings over a traditional phone system. Users can make free national and international calls and also avail other services.
- Organizations can enhance their relationship with customers by providing them free 24×7 customer support services.
- Co-ordinating with remote workers has become much easier with VoIP systems.
- Fax machines are now outdated, but still VoIP offers fax to email services for those who still prefer to use it.
- The infrastructure is less expensive and the system can be setup very easily.
- With a high-speed broadband Internet connection, a good VoIP service can provide excellent call quality with very little downtime.

Figure 5.27 Benefits of VoIP

Figure 5.27 summarizes the key benefits of VoIP technology.

5.9.4 Disadvantages of VoIP

- Some VoIP services do not work during power outages. The service provider also does not offer backup power.
- If users do not have high-speed internet connection then VoIP is of limited use.
- Poor internet connection can affect the quality of calls.
- VoIP services are vulnerable to cyber-attacks. Though reliable service providers and software systems implement tools and measures to protect against such vulnerabilities, the risk is always there.

5.10 WEB PAGE

A Web page is a document that is accessed through the Internet or other network using a Web browser. It is commonly written in HyperText Markup Language (HTML). A Web page may contain text, graphics, video and hyperlinks to other Web pages and files.

Usually, a Web page has a .htm or .html file extension. However, it may also have extensions like .cgi, .php, .pl,, etc.

> You can view the source code of the Web page.

To access a Web page, you must enter its URL address in the address bar of the Web browser. If you are not sure of the URL of the Web page then you can use a search engine to find the Web page or use the search on the website containing the Web page.

> The first Web page was created at CERN by Tim Berners-Lee on August 6, 1991. You can visit and browse the first website and first Web page at the http://info.cern.ch/ address.

Web pages can be either static or dynamic.

Static Web pages show the same content each time they are viewed.

Dynamic Web pages have content that can change each time they are accessed. For example, the Web pages that display date, time, current temperature, availability of seats in a train or flight, etc., fall under this category. Dynamic Web pages are written using scripting languages like PHP, Perl, ASP, or JSP. However, the information is returned as HTML code so that the browser can easily display them on the user's screen.

> A Web page is an individual document on a website.

5.11 WEBSITE

A website is a collection of related Web pages. It may contain one or more Web pages. In fact, a website may even have thousands of Web pages.

To access a website, we must enter its URL in the address bar of the Web browser. When no particular Web page is mentioned in the URL, the home page or the index page which is stored as index.htm is displayed on the screen by default. If you remember, home page is the first page or the starting page of a website.

However, to refer to a particular Web page on a website, the user must enter the complete path of the Web page. We have learnt in the previous sections that name and path of the file is mentioned as the last part of the URL (sub directory and filename).

> Any business, government, or person can create a website on the Internet. Today, there are billions of websites on the Internet that have been created by billions of different people.

For example, if we write, www.abc.com then the index.htm page on the abc website is displayed. But if we write www.abc.com/contacts/customer.htm, then the customer.htm Web page stored in the contacts folder is displayed.

A website is stored on a Web server (refer Fig. 5.28). A very large website may be spread over a number of servers in different geographic locations. For example, the website of IBM consists of thousands of files and Web pages that are spread out over many servers across the globe. However, one Web server can also store the files and Web pages of several small websites.

Computer Networks

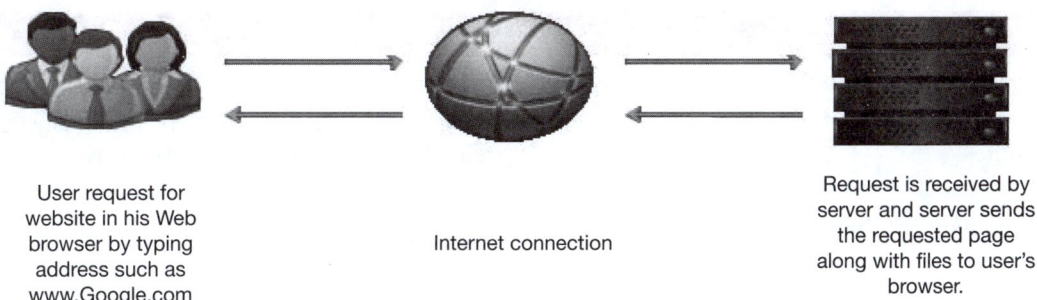

Figure 5.28 Web server stores and sends the requested Web pages

All websites hosted through the Internet constitute the World Wide Web (WWW). To be useful, a website must have well-structured information that is presented in a user friendly look and feel.

> Multiple pages of a large website can be stored on several servers. In contrast, a single server can host pages of several small websites.

5.11.1 Static and Dynamic Websites

Like static Web pages, we have **static websites**. A static website has all static webpages. That is, it has Web pages that always display the same content/information. For example, a company's website that provides details about the company's portfolio, contacts, future projects etc. A static website can be developed by anyone who has a basic knowledge of HTML.

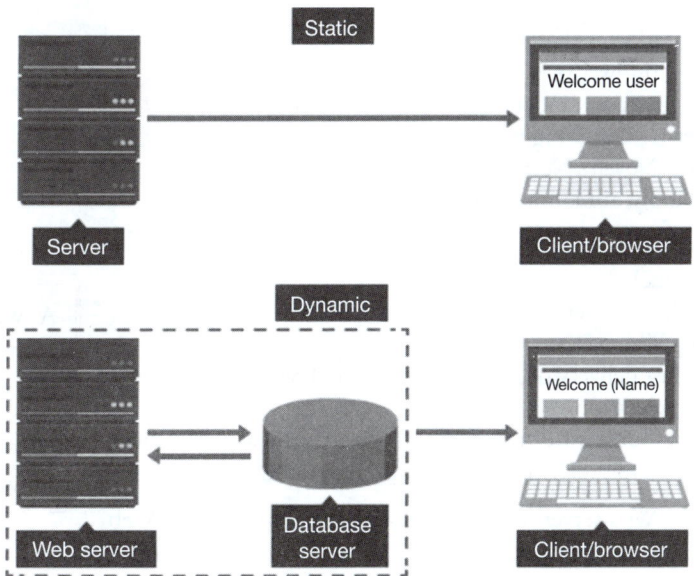

Figure 5.29 Static vs. dynamic websites

Dynamic websites, however, use database (a collection of tables) to store and create information as and when required or requested by the user. The information on a dynamic website changes automatically. Some examples of dynamic website that we frequently use are online shopping, airline/railway reservation, and social networking websites, to name a few. To create a dynamic website, one must know PHP, JSP, Perl, ASP or other technologies. Refer Fig. 5.29 and Table 5.3 to clearly understand the difference between the two types of websites.

Table 5.3 Difference between static and dynamic websites

Static Websites	Dynamic Websites
The same information is displayed always.	Information may change every time the user requests it.
A basic knowledge of HTML is sufficient to develop a static website.	A user must know ASP, JSP, PHP, Perl or any other technology in addition to HTML to create a dynamic website.
Information must be manually changed to update it.	Information changes automatically based on underlying logic.
Example, a website listing the profile, products, prices, contacts of key persons, etc.	Example, online shopping, online reservation websites.

5.12 WEB SERVERS

A Web server is a computer that uses protocols like HTTP, SMTP, etc. to respond to client requests made over the World Wide Web (WWW). Web server software controls how clients access files hosted on it. Usually, clients type URLs of the websites; it is the role of Web server to deliver the site's content to the client requesting it. The Web server stores all files related to the website, including HTML documents, images and JavaScript files. Web server is connected to the internet 24 × 7 to facilitate data to be exchanged with other connected devices.

Thus, the Web server works on the client–server model (Fig. 5.30). All computers that host websites must have Web server software. Some popular Web servers include Apache, Microsoft's Internet Information Server (IIS) and Nginx – pronounced *engine X*. Other Web servers include Novell's NetWare server, Google Web Server (GWS) and IBM's family of Domino servers.

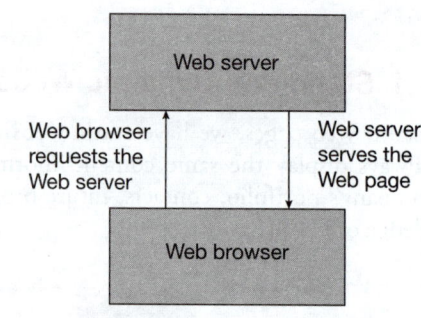

Figure 5.30 Relationship between Web browser and Web server

These Web servers are often used for:

- Sending and receiving emails.
- Handling requests for File Transfer Protocol (FTP) files.
- Building and publishing Web pages.
- Caching Web pages for fast delivery of frequently requested pages. This process is also known as Web acceleration.
- Limiting the speed of response to different clients to prevent a single client from dominating resources to satisfy requests from a large number of clients.

> A Web server can even be embedded in a device such as a digital camera to allow users to communicate with the device through any Web browser.

For choosing an appropriate Web server, the user must consider how well a Web server works with the operating system installed in his computer, how efficient it is in searching for relevant information, managing server-side programming and security characteristics.

A single Web server can host one or multiple websites using the same software and hardware resources. This is known as virtual hosting.

5.13 WEB HOSTING

Web hosting is an online service that enables users to publish their website or Web applications on the Internet. When opting for a Web hosting service, it means that the user wants to take some space on rent on a Web server to store all the files and data necessary for his/her website to work properly. Once the pages of a website are stored on the Web server, they can be accessed by other computers connected to the Internet.

The server runs 24 × 7 and has full protection against malicious attacks. Whenever someone types the URL in the address bar of the Web browser, the Web server transfers all the files necessary to serve that request.

Users must choose a hosting plan that best fits their needs. In fact, you can think of a Web hosting service as housing rentals (refer Fig. 5.31). Users have to pay the rental amount regularly to keep the server running continuously.

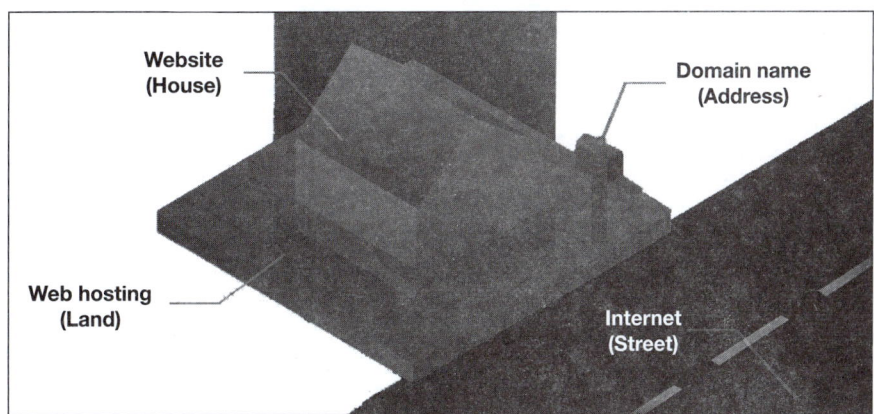

Figure 5.31 Web hosting components analogy

5.13.1 Types of Web Hosting Services

The different types of Web hosting services available are:

Shared Hosting: For a blogging website or for a website of a small business, Shared Hosting is the right choice. This service is quite affordable as it allows the Web server's space to be shared by other websites. However, since resources of the Web server are shared with other websites, the speed and performance of a website suffers. Moreover, users have minimal control over the server.

Pros	Cons
• Less expensive • Excellent option for small online business websites • Domain specific technical knowledge not required • Website Maintenance and server administration is done by the hosting company.	• Little or no control over server configuration • Increased traffic on one or more websites can slow down another website.

WordPress Hosting: This is a form of shared hosting created for WordPress site owners. The server is configured specifically for WordPress and the website has pre-installed plugins for crucial tasks, such as caching and security. This allows website to open much faster and run with fewer problems. WordPress hosting plans also include features like pre-designed WordPress themes, drag-and-drop page builders, and specific developer tools.

Pros	Cons
• Less expensive • User-friendly interface • One-click WordPress installation • Good performance for WordPress sites • Customer support services to deal with WordPress issues • Pre-installed WordPress plugins and themes.	• The hosting plan is optimized only for WordPress sites. • Hosting any other website on the server may pose several challenges.

Reseller Hosting: The reseller hosting plan allow users to rent out or re-sell the same hosting services provided by the parent hosting company.

Dedicated Hosting: Dedicated hosting gives users complete administrative control of server that is dedicated solely to their website. Users can manage their websites as per their requirements. They can choose the operating system and software to be used and set up the whole hosting environment according their needs.

Dedicated hosting is as powerful as owning your own server. Therefore, it is best-suited for large online businesses that deal with heavy traffic.

Pros	Cons
• Full control over server configuration • High reliability and security options • Root access to your server	• High cost, more oriented towards larger businesses • Technical and server management knowledge is a must.

VPS Hosting: VPS hosting is an advanced form of shared hosting. It assigns users, resources that are not shared with the other websites. These services are expensive as the Web server allocates an entirely separate partition for websites on that server. This means that users get a dedicated server space and a reserved amount of resources and memory. It is a great medium for businesses with a rapidly increasing traffic.

Pros	Cons
• Dedicated server space • Increase in traffic on other websites does not affect performance • Complete control and access to the server • Easy scalability and high customizability	• More expensive than other types of hosting • Technical and server management knowledge is a must.

Cloud Hosting: Cloud hosting is the most reliable solution on the market. It provides users with a cluster of servers. All files and resources are replicated on each server.

When one of the cloud servers is busy or encounters a problem, Web traffic coming to it is automatically routed to another server in the cluster. This results in little to no downtime of services. Hence, it is a preferred choice for busy websites.

Pros	Cons
• Little or no downtime • Server failures have no effect on your website • Allocates resources on demand • Pay-as-you-go pricing strategy – you only pay for what you use • More scalable than other Web hosting types	• Hard to estimate the actual costs • Root access is not always provided.

5.13.2 Selecting the Right Web Hosting Package

There are several Web hosting options available. The answer to which service a user must opt for varies from business to business. For example, the right option to be chosen depends on:

- The type of website – blogging website, an ecommerce portal, a news website, etc. that has to be hosted.
- The amount of Web traffic and robustness of the infrastructure required depends on the type of website chosen.
- Speed at which the online business will expand
- Storage space and bandwidth requirement
- Cost that the user can afford to pay.

5.14 WEB BROWSER

A Web browser or in short, a browser, is a software that is used to find, retrieve and display Web pages on the World Wide Web. A browser displays information including Web pages, images, video and other files.

We know that Internet is based on a client–server model. In this architectural framework, the Web browser is a client that runs on the user's computer and contacts the Web server using HTTP (Hyper Text Transfer Protocol) to request information. The Web server sends the information back to the Web browser, which it displays for users to see.

Many browsers have plug-ins to extend their functionalities so that they can display multimedia information (like music, video), perform tasks like video conferencing and offer other security features to the browser.

> Web browsers allow users to navigate through Web pages on the Internet.

5.14.1 Popular Web Browsing Software

Browsers available in the market today range in features from minimal, text-based user interfaces with a simple for HTML to rich user interfaces supporting a wide variety of file formats and protocols.

All major Web browsers have the following features.

- Allow users to open multiple websites at the same time, either on different browser windows or on different tabs of the same window.
- *Back* and *forward* buttons to go back to the Web page the user was viewing before and after viewing the current page respectively
- *Refresh* or *reload* button to reload the current Web page
- A *stop* button to cancel loading the Web page. In some browsers, this button is merged with the reload button.
- A *home* button to return to the user's home page (the first page when browser opens).
- An address bar to enter the URL of the website to be viewed
- A status bar to display progress in loading the Web page and also the page zooming capability.
- The ability to view the HTML coding of the Web page.

> Lynx is a text-only Web browser. It cannot support multimedia data.

Some popular Web browsers are Microsoft Edge, Microsoft Internet Explorer, Mozilla Firefox, Google Chrome, Apple Safari and Opera. When choosing a browser for your computer, you must give first preference to features like simplicity, speed and security. For this, it must have the following characteristics:

- Even a naïve user working on the browser must find it easy to surf the net
- It must download the pages in less than two seconds
- It must have a customizable toolbar
- It must have the ability to save bookmarks.
- It must have security features such as privacy settings, pop-up blockers and anti-spyware to allow users to surf the net safely without compromising their personal data
- It must have dedicated technical support ranging from FAQs to tutorials.

> Web browsers operate at the application layer of the OSI Model.

5.14.2 Add-on and Plug-in

Whenever we want to install a new software, we always want one that has maximum features. But even with multiple features, there is no guarantee that the software will have the features that you are looking for. It is impossible for any software to have all the features. Therefore, software developers usually provide all basic functionalities and allow users to further customize the software by installing add-ons or plug-ins.

Plug-in and Add-on are extensions that are used to extend the usability of the program. There is no hard-core rule as to what should be a part of the software and what should be included as an add-on. It just depends on the software developer team, what they want to make a mandatory functionality and what they would consider as a desirable functionality.

These extensions can be developed either by the company that developed the software or by any other company. Usually, we call an extension as a plug-in when it is a third-party software that is meant to interact with a certain program. For example, to view animations and videos, the Web browser must have a plug-in called flash player installed in it. Flash player is not native to any Web browser. It is made by another company in such a way that all popular Web browsers are compatible with it.

An add-on also extends the functionality of a software but it is meant only for a particular software and not all. For example, an add-on developed for Firefox browser will not work for any other browser. The most commonly used add-ons for browsers are toolbars which take a bit of space but give instant shortcuts to certain online services. Add-ons are also extensively used in online games like World of Warcraft, in which players can create their own add-ons to help other players who have little knowledge about that game.

Activity: To remove an extension from Google Chrome (Fig. 5.32)
Step 1: Double click on Google Chrome icon to open it.
Step 2: Click on three vertical dots in the upper-right corner of the Chrome window.
Step 3: Click on More Tools option.
Step 4: Click on Extensions.
Step 5: Click the Remove button on the extension that you want to remove.
Step 6: Confirm deletion by clicking on **Remove**.

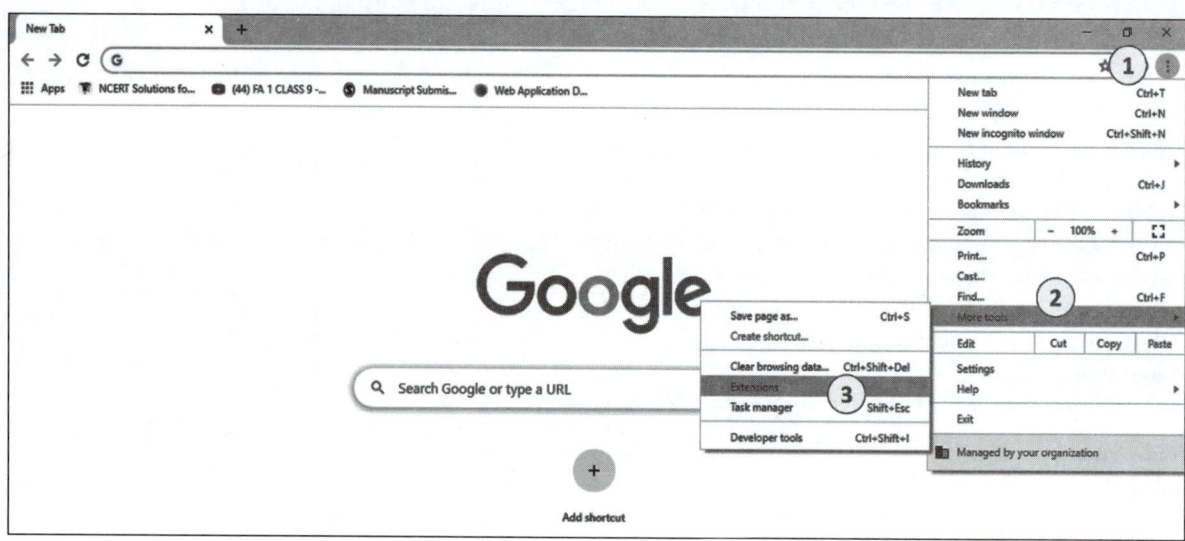

Figure 5.32   Removing an extension from Google Chrome

5.15 HTTP COOKIE

Also known as a Web cookie, an Internet cookie or a browser cookie indicates information that is stored on a computer by a Web server. The browser stores each message in a small file, called **cookie.txt**. The computer is supposed to send this information back to the server each time the user visits that website. The computer does not change the information it receives from the Web server.

Cookies are files that contain information like a username and password that are exchanged between a user's computer and a Web server to identify a particular user and improve his overall browsing experience.

For example, cookies allow websites to retain the user's login credentials and preferences, such as colors, themes, sports, news, etc. The computer remembers cookies using the **name=value pair**. When the user re-visits the website in future, the Web browser automatically returns the user's information previously stored on the Web server in the form of a cookie.

5.15.1 Types of Cookies

There are two types of cookies.

Session Cookies are used only while navigating a website. They are stored in RAM and are never written to the hard drive. Therefore, as soon as the session ends, these cookies are automatically deleted. In this way, session cookies maintain user privacy.

Persistent Cookies are stored on the computer's hard disk and are thus retained even after the session ends. Usually, these cookies have an expiration date and are automatically removed when that date is reached.

Persistent cookies are used for two main reasons:

Authentication: Cookies track the username and password with which a particular user has logged in to the website. They are a big help to users as they have to no longer remember passwords for that site. (Note that when you click on the Save Password on this computer option, the username and password are actually stored as cookies on the computer).

Tracking: Cookies can also be used to track multiple visits to the same site over time. Some online websites use cookies to track pages visited by a particular user and products ordered or added to their wish lists. This information is then used to suggest other products in which the user may be interested.

5.15.2 Security Concerns

- Usually, cookies cannot transfer viruses or malware to the user's computer.
- Cookies cannot pass any confidential information to the Web server as cookies are the information sent by the server and this information cannot be changed in any way. Because the data in a cookie does not change when it travels back and forth, it has no way to affect how your computer runs.
- Computer cookies not only keep track of data for websites, but also hold a host of personal information.
- Some cyber-attacks can hijack cookies and get all information regarding the user's browsing sessions.

5.15.3 Removing Cookies

Deleting or prohibiting all sorts of cookies will make some navigation to websites difficult. Without cookies, users may have to re-enter their data for each visit. Before removing cookies, users must evaluate the ease of use expected from a website that uses cookies because cookies always improve the Web experience. Users can just handle them carefully to make a balance between ease and security concerns.

> Zombie cookies are used by Web analytics companies to track unique individuals' browsing histories or even to ban specific users.

However, we can practise some control over third-party and tracking cookies to protect our privacy.

Third-party cookies pose serious security threat as they are generated by websites other than those that the user is currently surfing. These websites may be linked to ads on Web page(s) being visited by users. Therefore, visiting a site with 10 ads may generate 10 cookies, even if users do not even click on them.

Some third-party cookies may be zombies. **Zombie cookies,** also known as flash cookies, are permanently installed on users' computers, even when they opt not to install cookies. They also reappear after they have been deleted, so it is very difficult to remove them.

5.16   WEB BROWSER SETTINGS

When we buy a computer, one or more Web browsers will always be installed in it. Every Web browser has its own default settings. Although there is no harm in working with the default settings, in case you to add some more features (like security) or change the default settings as per your preference, then you must configure it.

For example, in the Google Chrome window follow the steps given below to enable, disable and clear cookies (Fig. 5.33).

Step 1: Click on the three dots on the upper right-most corner of the Chrome window.
Step 2: Click on Settings.
Step 3: Click on Privacy and Security option in the left panel of the Chrome window.
Step 4: Move to the Privacy and Security group in the right panel.
Step 5: Click on the desired arrow to change the appropriate settings like,
      Clear Browsing Data
      Allow or Block Cookies
      Clear Cookies when you quit Chrome
      Allow trusted websites to save Cookies
      Never allow untrusted websites to save Cookies
      You can even go to Site Settings to block notifications from a particular website or block pop-ups.

Step 6: Close the Settings Tab.

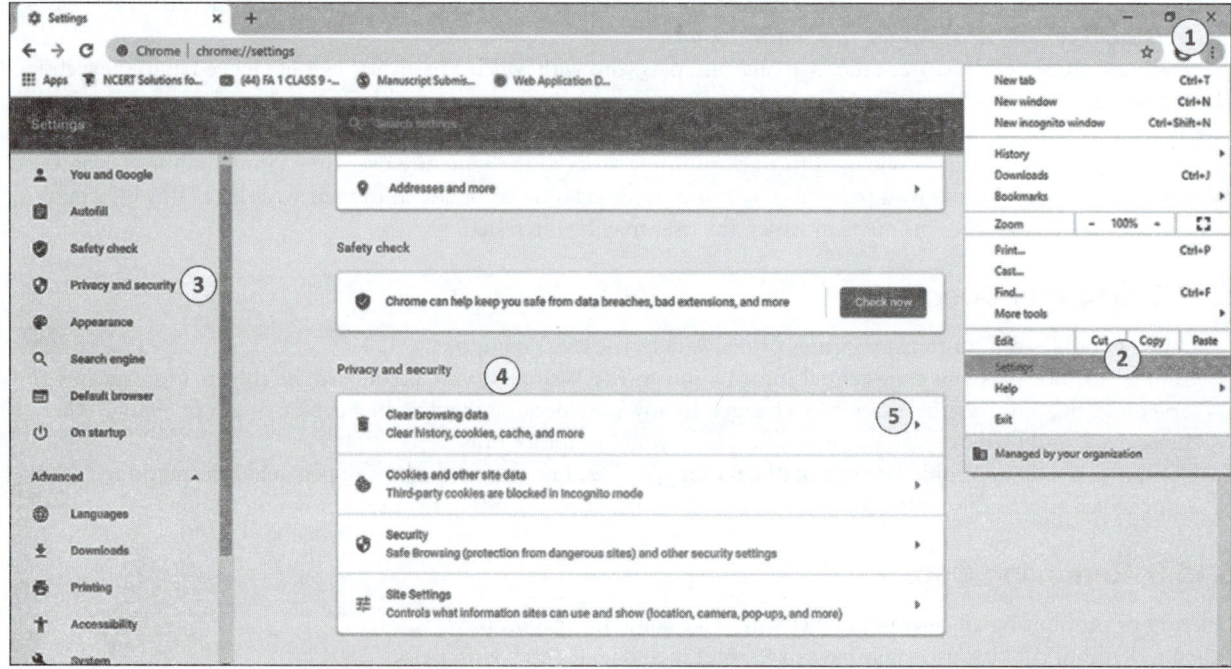

Figure 5.33 Managing cookies in Google Chrome

Key Terms

Computer network: A computer communication network or a computer network is a collection of computers and devices interconnected to facilitate sharing of resources (printer, CD-ROM), information and electronic documents among interconnected devices.

Internet: A network of networks.

Modem: A hardware device that allows a computer to send and receive data over a telephone line or a cable or satellite connection.

Modulation: The process of converting digital data into an analog signal.

Demodulation: The process which takes an analog signal and turns it back into a digital data that can be read by the receiving computer.

Repeaters: Network devices that works at first layer of the OSI Model. Its function is to amplify or regenerate an incoming signal before retransmitting it.

Switch: A high-speed intelligent network device that connects multiple computers through its ports.

Router: A network device that connects multiple computer networks together using either wired or wireless connections. It works at Layer 3 of the OSI model and moves data from one network to the other.

Gateway: A device that joins two networks using different protocols (set of rules followed for data transmission).

Network topology: An arrangement of computers or other computing devices. Topology describes the pattern in which different devices on the network are connected and the way data flows between them.

Internet: A global network that connects billions of computers all over the world.

World Wide Web (WWW): All the resources and users on the Internet that are using the hypertext transfer protocol (HTTP).

Web page: A document that is accessed through the Internet or other network using a Web browser.

Inbox: Inbox is the folder in which all the incoming emails (emails that are received) are stored and can be accessed.

Outbox: Outbox is the folder in which all the emails sent are stored temporarily when it is not fully sent. This means that Outbox keeps the email which is pending to be delivered or not sent because of any reason like non-availability of Internet connection, etc.

Draft: It is the folder in which email messages that are composed (or written) but not sent or queued to be sent are stored.

Junk: Also known as Spam, it is the folder in which all fake and spam kinds of email messages are stored. Such messages may contain virus, malware or spyware that can steal data from our system.

Sent items: It is the folder that stores all the email messages that were successfully delivered.

Deleted items: Also known as Trash, it is the folder that stores all the email messages that have been deleted so that you can reuse, send, forward or print them if the need arises.

Website: A Website is a collection of related Web pages.

Web server: A computer that uses protocols like HTTP, SMTP, etc., to respond to client requests made over the World Wide Web (WWW).

Web hosting: An online service that enables users to publish their Website or Web applications on the Internet.

Web browser: Software that is used to find, retrieve and display Web pages on the World Wide Web.

Zombie cookies: Also known as flash cookies, they are permanently installed on users' computers even when the user opts not to install cookies. They also reappear after they have been deleted, so it is very difficult to remove them.

Chapter Highlights

- LAN (Local Area Network) supports communication between two computers or more computers/computing devices in a limited geographical area such as home, school, computer laboratory, office building, or closely positioned group of buildings.
- Owing to limited scope and cost of operation, LANs are typically owned, controlled and managed by a single person or organization.
- WANs (Wide Area Network) span a large geographic area such as a city, country, or even intercontinental distances, using a communication channel that combines many types of media such as telephone lines, cables and air waves.
- The Internet is a public WAN, but organization can also form a private WAN, which is basically two or more LANs connected to each other.
- MAN (Metropolitan Area Network) is a network that interconnects computers and other devices in a geographic area or region larger than that covered by LAN but smaller than that covered by WAN.
- CAN or Campus Area Network is almost entirely owned by the campus of an enterprise, university, government, military bases, etc. The size of the area that CANs cover is larger than that of LAN and smaller than that of MAN or WAN.
- PANs (Personal Area Networks) are used to communicate with personal devices.
- Unlike switches, hubs do not have the intelligence to filter data. Hence, every device picks the message but only the destined device processes the packet and all the other computers just discard it.
- Speed of a modem signifies the number of bits that a modem can send or receive in one second.
- In the star network topology, a central computer, also known as the hub or the server, is directly connected to all other computers or computing devices.
- In the ring topology, every computer is connected to two of its neighbors – one on the left and the other on its right, thereby forming a closed loop. The last computer is connected to the first.
- The mesh network topology links all computers or computing devices nodes directly to all other devices on the network.
- A tree topology is also known as a hierarchical topology because all the computers are connected by forming a hierarchy. This topology has at least three levels to the hierarchy.
- A uniform resource locator (URL) specifies the unique address for a file that is accessible on the Internet.
- On the Web, all the documents are formatted in a special markup language called Hypertext Markup Language (HTML) that supports links to other documents, graphics, audio, and/or video files. This feature enables users to jump from one document to another by simply clicking on hot spots.
- VoIP is a technology that allows users to make voice calls using a broadband Internet connection instead of a regular (or analog) phone line.

- VoIP applications integrate voice, video and text chat. Apple's FaceTime, Zoom, Google Meet and WhatsApp are all examples of VoIP applications.
- Web pages can be either static or dynamic.
- Plug-in and Add-on are extensions that are used to extend the usability of a program.
- Cookie also known as a Web cookie, an Internet cookie or a browser cookie indicates information that is stored on a computer by a Web server. The browser stores each message in a small file called cookie.txt.

Review Questions

1. Define a computer network and give its advantages.
2. Besides the advantages there some serious concerns about computer networks. What are these concerns?
3. Draw a comparison between LAN and WAN.
4. Write a short note on the following network devices.
   a. Repeater b. Switch c. Router d. Gateway e. Modem
5. We have a router at home for broadband connection, which can still communicate a variety of protocols over the internet. How has this been possible, explain.
6. What do you understand by the term network topology? Explain any three topologies.
7. Why is the Internet said to be based on a partial mesh network?
8. With the help of an example explain the significance of URL.
9. Explain the relationship between WWW and the Internet.
10. Write a short note on any two ways of communicating with other users over the internet.
11. Give some advantages of email over the traditional mail.
12. Discuss VoIP as game changer in tele-calling services.
13. Differentiate between static and dynamic websites.
14. Discuss the role of Web server in the process of information sharing.
15. Highlight the different types of Web hosting services.
16. Differentiate between add-ons and plug-ins.
17. How is a session cookie different from a persistent cookie?
18. Give at least two pros and cons of using cookies.

Fill in the Blanks

1. A _____ is a collection of computers and devices interconnected to facilitate sharing of resources, information and electronic documents among interconnected devices.
2. _____ are typically owned, controlled and managed by a single person or organization.
3. Wireless LANs use _____ waves for communication.
4. _____ is the largest WAN.
5. _____ is a network that covers a geographic larger than that covered by LAN but smaller than that of WAN.
6. _____ Area Network is smaller than MAN but larger than LAN.
7. Bluetooth PANs are also called _____.
8. _____ converts digital data into an analog signal.
9. _____ Modems are the modems which are built onto the computer motherboard.
10. _____ works on the second layer of OSI model to connect multiple computers via their ports.
11. _____ works on the 7th layer and, in fact, any layer of the OSI model.
12. _____ specifies the arrangement of computers or other computing devices.
13. _____ topology creates multiple paths between two devices and provides connectivity even if one or more devices fail.

14. _____ URL contains only the one field, which is the domain name.
15. Email address has two parts that are separated by the _____ symbol.
16. _____ software is used to find, retrieve and display Web pages on the World Wide Web.
17. The URL of the website to be viewed is entered in the _____ of the Web browser window.
18. _____ and _____ are extensions that are used to extend the usability of a program.
19. _____ cookies are stored in RAM and are never written to the hard drive.
20. _____ cookies are permanently installed on users' computers, even when they opt not to install cookies.

State True or False

1. WAN supports communication between two or more computers in a limited geographical area such as home, school, computer laboratory or office.
2. PAN typically covers an area of range between 5 and 50 km.
3. LANs can be wired or wireless.
4. The Internet is a private WAN.
5. A private WAN can be created by combining two or more LANs.
6. When compared to WANs, LANs have a higher data rate.
7. The speed of a broadband modem is slower than that of a dial-up modem.
8. A repeater cannot differentiate between actual signal and noise.
9. Hubs are intelligent network devices that filter data.
10. In a star topology, every computer is connected to a single cable.
11. Tree topology is a combination of two or more topologies.
12. An absolute URL specifies the complete URL containing all three fields – protocol, domain and path.
13. While you are writing an email message, it is automatically being saved in drafts folder.
14. We can create dynamic Web pages using HTML.
15. A single Web server can host one or multiple websites.
16. Internet is based on a client–server or request/response model.
17. Web browser performs the role of a Web server on behalf of the user.
18. Web browsers operate at the application layer of the OSI model.
19. It is not possible to allow/disallow cookies form a particular website.
20. Add-on is a third-party software.
21. Persistent cookies are automatically deleted when a browsing session ends.
22. Cookies can transfer viruses or malware into the user's computer.

Multiple Choice Questions

1. Which of the following is a preferred area network for higher data transfer rates, smaller geographic range, and no leased telecommunication lines?
   a. LAN   b. MAN   c. WAN   d. CAN
2. A LAN can be easily connected to a WAN by using a special network device called _____.
   b. Hub   b. Bridge   c. Router   d. Switch
3. If there is a fault in the main cable, the entire network fails. This statement is true in case of which topology?
   a. Bus   b. Star   c. Mesh   d. Ring
4. In which topology, all data transmission is possible only through the hub?
   a. Bus   b. Star   c. Ring   d. Mesh

5. In which topology, data transfer is uni-directional?
   a. Bus   b. Star   c. Ring   d. Mesh
6. For *n* nodes, how many physical links are required for a mesh network?
   a. n   b. n – 1   c. n × (n – 1)/2   d. (n – 1)/2
7. Which topology is also known as a hierarchical topology or a *star of stars*?
   a. Bus   b. Tree   c. Ring   d. Mesh
8. Anything following the question mark (?) in a URL is _____.
   a. a variable   b. the value of a variable   c. Both of these.   d. None of these.
9. Which of the following is not a Web browser?
   a. Tencent Traveler   b. Maxthon   c. TheWorld   d. None of these.
10. Apple's FaceTime, Zoom, Google Meet, WhatsApp are all examples of _____ applications.
    a. VoIP   b. Chatting   c. Email   d. File Transfer
11. A Web page can be saved with _____ extension.
    a. .cgi   b. .php   c. html or .htm d. All of these.
12. Web client and Web server uses _____ for exchanging information.
    a. FTP   b. HTTP   c. TELNET   d. UDP
13. Which Web browser supports only textual data?
    a. Safari   b. Netscape   c. Lynx   d. Konqueror
14. _____ are files stored by a Web server on a user's computer to customize the user's browsing session.
    a. Add-on   b. Plug-in   c. Macros   d. Cookies
15. Which of the following is not true about a persistent cookie?
    a. Maintains user privacy   b. Has an expiration date
    c. Automatically removed when expiration date is reached   d. All of these.
16. Cookies are not used for _____.
    a. authentication   b. tracking
    c. customizing browsing session   d. providing additional functionality to the Web browser

Answers

Fill in the Blanks

1. computer network
2. LANs
3. radio
4. Internet.
5. MAN
6. Campus
7. piconets
8. Modulation
9. Onboard
10. Switch
11. Gateway
12. Network topology
13. Mesh
14. Relative
15. @
16. Web Browser
17. address bar
18. Plug-ins and Add-ons
19. Session
20. Zombie

State True or False

1. False
2. False
3. True
4. False
5. True
6. False
7. False
8. True
9. False
10. False
11. False
12. True
13. True
14. False
15. True
16. True
17. False
18. True
19. False
20. False
21. False
22. False

Multiple Choice Questions

1. a
2. c
3. a
4. b
5. c
6. c
7. b
8. c
9. d
10. a
11. d
12. b
13. c
14. d
15. a
15. d

Societal Impacts

Chapter Objectives

These days, the Internet is extensively being used for exchanging data or messages. Some data may be personal and thus confidential in nature. For example, when we do online banking or buy any product from a website, we send our password and credit card number through the Internet. Any person with malicious intentions can intercept (illegally access) our data and misuse it. However, the most common threats to Internet security comes either from the use of malware or through frauds such as phishing. In this chapter, we will therefore read about some very important topics including,

- Digital footprints
- Data protection
- Intellectual property right
- Software licensing
- Computer and Internet fraud
- Safely browsing the Web
- IT Act 2000
- Protecting one's identity
- Appropriate usage of social networks
- E-waste management
- Protecting oneself from side-effects of technology

6.1 DIGITAL FOOTPRINT

Digital footprints are footprints or traces that a user leaves when he/she is online. Whenever a user fills a registration form, sends an email, uploads pictures/videos or any other file, or searches for some information, he/she leaves traces of personal information about himself/herself on the Internet. Therefore, a digital footprint is the data generated as a result of actions and communications online that can be traced back to the user. There are two types of digital footprints – Active and Passive (Fig. 6.1).

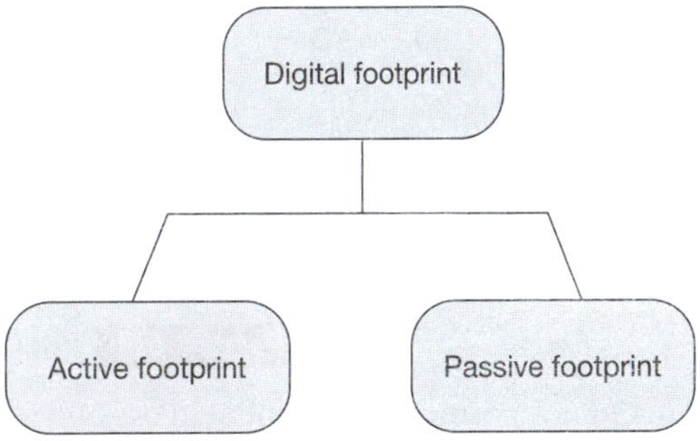

Active footprints are those footprints that a user leaves intentionally. For example, we leave active footprints whenever we post or like a comment on Facebook, tweet on Twitter, upload a file, send an email, chat and make phone calls (voice or video) over the Internet.

Figure 6.1 Types of digital footprints

Passive footprints are left by a user unintentionally. For example, whenever we visit a website, search for information or shop online, we leave behind information about ourselves. The websites keep a track of how many times we have visited a website and for what kind of information.

A digital footprint is relatively permanent and once the data is in public or even semi-public domain (like on Facebook), the user has very little control over how it will be used by others. Therefore, we should be very particular about our online activities.

Everyone who uses the Internet has a digital footprint. Though you don't have to worry about it, you must keep a check on what data you are leaving behind. For example, never post any irrelevant content that may lead you to trouble. Even if you delete your posts, tweets or emails, remember that it is still present on the Internet.

> While shopping online, websites record your movement from one webpage to another. They do this to keep a note of products you were looking for. This information helps them to do targeted advertisement (show advertisements of those products in which you are interested).

Moreover, digital footprints are of big interest to hackers who are looking to steal your identity. Remember that these days, digital footprints are also used by employers, schools, and other institutions or individuals (refer Fig. 6.2) to whom your clear identity and reputation matters. So, think before you write even a single word on social media. Figure 6.3 highlights some important points in this context.

To keep a check on what information about you is available online, just enter your name in different search engines and see what all information is displayed.

If you are on Facebook or on any other social networking site then you can control who can see your posts by making changes in the Privacy Settings. For example, Facebook allows you to limit posts merely to people in your Friends List.

However, remember that even after changing your privacy settings, the posts are still available on the Internet. There have been many complaints by Facebook users that "friends-locked" photographs can be seen as public images on Google Image Search. Therefore, keep the following points in mind while surfing the Internet.

Figure 6.2 Your parents, teachers, employers, future colleges, and police can easily find your digital footprints

 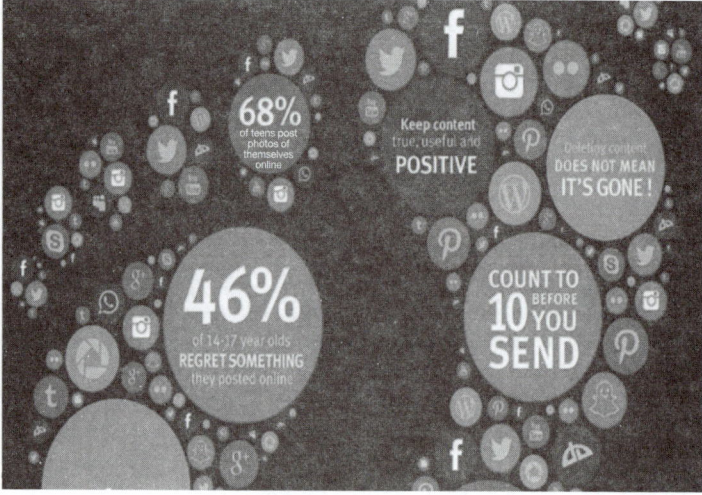

Figure 6.3 Before leaving digital footprints, we must think

Build a positive image online. Post only those things that contribute to the image of you that you want your parents, teachers, friends, relatives and employers (in future) to see.

Skip the negative tweets and un-tag yourself from posts or pictures on social networking websites that are either rude or controversial.

You can start blogging to showcase your work or a hobby about which you are really passionate.

6.2 NETIQUETTE

Netiquette, Network Etiquette, or Internet Etiquette (refer Fig. 6.4) is a set of rules that should be followed when a person is working on the Internet. These rules define a set of dos and don'ts while working on the Internet.

Netiquette has been defined to make the Internet experience pleasant and enjoyable for everyone. Some of these rules include:

- Do not reply to any unknown messages or messages that makes us uncomfortable.
- Do not exchange any personal information on Internet without your parent's permission.
- Always discuss your Internet activities with your parents.
- Avoid using Internet in the absence of your teachers or parents.

- Never share your passwords with anyone.
- Treat others as you would like to be treated. Do not write something that would hurt others' feelings.
- Do not write in capital letters as it is treated as shouting.
- Do not use too many emoticons.
- Do not send fake emails.
- Do not talk to a stranger. Never arrange for a meeting with a person you met on the Internet.
- For doing homework, do not just copy the contents from the Internet. That is cheating. Just take hints and write your own answers.
- Do not write messages in someone else's name.
- Do not write very long messages.
- Start your message with greetings.
- Never use rude, abusive or bad words in your message.
- Do not forward unnecessary emails especially those which prompt you to forward the mail to 10 people to change your luck in 24 hours, etc.

> Use nickname and not your real name for chatting. Also do not agree to meet with someone you have been interacting online.

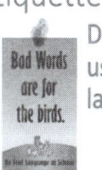

Figure 6.4 Online etiquette

6.3 ETHICS IN COMPUTING

Ethics is a set of moral values that govern the behavior of a person (refer Fig. 6.5). Ethics in computing refers to a set of moral values that regulate the use of computers. Let us take two examples to understand the term computer ethics.

- It may be easy for an individual to duplicate copyrighted electronic content but computer ethics states that it is wrong to do so without the author's approval.
- It may be possible to access someone's personal information on a computer, but computer ethics states that one should not do so. We must always respect others' privacy.

Figure 6.5 Ethics deals with judging whether an act is good or bad. Some of the ethical rules have been converted into laws

6.4 DATA PROTECTION

Before reading about terms like privacy and data protection, let us first understand what is personal information. Personal information means recorded information or opinions, whether true or not, that helps someone to identify whose information or opinion it is. For example, it can be name, address, sex, age, financial details, marital status, education, criminal record, employment history, etc.

Privacy is a fundamental right. It is essential to autonomy and the protection of human dignity. Privacy is an important issue as it protects us and the society against arbitrary and unjustified use of power. Strict privacy laws protect us from others who may wish to exert control on us. We can protect what can be known about us and done to us. We can limit who has access to our communications and information.

Privacy serves as the foundation upon which many other human rights are built. It creates barriers and helps us to protect ourselves from unwarranted interference in our lives. When there is undue interference, we are compelled to compromise on who we are and how we interact with the world around us.

Privacy laws give us a space to be ourselves without judgement and allows us to think freely without discrimination. When we talk of ensuring privacy, we must consider the following issues:

- the ethics of modern life
- the rules governing the conduct of commerce; and,
- the restraints placed on use of information.

Today, with advancements in technology, capabilities to protect privacy are greater than ever before, but the capabilities for surveillance has improved manifold.

These days, it has become very easy to uniquely identify individuals amidst mass data sets and streams. It is now possible for companies and governments to monitor every conversation we conduct, each commercial transaction we make and every location we visit. These capabilities may adversely impact individuals, groups and even society as such surveillance may call for action against them.

The biggest challenge to privacy is that the right can be compromised without the individual being aware about it. Moreover, we are neither informed about the monitoring we are placed under nor given the opportunity to question these activities.

In many countries, secret surveillance and lack of accountability has resulted in a risk to democratic life. Therefore, it is very important in the modern world to develop laws and technologies to strengthen the ability to freely enjoy this right.

Data Protection and Right to Privacy gives individuals legal rights over the personal data that is held about them. It gives individuals the right to

- be informed about the data held about them
- access data stored about them
- rectify incorrect data (if any)
- get their data erased
- port their data, that is, to transfer to a different service
- object to the misuse of their personal data
- object to using their data for automatic decision making and profiling.

6.4.1 Key Information Privacy Principles

Information privacy principles state that when an organization collects personal information, it should:

- Collect only the information that is needed. It should not intrude unreasonably. People should know what information about them is collected and for what purpose.
- Clearly state the purpose for which the information is being collected.
- Let people see their information and allow them to correct if required.
- Use the information collected only for the purpose that was stated or for any other related purpose which the person may reasonably expect.
- If possible, provide the option of not identifying people especially when they are giving information about some controversial issue.
- Ensure the protection of people's private information when it is transmitted anywhere outside the organization.
- Avoid collecting confidential or personal information about people like their ethnic background, political views, etc.

If an organization is found guilty of not following Information Privacy Principles, then it might have to make an apology, change a procedure, correct or delete personal information or even have to pay compensation

6.5 INTELLECTUAL PROPERTY RIGHTS (IPR)

Intellectual Property Rights (or IPR) are rights that are applicable to creative work which can be treated as an asset or physical property. They can be categorized into four main areas – copyright, trademarks, design rights and patents. Each of these are applicable in various situations and with its own set of technical rules. To protect your idea(s) effectively when launching a new product or doing any other important business activity, you may have to utilize one or more of the IPR types before commencing those activities.

Ⓒ Copyright

Copyright applies to items including literary, artistic, music and drama as well as in films, sound recordings, drawings, paintings, photography, typographical arrangements or any work that is recorded in some way. These rights protect the author's work by prohibiting unauthorized actions by others that may compromise the author's credibility and right to his/her work. The author is empowered to take legal action against instances of infringement or plagiarism.

Therefore, while obtaining permission to use creative works, we are talking about copyright law. To use someone else's work, we must first take the author's permission.

Trademarks

A trademark can be a name, word, slogan, design, symbol or any other item that is used to identify a product or organization. Trademarks which are unique for a product or company are to be registered with an appointed government body. The process of registering trademarks may take up to two years in India. However, once registered, a trade mark is valid for ten years and can be renewed thereafter indefinitely for further ten-year periods

Once registered, trademarks are identified by the abbreviation 'TM', or the '®' symbol. In most countries, the national patent office also administers trademarks. You must have observed that all big brands have a trademark (Fig. 6.6).

Design Rights

Designs (Fig. 6.7) must also be protected by both copyright and design rights. They may also be registered like patents. Once registered, designs are valid for a maximum of ten years and renewable for a further five years.

Figure 6.6 Popularly used trademarks

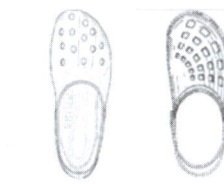
Crocs D'517,789   Infringing

Apple D'604,305   Infringing

Figure 6.7 Copying popular designs

> Unlike copyrighted works, trademarks have different degrees of protection depending on factors including the consumer awareness of the trademark, the type of service and product it identifies, and the geographic area in which the trademark is used.

Patents

Patents are applied for industrial processes and inventions. They also protect the item against the unauthorized implementation of the invention. In general terms, patents are grants made by national governments that give the creator of an invention an exclusive right to use, sell or manufacture the invention. All patents must be registered. The process of registering, however, may take 2 to 3 years to complete.

In India, the regulatory authority for patents is the Patent Registrar under the office of the Controller General of Patents, Designs and Trade Marks, which is part of India's Ministry of Commerce and Industry. Once registered, patents are valid for 20 years from the date of filing an application (subject to an annual renewal fee).

India's patent law operates under the 'first to file' principle which states that if two people apply for a patent on a similar invention, then the first one to file the application is awarded the patent.

> Internet piracy of films, music, games and software is an issue in India, as is unauthorised copying of physical books.

Right of Publicity

A patchwork of state laws known as the right of publicity protects the image and name of a person against unauthorized use for commercial purposes. For example, no company can use a celebrity's or even a common man's name and picture to advertise its product.

Trade Secrets

The Trade Secret laws provide protection against sensitive business information. For example, a marketing plan or launch of a new product must be kept confidential as it gives the business an advantage over its competitors (Fig. 6.8).

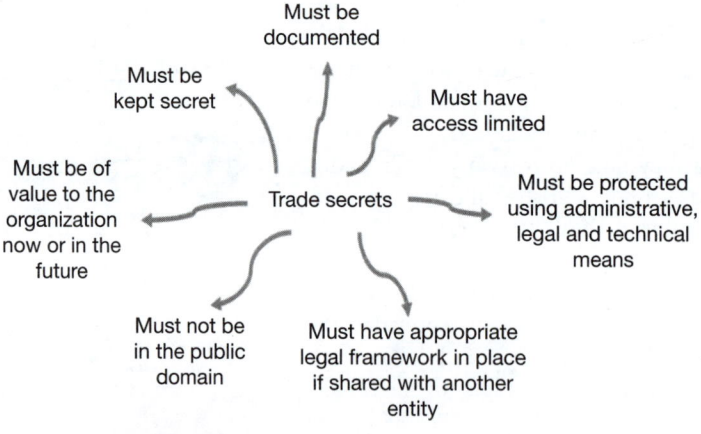

Figure 6.8 The 7 'Musts' of trade secrets

Table 6.1 summarizes these techniques.

Table 6.1 Summarizing protection of IPR techniques

		Protects	Infringement	Registration Process	Term	Comparative Costs
Patent	Utility patent	Functional aspects	Make, use, offer, sale, import	Yes	20 years upon filing	Expensive
	Design patent	Ornamental features	Make, use, offer, sale, import	Yes	15 years upon filing	Moderate
Trademarks		Brands	Used in commerce	Optional	Potentially indefinite, limited by use	Inexpensive
Copyrights		Works of authorship	Copying, etc.	Optional	Life plus 70 years	Inexpensive
Trade secrets		Information	Misappropriation	No	Potentially indefinite, limited by secrecy	Depends

6.6 PLAGIARISM

Plagiarism is an act of fraud that involves both stealing someone else's work and lying about it afterward. The term also includes the following activities:

- to steal and pass off someone else's work as one's own
- copying words or ideas from someone else without giving credit
- to commit literary theft
- to present an idea or a product as new and original when it has been derived from an existing source
- giving incorrect information about the source of a quotation
- changing words but copying the sentence structure of a source without giving credit
- copying several words or ideas from a source that it makes up the majority of your work. It is plagiarism even if you give credit to the source.
- using an image, video or piece of music as your own work without taking permission from its author or without providing appropriate citation
- re-mixing or altering copyrighted images, video or audio, even in an original way.

Note that the expression of original ideas that are recorded in some way (such as a book or a computer file) is an intellectual property that is protected by copyright laws. So, copying them is considered to be an act of plagiarism (Fig. 6.9).

Based on the above discussion, plagiarism can be categorized into following types.

- **Blatant or Direct plagiarism:** In this type of plagiarism, you purposefully use another person's words and try to pass them as your own work. Paying someone to do a work for you and submitting it as your own work is also a form of direct plagiarism
- **Self-plagiarism**: In this, you reuse your own work done previously.
- **Paraphrased plagiarism:** Here, you make few changes to someone else's work and then pass it as your own. In this case, do not forget to cite the source.
- **Mosaic plagiarism:** It is a combination of direct and paraphrased plagiarism. In this, you change certain words, phrases, and sentences without providing quotation marks or attributions.
- **Accidental plagiarism:** In this, we are not sure when to cite, paraphrase or quote. This occurs when citations are either missing or given incorrectly

Figure 6.9 Plagiarism – Copying others' work

We can avoid plagiarism can by correctly citing the sources. Simply acknowledging the source from which the content is borrowed so that the reader gets the necessary information necessary to go through the source is enough to prevent plagiarism.

We must take plagiarism very seriously because if we are caught doing so then we may have to bear serious consequences which may include:

- Imprisonment
- Heavy fines
- Destroyed student/professional reputation
- Legal repercussions
- Monetary repercussions
- It may also result in a failing grade, a suspension, or an expulsion.

> Plagiarism by students must be suppressed because this prevents them from tapping into their capabilities to do better work.

Therefore, before submitting your work, you must check to ensure that it is not plagiarised, even accidentally. This can be done by using a good Plagiarism Checker tool. Some of these online tools are available for free and other sophisticated ones are available at a cost. These tools help us to detect plagiarized and paraphrased content using highly advanced AI technology. If the content is copied, the tool will highlight those words or lines or paragraphs and also tell you the source from which it has been copied.

Many school and university students plagiarize by:

- Copying answers for assignments from websites
- Copying answers from their friends
- Copying someone else's work (from books or any other source) without giving them credit
- Giving incorrect information about the source of a quotation, thus preventing the users from getting a true copy of the source

- Copying the structure of the sentence but changing a few words, not giving the credit to source and presenting it as one's own work.
- Copying a major part from a source, irrespective of whether he/she is giving it the credit or not.
- Self-plagiarizing the content. Many a time, students plagiarize their own work to get two or more grades or awards for the same piece of work created by them.
- Summarizing or rewording someone else's ideas without providing a citation.

Some guidelines to escape plagiarism

- Write your answers yourself in your own style.
- Do not copy long paragraphs. When copying a definition or any information that cannot be and should not be changed, use quotation marks to illustrate that it is a direct quote.

6.7 SOFTWARE LICENSING

A software license is an agreement between the consumer and the creator of a software program that allows the consumer to do certain things that would otherwise be a violation of copyright laws. It provides legally binding guidelines for the use and distribution of software.

A software license gives an individual or an organization, the permission to use the software. However, in most situations, it is illegal to purchase one copy of software and then use it on multiple computers. In such a situation, the companies can purchase site licenses rather buying tens, hundreds, or thousands of individually licensed copies of a program.

The software license gives vital information regarding

- where and how and how often can the software be installed
- the consumer's right to copy, modify, or redistribute the software
- the consumer's right to access the underlying source code of the software.

Often, the license agreement also mentions the price of the software and the licensing fees (if any).
Before using a software, we must carefully read it to know how long the license lasts. A perpetual license does not expire. This means that once the software is purchased, it can be used any number of times. However, a term license expires after a specified period of time (often one year) and must be periodically renewed.

Types of Software Licenses

Based on the number of users, there are three types of software licenses. They are:

- **Single-user license:** The software is licensed for a single user and can be installed on a single computer.
- **Multi-user license**: This license allows users to install the software on multiple (fixed) computers so that it can be used by multiple users. For example, a five-user multi-user license allows the software to be used by up to five people.
- **Site license:** Software can be installed on an unlimited number of computers, as long as they are at the location of the site license. Site licenses are usually for schools and businesses.

6.8 FREE AND OPEN-SOURCE SOFTWARE (FOSS)

The licensee of a free software may copy, modify and distribute creative works. But, with proprietary software, the original copyright owner maintains ownership. The copyright owner is just renting or leasing copyrighted materials to licensees.

The term 'open source' refers to something that allows users to modify and share because its design is publicly accessible. Therefore, as compared to proprietary software, free and open-source software has fewer restrictions. Such a license frees users from using the software without seeking anyone's permission. The users can copy and redistribute the software to others for future development or use.

> Software licensing describes the legal rights for authorized use of digital material. Infringing software license agreement incurs criminal charges related to licensed intellectual property (IP) and copyrighted material.

6.8.1 Difference Between Open-source Software and Other Types of Software

As discussed in the previous section, the source code of proprietary software is accessible only to the organization that created it. The organization maintains exclusive control over it and can inspect or modify it (if required). To use proprietary software, computer users must comply with a license and agree to certain terms and conditions expressed by the organization that created it. Microsoft Office and Adobe Photoshop are examples of proprietary software.

The source code of open-source software is freely available to users; they can view the code, copy it, learn from it, alter it, or share it. LibreOffice, Gambas, GIMP, Firefox, Chrome, OpenOffice, Linux, and Android are some popular examples of free and open-source software.

Like proprietary software, users of open-source software must also accept the terms of a license. Open-source licenses affect the way people can use, study, modify and distribute software. Some open-source licenses, also known as "copyleft" licenses in contrast to copyright licenses, say that anyone who releases a modified open-source program must also release the source code (all the instructions or lines of code that makes the software do its intended task) for that program alongside it. Some open-source licenses also state that anyone who alters and shares a program with others must also share that program's source code without charging a licensing fee for it.

6.8.2 Benefits of Open-source Software

People prefer to use open-source software to proprietary software because of the following reasons.

Control: Computer programmers have more control over open-source software as they can examine the code to understand its logic and make changes to it as and when required.

Training: Open-source software helps programmers to improve their programming skills. They can access the code, study it and make a better software on their own. Programmers can also share their software with others, inviting comment and critique, as they develop their skills. When other more experienced programmers see their code, they can identify errors in them (if any) and also correct them.

Security: Open-source software is more secure than proprietary software. This is because anyone can view, update and upgrade the code to improve it and correct errors in it.

Stability: Open-source software is more stable than proprietary software. This is because in long-term projects, computer users are sure that the code has been distributed and many programmers are openly working on the code to maintain and update it. They can easily rely on such software for critical tasks as they can be sure that it will not fall into disrepair if their original creators stop working on them.

Community: Open-source software often inspires a community of users and developers to form around it. These users and developers collectively produce, test, use and promote the software.

> The term "free" indicates that the software does not have constraints on copyrights. Users have freedom to use it. And the term "open source" means that the source code is openly available for everyone to see it, edit it or share it.

Transparency: Computer programmers and users can clearly see what kinds of data are moving where and what changes have been done in the code. This is not possible in proprietary software.

Reliability: Proprietary software can be updated only by the organization that created it. But open-source software is not confined to an individual organization; it spans countless programmers and is constantly updated through active open-source communities. Open standards and peer review ensure that open-source code is appropriately tested quite often.

Flexibility: Open-source software can be customized for a particular application.

Lower Cost: Although open-source software is free, users have to pay a fee for technical support, security and managing interoperability.

No Vendor Lock-in: Open-source software can be used in anyway the user wishes. There are minimal or no restrictions for using it.

6.9 COMPUTER FRAUD

Since computers and the Internet are used for a wide variety of tasks today and in many ways, they have become indispensable, frauds related to computers have been increasing at a faster rate than ever before.

Computer fraud occurs when a person makes use of the Internet and a computing device to obtain something of value to the individual. This something of value can be information, but some take money or bank and personal information for later use.

For example, hacking is a common form of computer fraud in which a hacker uses technological tools to remotely access a protected computer or system. Another common form of computer fraud includes the interception of an electronic transmission unintended for the interceptor, such as passwords, credit card information, or other types of identity theft. Other types of computer fraud include:

- Emails requesting money
- Messages seeking personal information such as account numbers, social security numbers, and passwords
- Using someone else's computer to access personal information to perform fraudulent activity
- Installing spyware or malware on someone else's computer
- Violating copyright laws by copying someone else's information and using it in one's own name
- Illegally using someone's computer to change information, such as grades, work reports, etc.
- Denial-of-service attack in which the attacker prevents other innocent users to access a network
- Crimes intended to transmit or provide false or misleading information. Sending spam emails or participating in online auction fraud are examples of this type of computer fraud crime. The goal is often to convince people to part with money by misleading them.
- Crimes intended to obtain unlawful use of a computer or of a computer system. Botnet crimes are an example of this type of computer fraud.
- Providing misleading information to obtain unlawful access. For example, unlawfully obtaining funds or information by pretending to be someone else.
- Emails promoting *too-good-to-be-true* investment opportunities or goods for sale
- Spreading false news for influencing people's opinions on current events.

While most of the computer fraud is done for gaining money, some also do it for bringing bad name to an organization by revealing their confidential data and spoiling their credibility.

Although there is no way to protect confidential data, organizations must take some steps to minimize the probability of such fraudulent activities. Hence, one should take the following steps to protect their personal data:

- Be alert to the scams that are circulated over the Internet.
- Individual users and organizations should not publish personal details or other important data on the websites or forums.
- The organization/firms should not broadcast much of their business details on the Internet.
- Organizations must follow security policies and procedures.
- People working from homes should ensure that any message seeking organization's confidential data is valid and coming from the correct source (by checking its digital signatures).

6.10 INTERNET FRAUDS AND SCAMS

The downside of using Internet services includes stealing personal information, conduct of fraudulent transactions transmitting the proceeds of fraud to financial institutions. Such frauds can occur in chat rooms, email, message boards, or on websites (Fig. 6.10). Some common Internet frauds are discussed below.

Purchase Fraud: occurs when a criminal purchases a product or service online and pays for it through fraud, for example, using a stolen or a fake credit card. As a result, merchants do not get paid for the transaction and lose money.

Online Auction Fraud: occurs when a fraudster starts an online auction of high-priced items on a website. He/she then accepts payment from the auction winner, but either does not deliver the product or delivers a product that is less valuable than the one offered. This is the most common fraud on the Internet.

Online Retail Fraud: is similar to the auction fraud; in this, after receiving the payment for retail purchases, either the product is not delivered or an inferior product is delivered.

Work from Home: scam occurs when business opportunities are advertised on the Internet and users are asked to pay nominal to substantial sums of money to get themselves registered. The fraudster collects thousands of dollars but never delivers the promised material or adequate information to the subscribers; rather, he/she sends advices on how to place ads similar to the one through which the victim got recruited. In another scenario, the scammer accepts services from the victims (like writing directories, data entry, reading books, etc.) but then refuses to reimburse them by rejecting their work considering it sub-standard.

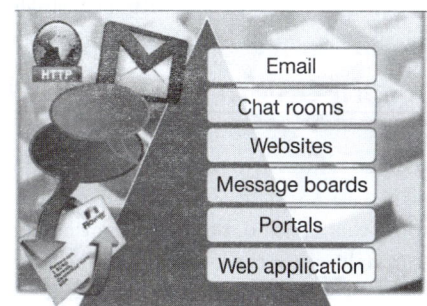

Figure 6.10 Tools used for Internet frauds

Phishing: is a fraudulent activity in which a person or a business pretends to be trustworthy when actually it is not. It is basically done to acquire sensitive information like passwords, account numbers and credit card details. Phishing is usually done through official electronic notifications or messages, such as emails or instant messages.

For example, a phisher will ask a potential victim to enter his/her password by displaying messages like "verify your account", "confirm billing information" or "enter your credit card number". Once the victim gives the details, the attacker could access the victim's information and use it for criminal purposes such as spamming or transferring money in his account or shopping online with the victim's credit card number.

While sending fraudulent messages or emails, the fraudsters copy the code and graphics from legitimate websites to give victims a look and feel of a legitimate mail from the trusted website so that victims can comfortably provide them their private and confidential information. Scammers may also provide links to cloned websites that appear identical to legitimate websites.

Pharming: occurs when a hacker exploits vulnerability in the Domain Name System (DNS) to redirect website traffic from a legitimate website to his fraudulent website. This process of making the victim's computer to communicate with the wrong server is called domain hijacking.

The fraudster constructs a fake website that looks similar to the legitimate site and asks for the user's personal information. For example, a copy of a bank's website may ask the user to enter his/her password, PIN number, bank account number, credit card number, etc. to steal the information and misuse it. This combination of domain hijacking with a phishing website constitutes pharming.

Stock Market Fraud: includes attempts to manipulate securities prices on the market for the personal profit of the scammer. The scammer usually follows any of the two methods to do this fraud. First is the pump-and-dump scheme in which false information is spread to cause a dramatic increase in price of thinly traded stocks in chat rooms, forums, Internet boards, or email (as spam). This is called the "pump". The moment prices reach the desired level, scammers sell their stocks (called "dump") to innocent victims, thereby making a substantial profit. Later, when the prices again fall to their usual prices, the victims realize that it was all a fraud.

In the second technique, called short-selling or scalping, the scammer spreads false information that causes dramatic decrease in prices. Once the stock price falls to the desired level, the scammer buys them in bulk and then reverses the false information or waits for the company to disapprove the information in the media. Once the stock regains its original price, the fraudster sells it making high profits.

Online Intellectual Property Theft: Individuals all over the world who share their notes and information on the Internet have exclusive rights on their material. But many people or students just copy and use it without taking permissions from the author. Some people also copy others' text, images and multimedia data and put them on their own website. Some may even go a step ahead and copy someone else's program code or material and distribute it for free when the programmer wanted to sell it. This process of copying and using someone else's online material is called online intellectual property theft.

Spam Email: is a common form of fraud in which the fraudster sends bulk emails to millions of email addresses to corrupt the receivers' computers, steal their identity or fool them to paying for fraudulent products or services. These emails offer false dealings to recipients like low-interest loans, winning lottery, fancy business proposals, free credit report checks, relationships with local singles, etc. Spam emails require recipients to open the email and click on a link which may also open up the computer to a virus, worm or other bugs that will corrupt the computer.

6.11 INFORMATION TECHNOLOGY ACT 2000

High-speed Internet connectivity has no doubt brought about a communication revolution. However, on the flipside, it has led to an increase in online crimes. A rise in these offences necessitated effective laws for protection online. Keeping this in mind, the Indian Parliament passed the Information Technology Act 2000 (No. 21 of 2000). This was conceptualized on the United Nations Commissions on International Trade Law (UNCITRAL) model.

The Government of India enacted the Information Technology (IT) Act with the objective to deliver and facilitate lawful electronic, digital, and online transactions, and mitigate cybercrimes. It defines the offences, along with the penalties for each category of offence, in detail.

The IT Act of India provides legal recognition for transactions involving exchange of electronic data and other means of electronic communication, commonly referred to as electronic commerce (or e-commerce). E-commerce involves alternatives to paper-based methods of communication and storage of information.

Salient Features of IT Act

Some of the key features of the IT Act are listed here:

1. Digital signatures have been replaced with electronic signatures.
2. A detailed note on offences, penalties, and breaches is given.
3. It talks about the justice dispensation systems for cybercrimes.
4. It provides details for the constitution of the Cyber Regulations Advisory Committee.
5. The Act is based on The Indian Penal Code 1860, The Indian Evidence Act 1872, The Bankers' Books Evidence Act 1891, The Reserve Bank of India Act 1934, etc.
6. It adds a provision to Section 81, which states that *nothing contained in the Act shall restrict any person from exercising any right conferred under the Copyright Act 1957*. Some important sections of the Act are given in Table 6.2.

Table 6.2 Cyber crimes and punishment as per IT Act 2000

Sections	Particulars	Punishment for the Offence
Section 43	Damage to computer system etc.	Compensation to the person affected
Section 66	Computer related offence	Imprisonment for term of 3 years or fine for 5 lakh rupees or both
Section 67	Publication or transmission of obscene material in e-form	Fine of 5 lakh rupees, and imprisonment of 3 years and double conviction on second offence
Section 68	Not complying with directions of controller	Fine up to 1 lakh or imprisonment of 2 years or both
Section 70	Protected system	Imprisonment up to 10 years and shall also be liable for a fine
Section 72	Breaking confidentiality of the information of computer	Imprisonment for term of 2 years or fine of 1 lakh rupees or both
Section 73	Publishing of false digital signatures	Imprisonment for term of 2 years or fine for 1 lakh rupees or both
Section 74	Publication of digital signatures for fraudulent purpose	Imprisonment for term of 2 years or fine for 1 lakh rupees or both

6.12 HACKING

Hacking means the act of identifying weakness in a computer system or even a network. Once the weakness is identified, it is exploited to gain access to that computer. For example, if someone has set a very weak password then a hacker (people who hack) can break the password to access the system.

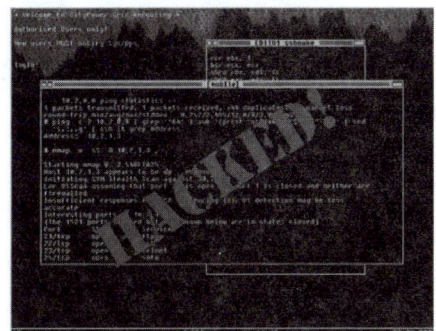

Hacking is a very serious problem today as computers have become a must-have device for all of us and a standalone computer without being connected to any network or the Internet is just not enough in today's era. We need to be connected for more information, for better ways to do the routine tasks, to socialize and to run a successful business. But this exposes our computers to hackers. *Hackers hack computer systems to commit fraudulent acts such as fraud, privacy invasion, stealing corporate/personal data, etc.*

Hacking can either be ethical or unethical. Ethical hacking is done when someone deliberately accesses the computer but not to break its security and steal data. It is done only to identify any weakness in the system so that they can be overcome. Ethical hackers are usually experts in computer technology who have a sound knowledge of computer hardware and software.

Unethical hacking, on the other hand, is done by hackers who gain unauthorized access to the computer system and also to the secured accounts. These hackers always have wrong intentions and they gain access, usually by cracking passwords and other security codes. Therefore, unethical hackers are also known as crackers.

Preventive Measures

- Create complex passwords. Password should consist of a combination of numbers, upper- and lower-case letters, and special characters that are difficult to guess. Figure 6.11 clearly states features of a strong password.
- Create a different password for every account. This ensures that even if the hacker has broken your password of one account, at least the others are safe.
- Never share your passwords with anyone. Not even with your close friend. Do not even write it down on the last page of your notebook or at places which can be easily accessed by others.
- Change your passwords often. You must change it at least once in every 4–5 months.
- Do not repeat your password. Always set a new one. Websites like Gmail never allows you to choose a previous password.
- After checking your emails and using your other accounts, do not forget to log out.
- Install anti-virus software and firewalls.

Figure 6.11 Features of a strong password

Include	Do not include
More characters	Dictionary words
More numbers/symbols	Repeated words
Memorable combinations	Personal information
Uppercase & lowercase	The word "Password"

6.13 SPREADING RUMOUR AND CYBER BULLYING

Cyber bullying or Internet bullying is a form of teen violence that has already caused lasting harm to young people. Some teens use Internet to bully or harass another person (classmates or neighborhood friends). As a result, the victim goes into depression or develops anxiety problems. In many cases, victims have even committed suicide (Fig. 6.12).

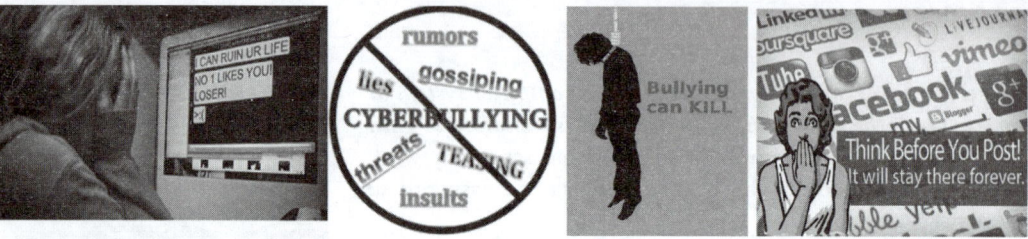

Figure 6.12   Cyber bullying and its effects

In cyber bullying, teens have been found involved in the following activities. We have laid special emphasis on this point so that students can understand the sensitivity of the matter and avoid such practices.

- Sending threatening messages through smart phones or emails
- Spreading rumors through social networking websites or through group messages.
- Stealing someone's email id and password and using it to send threatening or damaging messages to a third person
- Taking pictures of someone and spreading it through the Internet.
- Sexting, or circulating sexually suggestive pictures or messages about a person.

SERIOUS NOTE: Teens often think that cyber bullying is only for fun. But remember that such activities can get you out of your school, affect your admission in college and in getting a job in a reputed organization. Parents of such children can face legal charges for cyber bullying.
If cyber bullying involved sexting, then the offender can be registered as a sex offender.
Even if teens use fake email ids, there are many ways to find out who had sent these messages.

Preventive Measures for Cyber Bullying

- Make children aware of the serious consequences of cyber bullying.
- The victim should discuss the matter with his/her parents and teachers.
- The victim should keep all bullying messages as a proof that can be shown to the teachers, parents of the bully and may be to the police if the bully does not stop sending such messages. Never delete them.
- Block the bully's number as well as email address. Parents should ensure that teens do not use personal mobile phones, email addresses or accounts on social networking websites.
- Parents should also ensure that children always use the computer in the living room and not in their personal rooms so that they can keep a check on what the children are doing.

6.14   PHISHING

Phishing is the act of sending an email or messages to a user falsely claiming to be a legitimate authority. Phishing is done to scam the user to get his personal information (this is an example of identity theft).

Phishing emails usually ask the user visit a website (that is actually bogus) to update his/her personal information like password, credit card number, social security number, or bank account numbers (refer Fig. 6.13). All this information is already available with the legitimate website. The bogus website captures the details entered by the user and the fraudster uses it to commit a crime.

The bogus website is created in such a way that it looks exactly like the original website. This is done so that user does not suspect the website before entering the information.

Figure 6.13   Phishing attack to steal information

Preventive Measures

- If you get an email from a company with which you are not associated, do not give any personal information.
- Bogus websites will have spelling and grammar errors. Always check for such errors as they indicate a phishing attack.
- If a bank website is asking for your account number, then it would have at least specified the other details correctly. But bogus websites do not display any information, it only asks for your details.
- Bogus website will give you very short deadlines to fill the information (like within 24 hours) but a genuine one will give you ample time. So, beware.
- The bogus websites will have a different URL that can be easily identified. So, if a website is asking for personal information, do not forget to check its URL.
- If you have got an email asking for your personal information, do not fill it at once. Rather, contact the company directly through their email address or phone.
- A phishing email always states that the user's account or password or credit card number is expiring, the user's account is being hacked and that the account information needs to be changed. It may say that the credit card number has been duplicated and he or she needs to log in to confirm recent orders or transactions. Remember this and do not become a prey.
- Never respond to emails coming from an unknown person, especially from a foreign country.
- Never respond to emails that threaten to harm unless a huge amount of money is paid.
- A legitimate email asking for your details will always have your name but a fraudulent email will have generic greetings "Dear Customer".

6.15 E-WASTE MANAGEMENT

With technology becoming an integral part of our lives, semiconductors and sensors used in wearable devices, monitors, smart homes, TVs, etc., all produce e-waste (refer Fig. 6.14).

Moreover, the life span of devices has become shorter. With cheaper technology and rapid advancements, people throw away their gadgets as soon as their batteries die and buy new ones. Even companies intentionally motivate this behavior by making their products obsolete every 2–3 years (by updating the design or software and discontinuing support for older models) so that they continue to profit from steady sales.

Figure 6.14 Huge amount of E-waste generation

In 2016, the world's population generated 49 million tons of e-waste, which is approximately equal to about 4,500 Eiffel Towers. It is estimated that by 2025, 63 million metric tons of e-waste will be produced.

Electronic waste or e-waste typically includes discarded computer monitors, motherboards, mobile phones and chargers, CDs, headphones, TVs, ACs and refrigerators. Apart from precious metals like gold, cobalt, silver, copper, platinum, palladium and lithium, e-waste also contains heavy toxic metals like lead, mercury, cadmium and beryllium, polluting PVC plastic, and hazardous chemicals, such as brominated flame retardants, which can harm human health and the environment.

With ever-increasing demand for electronic equipment, manufacturers are beginning to face shortages of the raw materials needed to make their products, so reclaiming and reusing the materials from discarded products and waste, makes economic and environmental sense. A recent study (https://www.sciencedaily.com/releases/2018/04/180404093956.htm) in China stated that mining copper, gold and aluminium from their native ores cost 13 times more than recovering the metals through mining of e-waste.

Global E-Waste Monitor 2017 reported that India generates about 2 million tonnes (MT) of e-waste annually. India ranks fifth among e-waste producing countries, after the US, China, Japan and Germany.

In 2016–17, India treated only 0.036 MT of its e-waste. Moreover, about 95% of India's e-waste is recycled in the informal sector. Globally, only 20% global e-waste is recycled. A report by UN indicates that due to poor extraction techniques, the total recovery rate of cobalt from e-waste is only 30 per cent. Cobalt is a metal which is in great demand for laptop, smart phone and electric car batteries.

The report also states that one recycler in China produces more cobalt by recycling than by mining in one year. Recycled metals are also 2-to-10 times more energy-efficient than metals obtained from their ores.

The UN report also suggests that reducing the amount of e-waste and improving lifespan of electronic gadgets are essential for building a more circular economy. In such an economy, waste is reduced, resources are conserved and fed back into the supply chain for developing new products.

Inspired by the report, the organizing committee of Tokyo Olympic Games that were supposed to be held in 2020 had ordered to make medals with 50,000 tonnes of e-waste. For this, nearly 8 tonnes of gold, silver and bronze were extracted by November 2018 to make 5,000 medals.

In India, laws to manage e-waste are already in place since 2011. It allows only authorized dismantlers and recyclers to collect e waste. These laws were strengthened in 2016 and over 21 products were included under the purview of the rule. It also ensured the take-back of the end-of-life products.

A new arrangement called Producer Responsibility Organisation (PRO) has further strengthened the guidelines by making it mandatory for producers to manage 20% per cent of the waste generated by their sales. The law also states that the responsibility of producers is not confined to waste collection, but extends to ensure that the waste reaches the authorized recycler/dismantler.

Even after upgrading the laws, massive amounts of e-waste are still being generated at huge health and environmental cost by the informal sector, polluting ground water and soil.

E-waste is growing at a compound annual growth rate (CAGR) of about 30 per cent in the country. It is estimated that e-waste generation was 1.8 MT in 2016 and would be approximately 52.2 MT by 2021.

> Electronic devices are made of a complex mix of materials that include gold, silver, copper, platinum, palladium, lithium, cobalt and other valuable elements. These precious materials can be reclaimed through recycling.

Though India has more than 178 registered e-waste recyclers, many of them are not recycling waste at all. This is because some of these recyclers are found to be working in hazardous conditions while others do not have the capacity to handle such waste.

The Ministry of Electronics and Information Technology (MeitY) started an e-waste awareness programme under Digital India, along with industry associations from 2015, to create awareness about the hazards of e-waste recycling by the unorganized sector, and to educate them about alternative ways of disposing it.

The program's main focus is to adopt best practices for environment friendly e-waste recycling practices. This would help to generate jobs as well as viable business prospects for the locals.

6.15.1 Development of Waste Recycling Technologies

The MeitY has also developed affordable technologies to recycle valuable materials and plastics in an environmentally friendly way. One of them can recycle 1000 kg/day (~35 MT e-waste). This could then be made suitable for creating an eco-park in the country. Even a majority (76 per cent) of the waste plastics can be converted into suitable materials that can be used in all ways as original plastics is used. The technology has already been transferred for commercialization.

Professor Veena Sahajwalla suggests setting up micro-factories in India that can transform e-waste into reusable material to be converted into ceramics and plastic filaments for 3D printing. And metals like gold, silver, copper and palladium found in the e-waste can be separated for re-sale in conditions that are totally safe.

There is an immense potential in e-waste recycling in the country. But before that there is a need for skill development and introduction of technology that adopts adequate safety measures in the country's informal sector.

Since India is highly deficient in precious mineral resources, there is need for a well-designed, robust and regulated e-waste recovery regime which would generate jobs as well as wealth.

6.15.2 Formal vs. Informal Recycling

Recycling e-waste is practiced both formally and informally. Formal e-waste recycling involves disassembling the electronic gadgets, separating and categorizing the contents by material and cleaning them. Items are then separated for further sorting. However, the companies involved must adhere to **health and safety rules**. They must also use **pollution-control** techniques to minimize environmental hazards of handling e-waste. All this makes formal recycling **expensive**. As a result, many companies and countries illegally export their e-waste to developing countries where recycling is cheap. For example, US is the second largest producer of e-waste after China, but recycles only 40% of the e-waste and exports the rest to developing countries (in Asia) where informal recycling is typically cheap, unlicensed and unregulated.

At these informal recycling workshops, workers including women and children recover valuable materials by burning devices to melt away non-valuable materials. For example, they melt toxic material like mercury and use acids to recover gold. They also dismantle devices by hand to reclaim other materials of value. These people do not wear protective equipment and are unaware that they are handling dangerous materials. Inhaling toxic chemicals and direct contact with hazardous e-waste materials increases lead levels in blood, triggers spontaneous abortions, stillbirths, premature births, reduces birth weights, causes gene mutations, affects lung function, causes congenital malformations, abnormal thyroid function, and neurobehavioral disturbances. Moreover, e-waste toxins contaminate water, air and soil. In addition to the health and environmental hazards, informal recycling can pose security risks. While formal recyclers usually wipe all data from the devices, informal recycling does not. Criminals search e-waste for credit card numbers and other financial information.

(a) (b)

Figure 6.15 (a) Formal; (b) Informal recycling

Figure 6.15 shows a typical set-up where such e-waste recycling is done. *Sources:* https://phys.org/news/2009-10-increasingly-states-e-waste-recycling.html; https://www.downtoearth.org.in/blog/waste/new-e-waste-draft-rules-promise-a-broader-scope-49513

Looking into these hazards, people in developing countries prefer to earn by dismantling, refurbishing, repairing and reselling used electronic devices. In China (also known as the e-waste capital of the world), 75 percent of households are involved in the recycling business. Informal recycling is practiced in India, Nigeria, Ghana and the Philippines.

6.15.3 Alternative Solutions of Disposal

With flooding e-waste material around the world, recycling alone is not enough. Therefore, some alternative solutions are being researched and practiced around the world. Some of these solutions are given below:

Design Better Electronic Products: that are safer, more durable, repairable and recyclable. Use of toxic materials should be minimized. Moreover, chemical engineers at Stanford University are working to develop the first fully biodegradable electronic circuit using natural dyes that dissolve in acid with a pH 100 times weaker than vinegar.

Companies should also manufacture phones that enable consumers to upgrade parts of their phones instead of having to entirely replace them. Google, LG and Motorola released modular models, but they were not well received in the market as it was clumsier and more costly. But now that people are well aware of the e-waste problem, companies design a modular phone that has market appeal.

We must repair and reuse the devices we have.

Extended Producer Responsibility: instructs companies manufacturing electronic products to take the responsibility for the management and disposal of their products at the end of their lives. This will help to turn waste materials into a resource for producing new products. In USA, manufacturers provide consumers with free and convenient e-waste recycling.

EcoATMs are extensively used in the US for e-waste recycling. EcoATM provides a convenient and safe way to recycle and sell e-waste at kiosks (Fig. 6.16). The EcoATM evaluates the old phones, TVs and other devices based on the model and condition and pays the right amount to the customer. Sold items are then either reused or responsibly recycled.

In China, the largest Internet company, Baidu, and the United Nations Development Programme developed a smartphone app that allows users to feed the item they want to recycle, its picture, size and the pick-up date along with their name and address. Within 24 hours, the item will be picked up for recycling.

Figure 6.16 EcoATM to collect E-waste

Giving Informal Recyclers Financial Incentives to Divert E-waste to Formal Collection or Recycling Centres. For example, informal recyclers could be paid more to deliver e-waste to a formal collection centre than they would get for dismantling it by hand themselves.

Like developed countries, developing countries must also devise sophisticated disposal schemes and high-cost systems, which are less hazardous to handle waste (Fig. 6.17).

In developing countries, the regulations that guide the disposition of e-waste is mostly fragmented and lack monitoring. These regulations should be made stringent and monitored effectively.

Figure 6.17 Dismantling and recycling e-waste

6.16 AWARENESS ABOUT HEALTH CONCERNS RELATED TO THE USAGE OF TECHNOLOGY

Technology may have made unprecedented positive changes in the world. However, everything in this world has two faces. The world has also experienced the negative effects of technology and its overuse. Although it is impossible to stay away from technology, we can take steps to ensure its mindful usage. We must make smart use of technology (TV, computers, smartphones, gaming devices, etc.) to enjoy its conveniences and overcome the side effects caused by its overuse. For this, we can consider the following symptoms linked to technology addiction.

6.16.1 Digital Eye Strain

When we look at the screen for long hours, we often forget to blink our eyes. Research has proved that digital eye strain reduces our blink rate by half. Reducing blink rate affects tears in our eyes. These tears protect our eyes. Moreover, reading smaller fonts on a smartphone or other portable device can intensify the strain.

Symptoms of digital eye strain include dry eyes, headaches, blurred vision, burning, itching, difficult to focus on something and pain in the neck or shoulders. For most people, eye strain may just cause a little discomfort without resulting in any long-term problems.

Reducing Digital Eye Strain: To minimize discomfort, doctors advocate the "20-20-20" rule which states, "Every 20 minutes, take a 20-second break and focus on something 20 feet away". Refresh your eyes frequently by blinking every time you breathe. Other tips to deal with digital eye strain include:

- Reducing overhead lighting to eliminate screen glare
- Using anti-glare coated eye glasses
- Staying at least one arm's distance away from the screen
- Increasing the font size of text on devices to make them easier to read
- Regular eye check-ups

6.16.2 Sleep Disorders

Many of us are so addicted to our devices that we often sleep with them. According to a research, 71 percent of smartphone users do so to ensure that they do not miss any notification. Another research concluded that over 40% of bedside smartphone users wake up to noises or lighting from notifications coming from their device.

Light coming from these devices suppresses the release of the sleep-promoting hormone melatonin, enhances alertness and shifts circadian rhythms to a later hour, thereby making it difficult to fall asleep (study by Charles Czeisler, MD, of Harvard Medical School and Brigham and Women's Hospital). Sleeping disorder is a serious concern as it affects us physiologically and psychologically.

Tips for Addressing Smartphone Addiction in Bed: Those facing sleeping disorders due to devices must consider avoiding these devices at bed-time and replacing them with sleep-conducive activities such as taking a bath or reading a book. Other tips to overcome device addition during bedtime include the following:

- Turn off your Wi-Fi or use an Internet blocker
- Listen to a podcast
- Keep the phone at a location where you can't reach but can still hear
- Track your usage and set a limit
- Turn off unnecessary notifications
- Set your screen to night mode.

6.16.3 Physical Inactivity

When using devices for work or entertainment, we are generally not exercising. In Thailand, a study covering college students revealed that students experiencing smartphone addiction participated in lesser physical activity as compared to those who moderated their use. Moreover, it has been found that physical inactivity and the blue light coming from these devices increase obesity (Fig. 6.18).

Also, everyday digital devices that we use have made our life sedentary and increased negative health effects including obesity, cardiovascular diseases, Type 2 diabetes and premature death.

Overcoming Physical Inactivity: One can use any fitness app that can help him/her to stick to an exercise routine, stay motivated and track progress.

Figure 6.18 People become obese due to overuse of technology

- Use health apps to track chronic illnesses and communicate vital information to doctors
- Use apps that help you track diet, exercise, and mental health information
- Use apps that facilitate storing and sharing online medical records so that you can access test results and follow prescriptions in a better way
- Follow a healthy and active daily routine.

6.16.4 Musculoskeletal Problems

When using smartphones and other devices, we usually hold our head in an unnatural forward-leaning position. This position puts a lot of stress on our neck, shoulders and spine. Even among teens, neck-shoulder pain and low back pain problems are constantly rising. Overuse of technology can also result in strain injuries of the fingers, thumbs, and wrists.

Managing Muscular Pain: To reduce strain injuries and pain, follow the tips given below.

- Stretch your body at regular intervals.
- Create an ergonomic workspace.
- Maintain proper posture while using your devices (Fig. 6.19).
- Take short breaks and walk around every hour to keep the muscles loose and avoid stress as well as incorrect posture.
- Sit upright so your back is against your seat and your abdominal muscles are engaged. Avoid slouching, whenever possible.
- Hold your devices straight out in front of your face and your head sitting squarely on your shoulders. This position may seem a little awkward at first, but it is necessary to avoid strain injuries.
- If you are sick of sitting all day, use a body-standing desk.
- If pain persists, see a doctor.

Figure 6.19 Right way of sitting in front of a computer

6.16.5 Mental Health

Every day, more than three billion people interact over social media. Over-using these services can impact our mental health and overall well-being. Social media addiction directly increases mental health disorders like depression, suicidal ideation, aggression, anxiety, and feeling of being isolated, particularly among the teenagers. Social networking sites like Facebook, Instagram and Twitter place high social pressures that sometimes results in cyberbullying and general feelings of discontent.

According to a research, teens and women who spent five or more hours daily on social media were twice more likely to experience depression-related symptoms than males.

Tips for Managing Social Media Use

Manage your time on social media.

- Log off and take regular social media breaks.
- Think twice or thrice before posting anything on social media.
- Use appropriate settings options to decide who should see your posts.
- Limit the number of profiles you have on social media.
- Delete apps that affect your productivity.
- Focus on real-world relationships rather than spending time over online friendships.

6.16.6 Technology Affecting Children

Children's brains are still developing and are more sensitive to the side-effects of technology overuse than adult brains (Fig. 6.20). Children overusing technology may be more likely to experience issues such as:

- deteriorating academic performance
- lack of concentration
- low creativity
- delays in language development
- delays in social and emotional development
- physical inactivity and obesity
- sleep disorders
- aggressive behaviors
- addiction to devices

Figure 6.20 People get involved with devices thereby ignoring real-world relationships

- increased likelihood of developing symptoms of attention-deficit hyperactivity disorder (ADHD).

The American Academy of Pediatrics recommend that children less than 1.5 years old should not see or use devices, 2–5-year-olds should not use them for more than 1 hour a day.

Key Terms

Digital footprints: Footprints or traces that a user leaves when he/she is online.

Active footprints: Digital footprints that are left by a user intentionally.

Passive footprints: Digital footprints that are left by a user unintentionally.

Netiquette: Also known as Network Etiquette, or Internet Etiquette, it is a set of rules that should be followed when a person is working on the Internet.

Ethics: A set of moral values that govern the behavior of a person.

Intellectual Property Rights (or IPR): Rights that are applicable to creative work which can be treated as an asset or physical property. They can be categorized into four main areas – copyright, trademarks, design rights and patents.

Trademark: A name, word, slogan, design, symbol or any other item that is used to identify a product or organization.

Plagiarism: An act of fraud that involves both stealing someone else's work and lying about it afterward.

Software license: An agreement between the consumer and the creator of a software program that allows the consumer to do certain things that would otherwise be a violation of copyright laws.

Phishing: A fraudulent activity in which a person or a business pretends to be trustworthy when actually it is not. It is basically done to acquire sensitive information like passwords, account numbers and credit card details.

Pharming: A fraudulent activity that occurs when a hacker exploits vulnerability in the Domain Name System (DNS) to redirect website traffic from a legitimate website to his fraudulent website.

Online intellectual property theft: The process of copying and using someone else's online material.

Spam emails: A form of fraud in which the fraudster sends bulk emails to millions of email addresses to corrupt the receivers' computers, steal their identity or fool them into paying for fraudulent products or services.

Hacking: The act of identifying weakness in a computer system or even a network.

Cyber bullying: Also known as Internet bullying, it is an unethical act that is done to bully or harass another person, thereby resulting in the victim going into depression or suffering from anxiety problems.

Chapter Highlights

- Personal information means recorded information or opinions, whether true or not, that helps someone to identify whose information or opinion it is.
- Privacy laws give us a space to be ourselves without judgement and allow us to think freely without discrimination.
- Product designs must also be protected by both copyright and design rights.
- Patents are applied for industrial processes and inventions. They also protect the item against unauthorized implementation of the invention.
- Right of publicity protects the image and name of a person against unauthorized use for commercial purposes.
- Trade Secret laws provides protection against sensitive business information.
- A free software license or an open-source license allows users to use the software without seeking anyone's permission. The users can also copy and redistribute the software to others for future development or use.
- Computer fraud occurs when a person makes use of the Internet and a computing device to obtain something of value to another person or group.
- Ethical hacking is done when someone deliberately accesses the computer to identify any weaknesses in the system so that they can be overcome. Unethical hacking, on the other hand, is done by hackers who gain unauthorized access to the computer system and also to the secured accounts.
- Electronic waste or e-waste typically includes discarded computer monitors, motherboards, mobile phones and chargers, CDs, headphones, TVs, ACs and refrigerators.
- Formal e-waste recycling involves disassembling the electronic devices, separating and categorizing the contents by material and cleaning them.

- 20-20-20 rule states that for every 20 minutes of screen time, we need to take a 20-second break and focus on something 20 feet away.
- Overuse of digital technologies has made our life sedentary, which has further increased negative health effects including obesity, cardiovascular diseases, Type 2 diabetes and premature death.

Review Questions

1. Define the term 'digital footprint'. Differentiate between active and passive digital footprints
2. Why should we think twice before posting anything on social media?
3. Define the term 'Internet Etiquette'. Also list some important points that one must consider while going online.
4. What do you understand by the term 'ethics' in the field of computing?
5. Explain the importance of privacy laws.
6. How does privacy laws help us to protect our data?
7. Differentiate between copyright, trademark, patent and trade secret.
8. Why do people plagiarize?
9. Why is plagiarism a serious concern?
10. Why is it necessary to read the terms of a software license before using it?
11. What do you mean by a FOSS?
12. List some advantages of using FOSS.
13. Explain the different types of computer frauds. How can one protect oneself from such frauds?
14. Discuss any three sections and punishments specified in IT Act 2000.
15. What is hacking? Differentiate between ethical and unethical hacking.
16. What important things we should remember in case of passwords?
17. Why is cyber bullying a serious crime even if done by children?
18. Define phishing. How can you identify a phishing attack?
19. What is e-waste management and why is it important?
20. Differentiate between formal and informal recycling. Which one of the two is better and why?
21. How has technology affected our health? Discuss ways to combat it.

Fill in the Blanks

1. _____ means footprints or traces that a user leaves when he/she is online.
2. A digital footprint can be traced back to the _____.
3. _____ are digital footprints that are left by a user unintentionally.
4. To see the footprints left by us, we must enter our name in different _____.
5. _____ defines a set of dos and don'ts while working on the Internet.
6. Writing a message in capital letters is treated as _____.
7. _____ laws give us space to be ourselves without judgement and allows us to think freely without discrimination.
8. _____ are rights that are applicable to creative work.
9. _____ are applied to industrial processes and inventions.
10. _____ protects the image and name of a person against unauthorized use for commercial purposes.
11. Changing words but copying the sentence structure of a source without giving credit is an act of _____.
12. Reusing your own work done previously is known as _____.

Societal Impacts **211**

13. The process of copying and using someone else's online material is called _____.
14. _____ is a form of fraud in which the fraudster sends bulk emails to millions of email addresses.
15. Section _____ deals with damage to computer systems.
16. _____ means the act of identifying weaknesses in a computer system or even a network.
17. _____ includes discarded computer monitors, motherboards, mobile phones and chargers, CDs, headphones, TVs, ACs and refrigerators.
18. _____ provides a convenient and safe way to recycle and sell e-waste at kiosks.
19. Physical inactivity and the blue light coming from these devices increases _____.
20. We must create an _____ workspace.

State True or False

1. Whenever a user fills a registration form, sends an e-mail, uploads pictures/videos or any other file, searches for some information, he leaves traces of personal information about himself/herself on the Internet.
2. Passive digital footprints are left intentionally by a user.
3. Everyone who uses the Internet has a digital footprint.
4. Patents provides protection against sensitive business information.
5. We can avoid plagiarism by correctly citing the sources.
6. Only for students and academicians, plagiarism in not a punishable crime.
7. The licensee of a free software may copy, modify and distribute creative works, provided a free license is obtained.
8. Spreading false news for influencing people's opinions on current events is an example of computer fraud.
9. Section 67 deals with breaking confidentiality of the information of computer.
10. Unethical hacking is done when someone deliberately accesses the computer but not to break its security and steal data.
11. We must create a different password for every account.
12. Informal e-waste recycling involves disassembling the electronics, separating and categorizing the contents by material and cleaning them.
13. We must have more overhead lighting to eliminate screen glare.

Multiple Choice Questions

1. Which of the following leaves an active digital footprint?
   a. Search information on Google
   b. Shop online
   c. Comment on Facebook
   d. Visit a website
2. What should we do when working online?
   a. Reply to any unknown messages or the messages that makes us uncomfortable.
   b. Exchange any personal information without your parent's permission.
   c. Treat others as you would like to be treated
   d. Use as many emoticons as possible to minimize the use of words
3. _____ is a set of moral values that govern the behavior of a person.
   a. Digital footprint   b. Ethics   c. Netiquette   d. Copyright
4. An organization's logo is protected using _____.
   a. Copyright   b. Trademark   c. Patent   d. Trade secret
5. _____ is a name, word, slogan, design, symbol or any other item that is used to identify a product or organization.
   a. Copyright   b. Trademark   c. Patent   d. Trade secret

6. _____ gives an individual or an organization, the permission to use the software.
   a. Software License   b. Patent   c. Copyright   d. Trademark
7. Software under which license can be installed on an unlimited number of computers?
   a. Single-user   b. Multi-user   c. Site license   d. All of these.
8. The term _____ means anyone can inspect, modify, and enhance the source code of the software.
   a. Free   b. Open Source   c. Proprietary   c. Shareware
9. Microsoft Office and Adobe Photoshop are examples of _____ software.
   a. free   b. open-source   c. proprietary   c. shareware
10. Which of the following is not an example of open-source software?
    a. LibreOffice   b. Gambas   c. GIMP   d. Photoshop
11. _____ is a fraudulent activity in which a person or a business pretends to be trustworthy when actually it is not.
    a. Phishing   b. Auction Fraud   c. Pharming   d. Spamming
12. Which Section of IT Act 2000 deals with publishing of false digital signatures?
    a. 43   b. 66   c. 73   d. 74
13. A strong password should not contain _____.
    a. alphabet   b. digit   c. special characters   d. None of these.
14. Spreading rumors, threatening and harassing someone are all examples of _____.
    a. plagiarism   b. hacking   c. cyber bullying   d. cyber stalking
15. Which of the following is not a disorder caused by overuse of technology?
    a. Obesity   b. Type-2 Diabetes
    c. Thumb and Finger Injury   d. None of these.
16. While using a device, we must not _____.
    a. hold the device in front of our neck   b. sit upright
    c. stretch our body   d. have at least one arm distance from it

Answers

Fill in the Blanks

1. Digital footprints
2. user
3. Passive footprints
4. search engines
5. Netiquette
6. shouting
7. Privacy
8. Intellectual Property Rights (IPR)
9. Patents
10. Right of Publicity
11. plagiarism
12. self-plagiarism
13. online intellectual property theft.
14. Spamming
15. 43
16. Hacking
17. Electronic waste or e-waste
18. EcoATM
19. obesity
20. ergonomic

State True or False

1. False
2. False
3. True
4. False
5. True
6. False
7. True
8. True
9. False
10. False
11. True
12. False
13. False

Multiple Choice Questions

1. c
2. c
3. b
4. b
5. b
6. a
7. c
8. b
9. c
10. d
11. c
12. c
13. d
14. c
15. d
16. a